A Programmer's Guide to Video Display Terminals

David Stephens

ATLANTIS PUBLISHING CORPORATION

DALLAS

Published by
Atlantis Publishing Corporation
P.O. Box 59467
Dallas, Texas 75229

ISBN 0-936158-01-8

Cover design by Peggy Holcomb

621.3987
S832p

Contents

Preface

When computers first began to appear the principal input/output device used was the Teletype®. This machine had long been used for sending and receiving coded messages by wire and was readily available in large numbers at reasonable prices. No great attempt was made to improve on it, since it was adequate for the low level of communications necessary to operate the system.

When the first microcomputer appeared the Teletype® was still the primary input/output device, again because it was readily available and relatively inexpensive. The early microcomputer users were served quite well by the Teletype®, since they were interested more in developing programs than displaying data.

The advent of the Video Display Terminal (VDT) was nearly as significant as the microcomputer itself. While the microcomputer brought cheap computing power to users who could not previously afford it, the VDT made possible spreadsheet and word processing programs that would not effectively run on hard-copy terminals.

The earliest VDTs were used as "glass Teletypes," displaying data line for line and scrolling when the screen filled. The true power of the VDT, however, was in its ability to display data anywhere on the screen in a random manner, something that no hard-copy terminal could do, and to display it at extremely rapid rates. This made it possible to design screen forms and allow a program to fill in the blanks. It also made possible word processing, where the screen was filled with text and editing could be done anywhere on the screen, with the screen redrawn as necessary.

The explosion of demand for VDTs resulted in many companies marketing terminals, and a wide range of features and control code sequences. The programmer was faced with the problem of designing a program which would run on a number of different terminals. While most VDTs operate in a similar manner, the code sequences necessary to direct their operation vary widely. A program designed to run only on one terminal will face a limited market, as computer users will have a variety of VDTs connected to their computers.

The computer user faces considerable frustration when he purchases a program and discovers that it does not support his terminal. He is left with the task of trying to "custom support" his terminal, or in extreme cases, finding that he cannot use the program at all without buying a different terminal. VDT manuals are as notorious as software documentation in that many people are unable to understand the code structure necessary to get a program running on their terminal.

Commercial programs support a limited number of terminals. It is impractical for most software developers to purchase all available terminals and test installation procedures on them. This manual evolved in response to many months of attempting to obtain control code sequences for a large number of terminals to be used in the installation routine for a software system.

Manufacturers' names were gathered from trade publications, directories, advertisements, and other sources. Most manufacturers were mailed requests for information at least six times and some as many as 27 times. A number of manufacturers consistently failed to respond and some requested that their VDTs not be listed. Some data sheets were completed by the publisher from direct observation or from third-party reports.

The results are contained in this manual, 146 VDTs and micro-computers. Some VDTs are listed more than once to reflect different configurations in different modes. Although there is a chapter on programming for VDTs, the essence of this manual is the data sheets. This manual is not intended to be a complete treatise on VDT programming, but offers a general orientation and some specific tips on programming for VDTs.

Programming for Video Display Terminals

Screen layout and nomenclature

Rows and columns

The typical video display terminal (VDT) has a screen layout consisting of 24 horizontal *rows* and 80 vertical *columns*. Other sizes are available, but less common. Other nomenclature exists for describing the rows and columns, principally x and y. The problem with using x and y is that different individuals and organizations assign different meanings to the coordinates. Some consider x to be a horizontal row, while others consider it to be a vertical column. For lack of more standard nomenclature, then, *rows* will be considered to run horizontally from top to bottom and *columns* vertically from left to right. See figure 1. *Line* is used interchangeably with *row* in this manual and in most VDT documentation.

Programs which use a pre-designed screen form, such as accounting programs, will find it necessary to use a standard size, such as 24×80, even if the terminal allows more rows and columns. Word processing and text editing programs, among others, may find it desirable to utilize a terminal's larger size or different configuration (portrait rather than landscape). In this case the programmer must allow for the number of rows and columns to be a variable amount.

Numbering rows and columns

It is crucial that a standard row and column numbering scheme be followed in any programming project. Terminal manufacturers are evenly divided on whether the top row is row zero or row one, and the left column is column zero or column one. It is immaterial which scheme is used as long the programmer maintains the scheme properly. Generally, terminals which transmit cursor coordinates in single-byte binary begin numbering with zero. Terminals which transmit cursor coordinates as two- or three-byte ASCII numerals generally begin numbering with one.

7

It is the programmer's responsibility to determine the scheme used for all terminals on which his program might run, and to make accommodations for the various schemes with his program. This will mean that the programmer must adopt one scheme or the other—he may use either zero or one as his starting point and make the necessary adjustments for different terminals. See *Cursor addressing*.

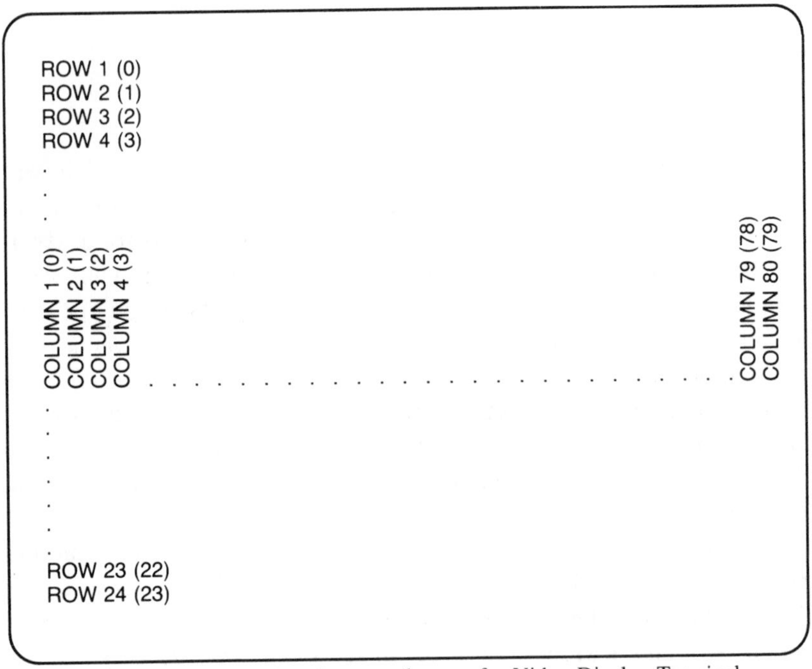

```
ROW 1 (0)
ROW 2 (1)
ROW 3 (2)
ROW 4 (3)
  ·
  ·
  ·                                                                        ∞  ∞
  ·          ⌢⌢⌢⌢                                                          ⌢  ⌢
           ⊙⌢⌢⌢⌢                                                          ⌢  ⌢
         O ⌢(0)(1)(2)(3)                                                  (78)(79)
      N 1 2 3 4                                                          79 80
   COLUMN COLUMN COLUMN COLUMN                                      COLUMN COLUMN
  ·  · · · · · · · · · · · · · · · · · · · · · · · · · · · · · · · · · · · ·
  ·
  ·
  ·
  ·
ROW 23 (22)
ROW 24 (23)
```

Fig. 1. Screen layout and nomenclature of a Video Display Terminal

Home

The *home* position is normally the upper left-hand corner, although on some terminals it might be some other position, frequently the lower left-hand corner. This may be switch or software selectable. When in doubt, the programmer might prefer to position the cursor explicitly using the cursor addressing sequence.

Clearing the screen

The most common erasure is clearing the screen, and almost all terminals have this function. Unfortunately, all do not accomplish it in the same manner. Some terminals position the cursor to the home position (upper left-hand corner) after clearing the screen, and some

8

leave the cursor at its previous position. Some terminals have no clear-screen function, but do have a clear-to-end-of-screen function.

For example, the DEC VT52 and IBM 3101 have almost identical control sequences. However, the 3101 has a clear-screen function (clear the screen and move the cursor home regardless of the original cursor position) while the VT52 does not. By using first the home sequence, then the clear-to-end-of-screen sequence, the desired effect is obtained on both terminals. This allows both terminals to use the same control code set.

Many of the manufacturers' data sheets and VDT manuals were vague on whether their clear-screen sequences left the cursor at the home position. Accordingly, it is good programming practice to always explicitly move the cursor home, either through a cursor-home or explicit move to row 1 (or zero), column 1 (or zero), then issue a clear-screen or clear-to-end-of-screen sequence.

Clearing the screen for any terminal

For terminals which have no clear-screen sequence at all, or in cases where a "standard" sequence is required (such as programs to be run before software is installed and configured for a terminal), the screen may be cleared by simply printing at least as many carriage return line feed combinations as there are rows on the terminal. On a standard-size VDT, printing 24 blank lines will effectively clear the screen. However, it also leaves the cursor at the lower left-hand corner.

Cursor addressing

The chief advantage of a VDT over a hard-copy printer is its ability to write data anywhere on the screen. To do this, a programmer must first position the cursor using the terminal's cursor addressing sequence. Cursor addressing is the programmer's chief concern in supporting a VDT, and occupies most of his time and effort in managing displays.

Cursor addressing sequences differ widely, although a few schemes will support a large number of terminals. The programmer must decide whether to use a few such schemes supporting most terminals, or to devote more programming effort and support the remaining terminals. This manual describes the cursor addressing sequences used by a number of terminals. It is the programmer's responsibility to incorporate them into his programs.

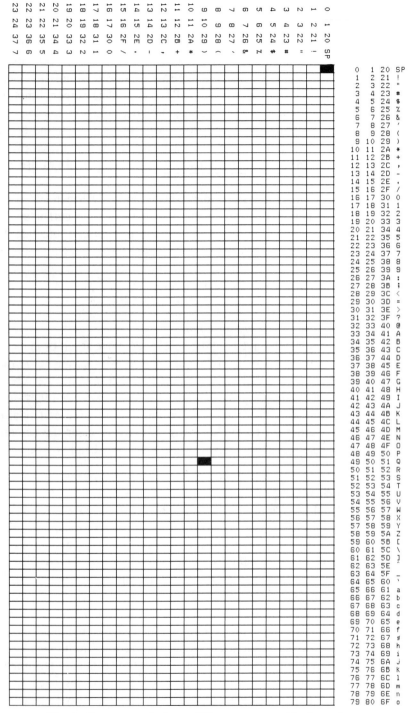

Fig. 2. Character equivalents of binary cursor positioning codes

The *lead-in sequence* is the character or group of characters which tells the terminal that the following data is to be used to position the cursor. The sequence is normally one or two characters in length.

Nearly all terminals use one of two forms for transmitting row and column information. These forms have many different names, varying among manufacturers, but are standardized for this manual.

Binary form

The *binary form* means that the row or column is expressed in binary notation and transmitted as a single-byte value. This single-byte value is frequently expressed as a character. For example, row 7 expressed in binary would be the ASCII bell code. Column 65 would be the ASCII character "A."

Terminals using the binary form almost always add an *offset* to the binary number. This offset is almost always 32 (20H). This has the effect of bringing the binary value into the printing ASCII range and eliminating the transmission of the ASCII control codes (00H–1FH). See figure 2.

It is here that the scheme used for numbering rows and columns becomes critical. Most manufacturers using the binary form begin numbering rows and columns with zero, referring to rows 0–23 and columns 0–79, rather than 1–24 and 1–80. Referring to figure 2 it is obvious that adding 20H to row 0 results in 20H, the correct character to be transmitted to designate row 0. However, a large number of manufacturers, while correctly giving 20H,20H as the coordinates for the top row, left column, gave erroneous coordinates (usually 2AH,52H) for the 10th row, 50th column. Figure 2 shows that the correct coordinates are 29H,51H.

This problem is common among terminal manufacturers and pro-grammers alike. There are well-known commercial programs which have failed to resolve this problem. If the numbering scheme begins with zero, then the 10th row is row 9, not row 10. The 50th column is column 49, not column 50. If the numbering scheme begins with one, then the 10th row is row 10, and the 50th column is column 50.

A number of manufacturers stated their numbering scheme as 1–24 and 1–80, but also stated the offset as 20H. When this was corrected and returned to them, a number of them still insisted that the correct offset was 20H. In these cases, the data sheets reflect the manufac-turer's insistence although this will almost certainly result in wrong cursor addressing sequences.

Wherever possible, however, this manual attempts to use the numbering scheme 1–24 and 1–80, and adjusts the offset to 1FH. Note that adding 1FH to row 1 gives the same result as adding 20H to row 0. It allows a more standard numbering scheme to be used, however, one that is compatible with almost all terminals using the ASCII numeral form discussed below.

Most VDT manuals contain a chart showing the characters to send the terminal to represent the row or column position. Few manuals explicitly state that these characters are obtained by adding an offset to the row or column position. In almost all terminals using the binary form the upper left position is designated by sending two spaces (20H,20H). Therefore, regardless of the method the programmer uses to refer to rows and columns, he must output these two spaces to position the cursor to this position.

Shown below are the sequences necessary to position the cursor to the two positions marked in figure 2 for representative terminals.

		Televideo Series	IBM 3101 & DEC VT52
Top row, left column	ASCII	ESC = SP SP	ESC Y SP SP
	HEX	1B 3D 20 20	1B 59 20 20
10th row, 50th column	ASCII	ESC =) Q	ESC Y) Q
	HEX	1B 3D 29 51	1B 59 29 51

Note that the only difference between the terminals is the second byte of the lead-in sequence. The method of referring to row and column positions is identical. This is true of a large number of terminals—while the lead-in sequence differs, the row and column values remain identical.

The following illustrates the method of arriving at the characters to be transmitted, assuming two different numbering schemes.

	Starting at zero			Starting at one		
	Actual Value	Add Offset	Output Value	Actual Value	Add Offset	Output Value
Top row	0	20H	20H	1	1FH	20H
Left column	0	20H	20H	1	1FH	20H
10th row	9	20H	29H	10	1FH	29H
50th column	49	20H	51H	50	1FH	51H

12

ASCII numeral form

The other principal method of transmitting row and column values is the *ASCII numeral form*. This method is simpler to understand and easier to read, but requires substantially more programming. Using this method, the row and column values are simply converted to ASCII numerals.

Some terminals might require that two bytes be transmitted for row and two for column, while others might allow variable-length numbers. For example, row 5 would be transmitted as 05 if two bytes were required, but just 5 if variable lengths were allowed. ANSI X3.64 allows variable lengths, and many ANSI terminals allow 132 columns, so row 5 might be transmitted as 5, 05, or 005, all with the same results. It is up to the programmer which method to use. If it is easier for the programmer to transmit a variable length of bytes, he may do so. However, if he wishes to transmit a fixed number (perhaps to "fill in the blanks" in a pre-reserved string) his only penalty will be the very small amount of time necessary to transmit the longer form.

No terminals in this manual show an offset when the ASCII numeral form is used. Almost all terminals using the ASCII numeral form begin numbering with one rather than zero. Therefore the 10th row is row 10 and the 50th column is column 50.

Since the row and column values might be differing lengths, terminals using the ASCII numeral form require a *separator sequence* and an *ending sequence* to separate the values and to designate the end of the entire cursor addressing sequence. This prevents confusion with data to be displayed as text or another control sequence. These sequences are typically one byte in length.

Shown below are the sequences necessary to position the cursor to the two positions marked in figure 2 for ANSI X3.64 terminals.

Top row, left column	ASCII	ESC [1 ; 1 H
	HEX	1B 5B 31 3B 31 48
10th row, 50th column	ASCII	ESC [1 0 ; 5 0 H
	HEX	1B 5B 31 30 3B 35 30 48

It is important to note that the ANSI X3.64 sequence to home the cursor is the cursor positioning sequence with no parameters, ESC [; H. This is equivalent to ESC [0 ; 0 H, which might lead the programmer to assume that the terminal begins numbering with zero instead of one. Experimentation with this notion, however, reveals that the sequences ESC [0 ; 0 H and ESC [1 ; 1 H are equivalent. The programmer should begin numbering with one rather than zero to avoid overlapping the first two rows.

Row or column first?

So far it has been assumed that the row is always transmitted before the column. While this is almost always the case, there are a small number of terminals that require the column value to be transmitted first, and at least one terminal series that allows either to be first (or either to be sent independently of the other). If the programmer desires to support as many terminals as possible he should allow his program to transmit either the row or column first, as required by the terminal being supported.

Delay after cursor positioning

Some terminals might require a slight delay after receiving a cursor positioning sequence in order to have time to respond and position the cursor. While most manufacturers either left this question blank or reported zero, some did specify a required delay. The programmer might wish to allow for a variable-length delay in his cursor positioning routine.

There are two basic methods of allowing this delay. The simplest is to transmit one or more nulls (00H) following the cursor positioning routine. This method has long been used following carriage returns on Teletype® and similar machines to allow time for the carriage to physically return to the left margin. Some VDTs however, might interpret these nulls as meaningful data and move the cursor or perform some other undesirable function.

The second method might be preferred if the VDT reacts unfavorably to nulls. This method requires putting the program into a "waste time loop" for a specified amount of time. This time should be variable so that the user can adjust it as necessary to fit his particular VDT, computer, modem or other communications line equipment, and other variables.

Note that even VDTs which state a required delay might not require an explicit delay routine. Quite often the time required by execution of instructions between the cursor positioning and writing of data will provide adequate delay, particularly if the program is written in a high-level language.

14

Scrolling

Since VDTs evolved as a direct replacement to the hard-copy Teletype® and similar machines, nearly all of them will scroll lines off the top as new ones are written on the bottom. This phenomenon is almost always overriden by the programmer who choses instead to use cursor addressing sequences to write data randomly on the screen. In text editing programs the programmer allows scrolling, but rigidly controls it using the same cursor addressing sequences.

However, there is one instance in which the programmer must pay close attention to the VDT's insistent desire to scroll. When a character is printed in the last column of a row the cursor will frequently return to the following line. While this might be irritating to look at, seeing the cursor jumping around the screen, it poses no problem as long as the programmer positions the cursor before writing the next character. When that row happens to be the bottom row, however, the screen might scroll unexpectedly when the rightmost column is printed.

On some terminals this may be controlled by switch or software selection. Controlling this phenomenon might have undesirable effects, however, on the terminal's scrolling for other applications, and the user might not want to change the terminal's configuration for a single program. A better solution might be to simply *never* write to the rightmost column of the bottom row. This is relatively simple for a program using a screen form, such as accounting, but might require more care in text-editing programs.

Carriage returns

A related problem is that of carriage returns (0DH) and line feeds (0AH). When sent to the terminal, these control characters normally do just what they say. A carriage return will return the cursor to the left column and may or may not line feed. A line feed will usually move the cursor down one row, and if it is the bottom row the terminal will probably scroll.

When sending control sequences, such as cursor addressing sequences, it is important that carriage return line feed sequences *not* be sent. Assembly language programmers should have no trouble with this, but BASIC and other high-level language programmers might find themselves wondering why their data is printing on row 5 column 1 when they specifically addressed row 4 column 50. The problem is that they unknowingly sent a carriage return line feed combination following their cursor addressing sequence.

This problem is avoided in BASIC by simply putting a semicolon after the cursor addressing sequence, for example:

```
100  PRINT CHR$(27)+"="+CHR$(4+31)+CHR$(50+31);
110  PRINT "ENTER YOUR NAME: ";
120  INPUT N$
```

The semicolon at the end of statement 100 is frequently left out. The result is that this statement is executed, then a carriage return linefeed sequence is sent, returning the cursor to the first column of the next row. The semicolon following statement 110 would not be necessary if an additional cursor addressing sequence were transmitted prior to statement 120.

The programmer must pay close attention to maintaining the cursor position. Another frequent mistake is transmitting CHR$(7) to ring the terminal's bell. If not followed by a semicolon (in BASIC) this single-character sequence will return the cursor to the first column of the next row, or scroll the entire screen if it is the right column of the bottom row.

Other high-level languages have similar methods of printing data without a carriage return line feed sequence.

Never hesitate to transmit the cursor addressing sequence even if you believe the cursor to be in the correct position. While the bell code (07H) should not move the cursor one space to the right, on some unusual terminals it might. Therefore, retransmitting the cursor addressing sequence following ringing the bell cannot hurt. The only penalty will be slightly larger program size and a very slight delay.

Cursor home

Most terminals have a unique *cursor home* sequence, designed to position the cursor at the top row, left column. If this sequence is not known then the programmer may simply send a cursor addressing sequence to position the cursor to row 0, column 0 or row 1, column 1, depending on his numbering scheme. Indeed, this method might be preferred, since the programmer can avoid asking the user to provide the cursor home sequence, simplifying VDT installation procedures.

Erasure

In addition to clearing the screen, a number of other erasures are permitted by many terminals. The programmer must use these erasures

16

carefully, however, as the results may not be what was expected. Despite attempts to standardize terminology on the data sheets, differences remain concerning erasures. For example, the data sheets contain an an erasure for the entire cursor line. Ideally, this erasure should fill the cursor line with blanks and leave the rest of the screen unchanged. Unfortunately, on some terminals this sequence might actually be a *delete line* command. This would delete the line and pull up all lines below, with disastrous effects if unexpected.

Some of the other erasures might also perform unexpectedly. The programmer might wish to use software routines to accomplish these desired erasures. For example, erase-entire-cursor-line may be performed by positioning the cursor to the left column of the line to be erased and printing a number of blanks corresponding to the width of the screen (normally 80). The programmer might also wish to allow the erase-entire-cursor-line sequence to be used optionally if the terminal supports it and it works as expected. It would be unwise, however, to assume this erasure to be standard on a large number of terminals and forego the software solution.

Video attributes

Many video display terminals and microcomputers now have *video attributes*. The most common attributes are *blinking, reverse video, underline, high intensity* and *half intensity*. With the exception of the standards of ANSI X3.64 terminals, there is a wide range of control code sequences used to obtain these attributes.

As with many other VDT features, there is a range of nomenclature concerning video attributes. High and half intensity, for example, mean different things to different terminal manufacturers. On some VDTs high intensity will be normal and half will be reduced, on others half will be normal and high enhanced, while still others might allow half, normal and high. Proceed with caution when using these attributes in combination.

Some terminals require a character position to be used for the attribute. To turn on blinking, for example, the character position before the blinking data is occupied by the code sequence that turns on blinking, and the character position following the blinking data is occupied by the code sequence that turns off blinking. Other terminals do not require such a character position, choosing instead to store the attribute as part of the displayed characters. This is of particular interest to the programmer. On a typical screen form used for

17

accounting, database, mailing list, etc., there will be pre-determined fields for the user to fill in. If these fields are to be highlighted with one or more attributes, it is relatively easy to allow the character position before and after the field for the attribute codes. In text editing applications, however, substantial problems arise. If the video attribute occupies a character position then that position appears in the middle of text as a blank. The user might be able to delete it as if it were a character, the cursor may or may not stop on it, and it is generally puzzling to the user. The programmer should therefore take great care in using video attributes, particularly in free-form screens, such as word processing or text-editing applications.

Some terminals and microcomputers, particularly those using memory-mapped video, use the high bit of each character to set the video attribute, rather than using specific code sequences before and after the highlighted data. These can cause problems for a programmer working in a high-level language, or other situations where non-ASCII characters are produced.

Cumulative attributes

In addition to the "standard" video attributes, many VDTs allow *cumulative* attributes. For example, a text-editing program might use underlining to accent a block of text. A block of text to be deleted might be in reverse video. When this underlined block is to be deleted it would then appear with underlining *and* reverse video. Another common combination is the use of reverse and blinking to flash error messages or warnings.

There are generally two ways of obtaining cumulative attributes. The simplest, although requiring more code to be transmitted, is to output the sequence for one attribute, then the sequence for the other. For example, assume ESC B turns on blinking and ESC U turns on underlining. Sending ESC B ESC U would then turn on blinking and underlining at the same time.

Not all VDTs allow such cumulative attributes, but instead have separate control sequences to turn on specific combinations. Continuing the above example, with ESC B as blinking, ESC U as underlining, blinking *and* underlining might be ESC X. ANSI X3.64 terminals allow either method (see ANSI X3.64 data sheet). Multiple attributes can be turned on one at a time until all desired attributes are in effect, or the programmer can use a specific sequence to turn on all desired attributes.

Turning off attributes

Attributes may have to be turned off individually or all at once. There may be a different code to turn of blinking, for example, than to turn off underlining. There may be one code sequence to turn off all attributes. If this is the case and blinking and underlining are both on, then this one sequence would turn both off, without allowing just one to be turned off.

Video attributes can be highly machine-specific and the programmer should give careful consideration to their use before including them in a program designed for wide distribution on a variety of VDTs.

Cursor control keys

VDT users will invariably push the "arrow" keys and expect the cursor to move. The result, unfortunately, can sometimes be disastrous. The cursor key might output a code sequence that the programmer has used for some other purpose. Many programs on the market today do not support the VDT's cursor keys.

WordStar®, a popular word processing program, and one of the first microcomputer programs to achieve wide distribution, was designed to run on as many terminals as possible, including those without cursor keys. The programmer elected to use control codes (those ASCII codes lying between 00H and 1FH), to move the cursor. The keys selected were control-S, control-E, control-D, and control-X, chosen because they form a diamond pattern on the keyboard. These same keys were used by dBase II®, a widely-distributed database management program, and something of a standard was born. A number of VDTs now use these codes for cursor control (the "up arrow" key outputs a control-E, etc.).

Another popular configuration is the control-H, J, K, L sequence (left, down, up, right), widely used on VDTs, but not supported by many programs.

The ANSI X3.64 standard uses escape sequences rather than control codes. The Escape [precedes the cursor key sequence, as it does in all ANSI X3.64 sequences. The letters A, B, C and D follow the lead-in sequence to produce up, down, right and left, respectively. A number of other terminals use the same sequences but drop the left bracket ([).

Problems in interpreting cursor control keys

Multiple-character cursor control keys can cause problems for the programmer. Unlike cursor addressing, video attributes, etc. which are

19

sent by the program *to* the VDT, cursor control keys send sequences *from* the VDT *to* the computer. A VDT's job is to receive and interpret data sent by the computer, and it is capable of doing it so fast that "handshaking" is often not required. The computer must respond to the terminal's input, and in many instances, such as a multi-user or multi-tasking system, it must respond to many other devices (terminals and printers) simultaneously.

There are two general areas of concern regarding this problem. The first is with the program itself. When receiving single-byte data, such as a control-E for cursor up, there is no timing problem, as the single-byte code is no different from any other ASCII code. If the operator strikes another control-E while the program is responding to the last, the worst that can happen is that it will be ignored, losing one cursor movement.

When the cursor control key outputs more than one byte there is substantial room for error. The program must recognize the lead-in sequence, normally an escape sequence, then stand ready to respond to the following character to designate direction. If the program has recognized the lead-in but is occupied with something else when the direction byte is received, then the program fails and the result is generally that the direction byte (usually A, B, C or D) is displayed on the VDT. If the operator holds down or repeats the cursor key a similar problem will result when the programmer's input buffer overflows.

Some VDTs might send the cursor control sequences too fast for the program to respond. If the input routine is overly long and complex it might not be fast enough to recognize and respond to every byte in the cursor control sequence. Typing the sequence one byte at a time might properly move the cursor, while depressing the cursor-up key might not work because the VDT sends the bytes faster than the input routine can handle them.

The second problem area is with the operating system. Regardless of how efficient and "bullet-proof" the applications program is, it still must operate under the control of the operating system. Even "standard" operating systems, such as CP/M®, have modifications made to them by the vendor which affect input and output. A program which properly recognizes the cursor control keys without fail, under all conditions, on one computer, might not recognize the keys at all on a similar computer running the same operating system. On some systems the program will recognize the cursor control keys most of the time, but will occasionally miss one, for no apparent reason.

The programmer should use considerable care in writing input routines to accept cursor control keys and should be prepared for a flood of complaints when the keys do not function as expected.

ANSI X3.64 standard

Many current-model VDTs comply to the ANSI X3.64 standard. This is a standard published by the American National Standards Institute which describes control sequences to be used by VDTs. The standard has gained acceptance with minicomputer companies, but remains largely unsupported by microcomputer companies and programs. If a program supports this standard it should run without modification on any VDT which conforms to the standard. The complete text of the standard may be obtained from the American National Standards Institute, Inc., 1430 Broadway, New York, New York 10018.

Data Sheets

Numeric Data

Number of rows and columns (items 3 and 4), top row (item 5), and left column (item 6) are stated in decimal notation. Delay times (item 16, 18–23) are stated in decimal notation and refer to milliseconds of delay. *All other numeric values are hexadecimal.*

Code Sequences

Code sequences are displayed in two lines. The top line is the ASCII graphic character, the control sequence (caret "^" followed by character), or the two- or three-letter representation of the ASCII control characters. See Appendix 1 for ASCII character set. Codes in the range 80H–FFH are not displayed on the first line since they are outside the ASCII character set.

The second line of the code sequence display is shown in hexadecimal notation.

Manufacturer Data

1. *Manufacturer.* This is normally the actual manufacturer of the terminal or microcomputer, but it could be an OEM selling the terminal under a brand name other than the original manufacturer, or a software house selling an operating system which makes the terminal or microcomputer operate in a manner different from its original manufacturer.

2. *Terminal.* One or more terminals may be listed. Where multiple terminals are listed, all must share the code structure shown on the data sheet, although they may have differing features such as screen size and color, character generators, auxiliary ports, keyboard configuration, set-up screens, etc. Manufacturers may group terminals or list them individually. Some manufacturers submitted multiple data sheets for a single terminal, showing code structures for various emulation modes.

Screen Layout

3. *Number of rows.* Rows are horizontal rows numbered from top to bottom. This item refers to the actual number of rows available to the user, exclusive of any status lines. A number of manufacturers included the status line in this count, and many status lines are available to the user, although they normally require special addressing.

A value here of 25 should be considered with caution, since it may include a status row not accessible without special addressing. Most terminals have 24 rows, and the 25th status row cannot be addressed like the other rows.

4. *Number of columns.* Columns are vertical columns numbered from left to right. The most common number of columns is 80, although many terminals allow 132 by software or hardware selection. In most cases a terminal allowing 132 columns is an 80-column terminal by default, and requires user or program action to convert to a 132-column terminal.

5. *Top row.* Some terminals, primarily those using binary cursor addressing (item 10), start numbering from the top row with row zero. Some terminals, primarily those using the ANSI X3.64 standard cursor addressing, start numbering from the top row with row one. For this manual, wherever possible, this value has been standardized as one by adjusting the offset (item 11) to be added.

6. *Left column.* Some terminals, primarily those using the binary cursor addressing form (item 10), start numbering from the left column with column zero. Some terminals, primarily those using the ANSI X3.64 standard cursor addressing form, start numbering from the left column with column one. For this manual, wherever possible, this value has been standardized as one by adjusting the offset (item 11) to be added.

7. *Printing in bottom right cause scroll?* When a character is printed in the rightmost column of the bottom row (normally row 24, column 80), some terminals will cause the screen to scroll. The top row will be lost and a blank row will be inserted as the bottom row. On some terminals, this does not occur—the screen remains the same. On some terminals this is controlled by switch or software selection. In this case this item is PROG or programmable. Many manufacturers left this item blank or did not understand the item. It is therefore good programming practice to consider that all terminals will scroll when the rightmost column of the bottom row is printed.

Cursor addressing

8. *Lead-in sequence.* This is the sequence of code that precedes the row and column values necessary to position the cursor. This is frequently an escape sequence.

9. *Row or column first.* Most terminals send the row value first, although some send column value first. A small number of terminals allow either to be sent first due to their unique addressing scheme. These terminals have expanded cursor addressing discussion in Notes.

10. *Numeric form of row and column.* The most common forms are binary and variable-length ASCII. Also acceptable are 2-byte ASCII and 3-byte ASCII. Binary means that the row and column values are converted into binary form, frequently with an added offset (item 11), and transmitted as a single byte of binary data. ASCII form means that the row and column values are converted into ASCII numerals. ANSI standard terminals allow one, two or three ASCII digits to be sent. Leading zeros are optional. Some terminals might require that two or three ASCII digits be sent, in which case the leading zeros would be required.

11. *Add offset to.* This value is almost always the same for both row and column, although some terminals have unusual cursor addressing schemes. This is an amount which is added to the row or column value before being transmitted. It is almost always added on terminals using binary form and no terminal in this manual uses an offset for ASCII form.

The most common offset is 20H (for terminals that start row and column numbering with zero), although to maintain consistency, this has been adjusted to 1FH, resulting in 20H as the binary value transmitted to position the cursor at the top row and left column. Note that this brings all row and column values into the printing ASCII character range, avoiding problems of transmitting control characters which might cause unexpected results particularly when communicating over a modem or other communications link.

12. *Separator sequence.* This is the sequence which separates row and column values. When using binary form for row and column values, this is not necessary and normally not used since the values occupy one byte each. In variable-length ASCII form, however, row and column values may occupy from one to three bytes each and it is necessary to separate them.

13. *End sequence.* This is necessary for variable-length ASCII form to distinguish the row and column values from text.

14. *Cursor to top row, left column.* This is a sample cursor addressing sequence showing how the elements are combined to actually position the cursor. The top row, left column are used here to further verify what notation the manufacturer uses to number rows and columns. In binary form, the most common values for this sequence are 20H for both row and column. For ANSI X3.64 terminals and most other terminals using ASCII form, the most common values here are one for both row and column.

15. *Cursor to 10th row, 50th column.* This is a another example designed to further verify the row and column numbering scheme. A large number of manufacturers reported erroneous values here, although their manuals showed the correct values. Many programmers fall into the same trap.

The 10th row is row 10 only if the top row is row one. The 10th row is row nine if the top row is row zero.

The 50th column is column 50 only if the left column is column one. The 50th column is column 49 if the left column if column zero.

This is discussed in more detail in the cursor positioning discussion elsewhere in this manual.

16. *Delay after positioning.* Some terminals require time to interpret the sequence and position the cursor following a cursor positioning sequence. This is stated here in milliseconds of delay. Most manufacturers left this blank or reported zero, although a few reported a delay time.

17. *Cursor home.* Most terminals have a sequence which will position the cursor to the home position. On terminals not having such a sequence, the sequence in item 14 will accomplish the same thing. Some terminals might allow ''home'' to be defined as somewhere other than the upper left corner.

Erasure

18. *Entire screen.* Some terminals clear the entire screen and home the cursor. Some clear the screen and leave the cursor where it was. Some terminals have only the capability to clear to end of screen, in which case this sequence might be a combination of cursor home and clear-to-end-of-screen.

19. *Cursor to end of screen.* This sequence clears from the cursor to the end of screen without moving the cursor.

20. *Beginning of screen to cursor.* This sequence clears from the beginning of the screen to the cursor without moving the cursor.

21. *Cursor to end of line.* This sequence clears from the cursor to the end of line (row) without moving the cursor.

22. *Beginning of line to cursor.* This sequence clears from the beginning of the line (row) to the cursor without moving the cursor.

23. *Entire cursor line.* This sequence clears the entire line (row) on which the cursor is located. As in clear screen, the cursor may or may not move to the beginning of the line (row). Some terminals do not have this function, and may accomplish it with a carriage return (without a line feed), then clear to end of line.

Note that this sequence is *not* the same as delete line. A delete line normally deletes the cursor line, then pulls up lines below the cursor to fill in the deleted line. The clear-cursor-line should erase the line and leave a blank line.

Delay. The required delay, in milliseconds, is shown for the selected erasure. This is the time the host should wait after the erasure before sending additional data or commands.

Video Attributes

24.–28. These are the sequences to turn on the specified attribute and to turn it off (or return to normal video). The off sequence is frequently the same for all attributes, and will usually be the same as item 31.

29. *Attributes occupy position.* On some terminals video attributes will occupy a character position to the exclusion of other data. These terminals require the programmer to allow for a blank character before and after the highlighted text.

30. *Attributes cumulative.* Many terminals allow multiple attributes to be in effect at one time. The simplest way to accomplish this, although requiring longer strings of code, is to turn on one attribute, then turn on another. For example, if ESC B turns on blinking and ESC U turns on underlining, then ESC B ESC U would turn on blinking and underlining at the same time. This concept works on ANSI X3.64 terminals although there is a shorter notation used.

Many terminals have completely separate codes for turning on multiple attributes. These are listed in Notes when provided.

31. *All attributes off.* This turns off all video attributes and returns to normal video.

Cursor Control (Arrow) Keys

32. *Cursor up.* The code sequence generated by the terminal and sent to the host when the Cursor Up (Up Arrow) key is depressed. This

26

same sequence sent by the host to the terminal will normally result in movement of the cursor up one row.

33. *Cursor down.* The code sequence generated by the terminal and sent to the host when the Cursor Down (Down Arrow) key is depressed. This same sequence sent by the host to the terminal will normally result in movement of the cursor down one row.

34. *Cursor right.* The code sequence generated by the terminal and sent to the host when the Cursor Right (Right Arrow) key is depressed. This same sequence sent by the host to the terminal will normally result in movement of the cursor right one column.

35. *Cursor left.* The code sequence generated by the terminal and sent to the host when the Cursor Left (Left Arrow) key is depressed. This same sequence sent by the host to the terminal will normally result in movement of the cursor left one column.

Character Set

36. *Full upper and lower ASCII.* Some terminals do not display the entire ASCII character set. If the answer to this item is NO, then exceptions should be listed in Notes.

37. *Generate all control codes.* Some terminals are not capable of generating all ASCII control codes (01H–1FH). If the answer to this item is NO, then exceptions should be listed in Notes.

38. *Bell or tone sequence.* Nearly all terminals produce a bell or electronic tone on receipt of a BEL (07H) code from the host. If the terminal recognizes a different sequence it is shown here.

Emulation

39. *Conform to ANSI X3.64?* If the terminal conforms to the ANSI X3.64 standard, the answer to this item should be YES. Note that many terminals have multiple modes, one of which might be ANSI X3.64. A manufacturer might answer YES to this item although the codes shown are not ANSI X3.64 compliant. In this case it is assumed that the ANSI mode is used to obtain ANSI X3.64-compliant operation.

40. *Terminals emulated.* Some terminals have a ''native'' mode in addition to emulating other terminals. Some terminals have no native mode and *must* emulate another terminal. Generally, the listed terminals emulated are in addition to the control codes shown on the data sheet.

41. *Information provided by.* If the manufacturer provided the information and/or approved the proofs, the information was provided by the MANUFACTURER. If the publisher obtained the information without the aid of the manufacturer the information was provided by the PUBLISHER. In the case of a dealer or user other than the publisher, the information was provided by a THIRD PARTY. OEMs selling terminals under private label are considered to be the MANUFACTURER. Software houses providing operating systems (such as CP/M® for the TRS-80®) are considered to be the MANUFACTURER of the software, but not the terminal or microcomputer.

42. *Program Function Keys.* Some terminals have program function keys which generate one or more characters. The codes produced by these keys are shown. Some terminals have programmable function keys which may be programmed by the user. If these keys have default or standard sequences, these are shown, although they may be changed by the user. There is space for only 16 keys, since this covers most terminals. Some terminals allow more function keys and these are usually described in Notes.

Notes

A numbered note refers to the item of the same number. For example, on many terminals which allow 80 or 132 columns, item 4 has a value of 80 and Note 4 mentions that 132 is optional. An unnumbered note is of general interest. Every effort was made to accommodate all terminal features within strict guidelines, but many terminals required additional explanation.

```
--------------------------------------------------------------------------
  1. Manufacturer:                    Altos Computer Systems
  2. Terminal:                        Altos II Terminal
--------------------------------------------------------------------------
```

SCREEN LAYOUT   VIDEO ATTRIBUTES
  3. Number of rows: 25   ON   OFF
  4. Number of columns: 80   24. Blinking:
  5. Top Row: 1   ESC [5   m   ESC [m
  6. Left Column: 1   1B 5B 35 6D   1B 5B 6D
  7. Printing in bottom right   25. Reverse video:
     cause scroll?   PROG   ESC [7   m   ESC [m
                                       1B 5B 37 6D   1B 5B 6D
CURSOR ADDRESSING   26. Underline:
  8. Lead-in sequence: ESC [4   m   ESC [m
            ESC [1B 5B 34 6D   1B 5B 6D
            1B 5B   27. High intensity:
  9. Row or column first: ROW   ESC [1   m   ESC [m
 10. Numeric form of row and column: 1B 5B 31 6D   1B 5B 6D
     VARIABLE-LENGTH ASCII   28. Half intensity:
 11. Add offset to: Row: 0
                          Col: 0
 12. Separator sequence: 29. Attributes occupy position: NO
            ;   30. Attributes cumulative: YES
            3B   31. All attributes off:
 13. End sequence: ESC [m
            H   1B 5B 6D
            48
 14. Cursor to top row, left column: CURSOR CONTROL KEYS
 ESC [1   ;   1   H   32. Cursor up:
 1B 5B 31 3B 31 48   ESC [A
 15. 10th Row, 50th Column: 1B 5B 41
 ESC [1   0   ;   5   0   H   33. Cursor down:
 1B 5B 31 30 3B 35 30 48   ESC [B
 16. Delay after positioning: 0   1B 5B 42
 17. Cursor home: 34. Cursor right:
            ESC [H   ESC [C
            1B 5B 48   1B 5B 43
                                      35. Cursor left:
ERASURE   DELAY   ESC [D
 18. Entire screen: 1B 5B 44
         ESC [2   J   0
         1B 5B 32 4A   CHARACTER SET
 19. Cursor to end of screen: 36. Full upper and lower ASCII: YES
         ESC [0   J   0   37. Generate all control codes: YES
         1B 5B 30 4A   38. Bell or tone sequence:
 20. Beginning of screen to cursor: ^G
         ESC [1   J   0   07
         1B 5B 31 4A
 21. Cursor to end of line: EMULATION
         ESC [0   K   0   39. Conform to ANSI X3.64?   YES
         1B 5B 30 4B   40. Terminals Emulated:
 22. Beginning of line to cursor:
         ESC [1   K   0
         1B 5B 31 4B
 23. Entire cursor line:
         ESC [2   K   0
         1B 5B 32 4B
```

CONTINUED ====>
```

41. Information provided by:
    MANUFACTURER

42. PROGRAM FUNCTION KEYS   NOTES
  1.   3. Optionally 40.
                                   4. Optionally 132.
                                 42. 16/32 programmable function keys.

  2.

  3.

  4.

  5.

  6.

  7.

  8.

  9.

 10.

 11.

 12.

 13.

 14.

 15.

 16.

```
--------------------------------------------------------------------------------
  1. Manufacturer:                         Ann Arbor Terminals
  2. Terminal:                             Ambassador
--------------------------------------------------------------------------------
```

SCREEN LAYOUT
3. Number of rows: 60
4. Number of columns: 80
5. Top Row: 1
6. Left Column: 1
7. Printing in bottom right
   cause scroll?   PROG

CURSOR ADDRESSING
8. Lead-in sequence:
            ESC [
            1B 5B
9. Row or column first: ROW
10. Numeric form of row and column:
    VARIABLE-LENGTH ASCII
11. Add offset to: Row: 0
                            Col: 0
12. Separator sequence:
            ;
            3B
13. End sequence:
            H
            48
14. Cursor to top row, left column:
ESC [1   ;   1   H
1B 5B   31   3B   31   48
15. 10th Row, 50th Column:
ESC [1   0   ;   5   0   H
1B 5B   31   30   3B   35   30   48
16. Delay after positioning: 0
17. Cursor home:
            ESC [H
            1B 5B   48

ERASURE   DELAY
18. Entire screen:
       ESC [2   J   156
       1B 5B   32   4A
19. Cursor to end of screen:
       ESC [0   J   0
       1B 5B   30   4A
20. Beginning of screen to cursor:
       ESC [1   J   0
       1B 5B   31   4A
21. Cursor to end of line:
       ESC [0   K   0
       1B 5B   30   4B
22. Beginning of line to cursor:
       ESC [1   K   0
       1B 5B   31   4B
23. Entire cursor line:
       ESC [2   K   5
       1B 5B   32   4B

VIDEO ATTRIBUTES
          ON   OFF
24. Blinking:
    ESC [5   m   ESC [m
    1B 5B   35   6D   1B 5B   6D
25. Reverse video:
    ESC [7   m   ESC [m
    1B 5B   37   6D   1B 5B   6D
26. Underline:
    ESC [4   m   ESC [m
    1B 5B   34   6D   1B 5B   6D
27. High intensity:
    ESC [1   m   ESC [m
    1B 5B   31   6D   1B 5B   6D
28. Half intensity:

29. Attributes occupy position: NO
30. Attributes cumulative: YES
31. All attributes off:
            ESC [m
            1B 5B   6D

CURSOR CONTROL KEYS
32. Cursor up:
            ESC [A
            1B 5B   41
33. Cursor down:
            ESC [B
            1B 5B   42
34. Cursor right:
            ESC [C
            1B 5B   43
35. Cursor left:
            ESC [D
            1B 5B   44

CHARACTER SET
36. Full upper and lower ASCII: YES
37. Generate all control codes: YES
38. Bell or tone sequence:
            ^G
            07

EMULATION
39. Conform to ANSI X3.64?   YES
40. Terminals Emulated:

CONTINUED ====>

Manufacturer: Ann Arbor Terminals
Terminal: Ambassador

41. Information provided by:
    MANUFACTURER

42. PROGRAM FUNCTION KEYS   NOTES
   1.   30. Blinking and reverse video:
                                     ESC [5 ; 7 m
                                 36. DEC mode option gives graphics
   2.   symbols.
                                 42. 12 programmable function keys.
                                     Total of 36 keys on 60 levels
   3.   are user-programmable.

   4.

   5.

   6.

   7.

   8.

   9.

  10.

  11.

  12.

  13.

  14.

  15.

  16.

----
1. Manufacturer: Ann Arbor Terminals
2. Terminal: Genie

SCREEN LAYOUT   VIDEO ATTRIBUTES
3. Number of rows: 30   ON   OFF
4. Number of columns: 80   24. Blinking:
5. Top Row: 1   ESC [5   m   ESC [m
6. Left Column: 1   1B   5B   35   6D   1B   5B   6D
7. Printing in bottom right   25. Reverse video:
   cause scroll?   PROG   ESC [7   m   ESC [m
                                       1B   5B   37   6D   1B   5B   6D
CURSOR ADDRESSING   26. Underline:
8. Lead-in sequence: ESC [4   m   ESC [m
           ESC [1B   5B   34   6D   1B   5B   6D
           1B   5B   27. High intensity:
9. Row or column first: ROW   ESC [1   m   ESC [m
10. Numeric form of row and column: 1B   5B   31   6D   1B   5B   6D
    VARIABLE-LENGTH ASCII   28. Half intensity:
11. Add offset to: Row: 0
                          Col: 0
12. Separator sequence: 29. Attributes occupy position: NO
           ;   30. Attributes cumulative: YES
           3B   31. All attributes off:
13. End sequence: ESC [m
           H   1B   5B   6D
           48
14. Cursor to top row, left column: CURSOR CONTROL KEYS
ESC [1   ;   1   H   32. Cursor up:
1B   5B   31   3B   31   48   ESC [A
15. 10th Row, 50th Column: 1B   5B   41
ESC [1   0   ;   5   0   H   33. Cursor down:
1B   5B   31   30   3B   35   30   48   ESC [B
16. Delay after positioning: 0   1B   5B   42
17. Cursor home: 34. Cursor right:
           ESC [H   ESC [C
           1B   5B   48   1B   5B   43
                                       35. Cursor left:
ERASURE   DELAY   ESC [D
18. Entire screen: 1B   5B   44
        ESC [2   J   156
        1B   5B   32   4A   CHARACTER SET
19. Cursor to end of screen: 36. Full upper and lower ASCII: YES
        ESC [0   J   0   37. Generate all control codes: YES
        1B   5B   30   4A   38. Bell or tone sequence:
20. Beginning of screen to cursor: ^G
        ESC [1   J   0   07
        1B   5B   31   4A
21. Cursor to end of line: EMULATION
        ESC [0   K   0   39. Conform to ANSI X3.64?   YES
        1B   5B   30   4B   40. Terminals Emulated:
22. Beginning of line to cursor:
        ESC [1   K   0
        1B   5B   31   4B
23. Entire cursor line:
        ESC [2   K   5
        1B   5B   32   4B

CONTINUED ====>

Manufacturer: Ann Arbor Terminals
Terminal: Genie

41. Information provided by:
    MANUFACTURER

42. PROGRAM FUNCTION KEYS   NOTES
    1.   30. Blinking and reverse video:
                                       ESC [5 ; 7 m
                                   36. DEC mode option gives graphics
    2.   symbols.
                                   42. 12 programmable function keys.
                                       Total of 26 keys on 36 levels
    3.   are user-programmable.

    4.

    5.

    6.

    7.

    8.

    9.

    10.

    11.

    12.

    13.

    14.

    15.

    16.

----

1. Manufacturer:	Ann Arbor Terminals
2. Terminal:	Genie+Plus

SCREEN LAYOUT
3. Number of rows: 60
4. Number of columns: 80
5. Top Row: 1
6. Left Column: 1
7. Printing in bottom right
   cause scroll?   PROG

CURSOR ADDRESSING
8. Lead-in sequence:
                ESC [
                1B 5B
9. Row or column first: ROW
10. Numeric form of row and column:
    VARIABLE-LENGTH ASCII
11. Add offset to: Row: 0
                            Col: 0
12. Separator sequence:
                ;
                3B
13. End sequence:
                H
                48
14. Cursor to top row, left column:
ESC [1   ;   1   H
1B 5B   31   3B   31   48
15. 10th Row, 50th Column:
ESC [1   0   ;   5   0   H
1B 5B   31   30   3B   35   30   48
16. Delay after positioning: 0
17. Cursor home:
                ESC [H
                1B 5B   48

ERASURE   DELAY
18. Entire screen:
        ESC [2   J   156
        1B 5B   32   4A
19. Cursor to end of screen:
        ESC [0   J   0
        1B 5B   30   4A
20. Beginning of screen to cursor:
        ESC [1   J   0
        1B 5B   31   4A
21. Cursor to end of line:
        ESC [0   K   0
        1B 5B   30   4B
22. Beginning of line to cursor:
        ESC [1   K   0
        1B 5B   31   4B
23. Entire cursor line:
        ESC [2   K   5
        1B 5B   32   4B

VIDEO ATTRIBUTES
          ON   OFF
24. Blinking:
ESC [5   m   ESC [m
1B 5B   35   6D   1B 5B   6D
25. Reverse video:
ESC [7   m   ESC [m
1B 5B   37   6D   1B 5B   6D
26. Underline:
ESC [4   m   ESC [m
1B 5B   34   6D   1B 5B   6D
27. High intensity:
ESC [1   m   ESC [m
1B 5B   31   6D   1B 5B   6D
28. Half intensity:

29. Attributes occupy position: NO
30. Attributes cumulative: YES
31. All attributes off:
                ESC [m
                1B 5B   6D

CURSOR CONTROL KEYS
32. Cursor up:
                ESC [A
                1B 5B   41
33. Cursor down:
                ESC [B
                1B 5B   42
34. Cursor right:
                ESC [C
                1B 5B   43
35. Cursor left:
                ESC [D
                1B 5B   44

CHARACTER SET
36. Full upper and lower ASCII: YES
37. Generate all control codes: YES
38. Bell or tone sequence:
                ^G
                07

EMULATION
39. Conform to ANSI X3.64?   YES
40. Terminals Emulated:

CONTINUED ====>

```
--------------------------------------------------------------------
      Manufacturer:                    Ann Arbor Terminals
      Terminal:                        Genie+Plus
--------------------------------------------------------------------
```

41. Information provided by:
    MANUFACTURER

42. PROGRAM FUNCTION KEYS   NOTES
    1.   30. Blinking and reverse video:
                                       ESC [5 ; 7 m
                                   36. DEC mode option gives graphics
    2.   symbols.
                                   42. 12 programmable function keys.
                                       Total of 36 keys on 60 levels
    3.   are user-programmable.

    4.

    5.

    6.

    7.

    8.

    9.

   10.

   11.

   12.

   13.

   14.

   15.

   16.

```
--------------------------------------------------------------------------
 1. Manufacturer:                        Ann Arbor Terminals
 2. Terminal:                            Guru (TM)
--------------------------------------------------------------------------

SCREEN LAYOUT                            VIDEO ATTRIBUTES
 3. Number of rows:              66           ON                    OFF
 4. Number of columns:          170     24. Blinking:
 5. Top Row:                     1      ESC [    5    m      ESC [     m
 6. Left Column:                 1      1B   5B  35   6D     1B   5B  6D
 7. Printing in bottom right            25. Reverse video:
    cause scroll?               PROG    ESC [    7    m      ESC [     m
                                        1B   5B  37   6D     1B   5B  6D
CURSOR ADDRESSING                       26. Underline:
 8. Lead-in sequence:                   ESC [    4    m      ESC [     m
              ESC [                     1B   5B  34   6D     1B   5B  6D
              1B   5B                   27. High intensity:
 9. Row or column first:      ROW       ESC [    1    m      ESC [     m
10. Numeric form of row and column:     1B   5B  31   6D     1B   5B  6D
    VARIABLE-LENGTH ASCII               28. Half intensity:
11. Add offset to:        Row:   0
                          Col:   0
12. Separator sequence:                 29. Attributes occupy position: NO
              ;                         30. Attributes cumulative:      YES
              3B                        31. All attributes off:
13. End sequence:                                    ESC [     m
              H                                      1B   5B  6D
              48
14. Cursor to top row, left column:     CURSOR CONTROL KEYS
ESC [    1    ;    1    H                32. Cursor up:
1B   5B  31   3B   31   48                            ESC [     A
15. 10th Row, 50th Column:                           1B   5B  41
ESC [    1    0    ;    5    0    H      33. Cursor down:
1B   5B  31   30   3B   35   30   48                  ESC [     B
16. Delay after positioning:     0                   1B   5B  42
17. Cursor home:                        34. Cursor right:
              ESC [    H                             ESC [     C
              1B   5B  48                            1B   5B  43
                                        35. Cursor left:
ERASURE                       DELAY                  ESC [     D
18. Entire screen:                                   1B   5B  44
         ESC [    2    J          210
         1B   5B  32   4A               CHARACTER SET
19. Cursor to end of screen:            36. Full upper and lower ASCII: YES
         ESC [    0    J          0     37. Generate all control codes: YES
         1B   5B  30   4A               38. Bell or tone sequence:
20. Beginning of screen to cursor:                   ^G
         ESC [    1    J          0                  07
         1B   5B  31   4A
21. Cursor to end of line:              EMULATION
         ESC [    0    K          0     39. Conform to ANSI X3.64?      YES
         1B   5B  30   4B               40. Terminals Emulated:
22. Beginning of line to cursor:
         ESC [    1    K          0
         1B   5B  31   4B
23. Entire cursor line:
         ESC [    2    K          6
         1B   5B  32   4B
```

CONTINUED ====>

41. Information provided by:
    MANUFACTURER

42. PROGRAM FUNCTION KEYS   NOTES
    1.   30. Blinking and reverse video:
                                      ESC [5 ; 7 m
                              36. DEC mode option gives graphics
    2.   symbols.
                              42. 12 programmable function keys.
                                      Total of 36 keys on 60 levels
    3.   are user-programmable.

    4.

    5.

    6.

    7.

    8.

    9.

   10.

   11.

   12.

   13.

   14.

   15.

   16.

```
--------------------------------------------------------------------------------
   1. Manufacturer:                     ANSI
   2. Terminal:                         ANSI
--------------------------------------------------------------------------------


SCREEN LAYOUT                           VIDEO ATTRIBUTES
   3. Number of rows:        24               ON                    OFF
   4. Number of columns:     80         24. Blinking:
   5. Top Row:                1         ESC [   5    m         ESC [     m
   6. Left Column:            1         1B  5B  35  6D         1B  5B  6D
   7. Printing in bottom right          25. Reverse video:
      cause scroll?          PROG       ESC [   7    m         ESC [     m
                                        1B  5B  37  6D         1B  5B  6D
CURSOR ADDRESSING                       26. Underline:
   8. Lead-in sequence:                 ESC [   4    m         ESC [     m
            ESC [                       1B  5B  34  6D         1B  5B  6D
            1B  5B                      27. High intensity:
   9. Row or column first:     ROW      ESC [   1    m         ESC [     m
  10. Numeric form of row and column:   1B  5B  31  6D         1B  5B  6D
      VARIABLE-LENGTH ASCII             28. Half intensity:
  11. Add offset to:        Row:   0
                            Col:   0
  12. Separator sequence:               29. Attributes occupy position: NO
            ;                           30. Attributes cumulative:      YES
            3B                          31. All attributes off:
  13. End sequence:                              ESC [     m
            H                                    1B  5B  6D
            48
  14. Cursor to top row, left column:   CURSOR CONTROL KEYS
  ESC [   1   ;   1   H                 32. Cursor up:
  1B  5B  31  3B  31  48                          ESC [     A
  15. 10th Row, 50th Column:                      1B  5B  41
  ESC [   1   0   ;   5   0   H         33. Cursor down:
  1B  5B  31  30  3B  35  30  48                  ESC [     B
  16. Delay after positioning:    0               1B  5B  42
  17. Cursor home:                      34. Cursor right:
            ESC [   H                            ESC [     C
            1B  5B  48                           1B  5B  43
                                        35. Cursor left:
ERASURE                      DELAY               ESC [     D
  18. Entire screen:                             1B  5B  44
            ESC [   2   J         0
            1B  5B  32  4A              CHARACTER SET
  19. Cursor to end of screen:          36. Full upper and lower ASCII: YES
            ESC [   J             0     37. Generate all control codes: YES
            1B  5B  4A                  38. Bell or tone sequence:
  20. Beginning of screen to cursor:              ^G
            ESC [   1   J         0               07
            1B  5B  31  4A
  21. Cursor to end of line:            EMULATION
            ESC [   K             0     39. Conform to ANSI X3.64?     YES
            1B  5B  4B                  40. Terminals Emulated:
  22. Beginning of line to cursor:
            ESC [   1   K         0
            1B  5B  31  4B
  23. Entire cursor line:
            ESC [   2   K         0
            1B  5B  32  4B
```

CONTINUED ====>

```
-----------------------------------------------------------------------
     Manufacturer:                    ANSI
     Terminal:                        ANSI
-----------------------------------------------------------------------

41. Information provided by:
    MANUFACTURER

42. PROGRAM FUNCTION KEYS          NOTES
  1.


  2.


  3.


  4.


  5.


  6.


  7.


  8.


  9.

 10.

 11.

 12.

 13.

 14.

 15.

 16.
```

```
--------------------------------------------------------------------------
1. Manufacturer:                          Beehive International
2. Terminal:                              ATL 008
--------------------------------------------------------------------------
```

SCREEN LAYOUT   VIDEO ATTRIBUTES
3. Number of rows: 24   ON   OFF
4. Number of columns: 80   24. Blinking:
5. Top Row: 1   ESC [5   m   ESC [m
6. Left Column: 1   1B 5B 35 6D   1B 5B 6D
7. Printing in bottom right   25. Reverse video:
   cause scroll?   PROG   ESC [7   m   ESC [m
                                       1B 5B 37 6D   1B 5B 6D
CURSOR ADDRESSING   26. Underline:
8. Lead-in sequence: ESC [4   m   ESC [m
          ESC [1B 5B 34 6D   1B 5B 6D
          1B 5B   27. High intensity:
9. Row or column first: ROW   ESC [1   m   ESC [m
10. Numeric form of row and column: 1B 5B 31 6D   1B 5B 6D
    VARIABLE-LENGTH ASCII   28. Half intensity:
11. Add offset to: Row: 0   ESC [2   m   ESC [m
                        Col: 0   1B 5B 32 6D   1B 5B 6D
12. Separator sequence: 29. Attributes occupy position: NO
          ;   30. Attributes cumulative: YES
          3B   31. All attributes off:
13. End sequence: ESC [m
          H   1B 5B 6D
          48
14. Cursor to top row, left column: CURSOR CONTROL KEYS
ESC [1   ;   1   H   32. Cursor up:
1B 5B 31 3B 31 48   ESC [A
15. 10th Row, 50th Column: 1B 5B 41
ESC [1   0   ;   5   0   H   33. Cursor down:
1B 5B 31 30 3B 35 30 48   ESC [B
16. Delay after positioning: 0   1B 5B 42
17. Cursor home: 34. Cursor right:
          ESC [H   ESC [C
          1B 5B 48   1B 5B 43
                                    35. Cursor left:
ERASURE   DELAY   ESC [D
18. Entire screen: 1B 5B 44
          ESC [2   J   0
          1B 5B 32 4A   CHARACTER SET
19. Cursor to end of screen: 36. Full upper and lower ASCII: YES
          ESC [J   0   37. Generate all control codes: YES
          1B 5B 4A   38. Bell or tone sequence:
20. Beginning of screen to cursor: ^G
          ESC [1   J   0   07
          1B 5B 31 4A
21. Cursor to end of line: EMULATION
          ESC [K   0   39. Conform to ANSI X3.64?   YES
          1B 5B 4B   40. Terminals Emulated:
22. Beginning of line to cursor: DEC VT100
          ESC [1   K   0   DEC VT52 (as a subset of VT100)
          1B 5B 31 4B
23. Entire cursor line:
          ESC [2   K   0
          1B 5B 32 4B

                              41   CONTINUED ====>

41. Information provided by:
    MANUFACTURER

42. PROGRAM FUNCTION KEYS
    1. P   P   ESC \
       50   50   1B   5C

    2. P   Q   ESC \
       50   51   1B   5C

    3. P   R   ESC \
       50   52   1B   5C

    4. P   S   ESC \
       50   53   1B   5C

    5. P   T   ESC \
       50   54   1B   5C

    6. P   U   ESC \
       50   55   1B   5C

    7. P   V   ESC \
       50   56   1B   5C

    8. P   W   ESC \
       50   57   1B   5C

    9. P   X   ESC \
       50   58   1B   5C

    10. P   Y   ESC \
        50 59   1B   5C

    11. P   Z   ESC \
        50 5A   1B   5C

    12. P   [ESC \
        50 5B   1B   5C

    13. P   \   ESC \
        50 5C   1B   5C

    14. P   ]   ESC \
        50 5D   1B   5C

    15. P   ^   ESC \
        50 5E   1B   5C

    16. P   _   ESC \
        50 5F   1B   5C

NOTES
 4. Optionally 132.
30. Also ESC [5 ; 7 m.
42. All function keys are preceded by
    a control string, which can be
    ANSI strings of APC, OSC, PM,
    DCS and SS3.

```
--------------------------------------------------------------------------
1. Manufacturer:                      Beehive International
2. Terminal:                          ATL 083
--------------------------------------------------------------------------
```

SCREEN LAYOUT   VIDEO ATTRIBUTES
3. Number of rows: 24   ON   OFF
4. Number of columns: 80   24. Blinking:
5. Top Row: 0   ESC ^X   ESC ^^
6. Left Column: 0   1B 18   1B 1E
7. Printing in bottom right   25. Reverse video:
   cause scroll?   NO   ESC ^N   ESC ^^
                                      1B 0E   1B 1E
CURSOR ADDRESSING   26. Underline:
8. Lead-in sequence: ESC ^O   ESC ^S
           ESC "   1B 0F   1B 13
           1B 22   27. High intensity:
9. Row or column first: COL   ESC ^Z   ESC ^^
10. Numeric form of row and column: 1B 1A   1B 1E
    BINARY   28. Half intensity:
11. Add offset to: Row: 20
                        Col: 20
12. Separator sequence: 29. Attributes occupy position: YES
                                      30. Attributes cumulative: YES
                                      31. All attributes off:
                                                ESC ^^
13. End sequence: 1B 1E

14. Cursor to top row, left column: CURSOR CONTROL KEYS
ESC "   SP SP   32. Cursor up:
1B 22 20 20   ESC f
15. 10th Row, 50th Column: 1B 66
ESC "   Q   )   33. Cursor down:
1B 22 51 29   ESC i
16. Delay after positioning: 0   1B 69
17. Cursor home: 34. Cursor right:
           ESC e   ESC h
           1B 65   1B 68
                                      35. Cursor left:
ERASURE   DELAY   ESC g
18. Entire screen: 1B 67
           ESC o   0
           1B 6F   CHARACTER SET
19. Cursor to end of screen: 36. Full upper and lower ASCII: YES
           ESC J   0   37. Generate all control codes: YES
           1B 4A   38. Bell or tone sequence:
20. Beginning of screen to cursor: ESC ?
                                                1B 3F

21. Cursor to end of line: EMULATION
           ESC K   0   39. Conform to ANSI X3.64?   NO
           1B 4B   40. Terminals Emulated:
22. Beginning of line to cursor: TD 830
           ESC D   ESC K   0   MT 983
           1B 44 1B 4B
23. Entire cursor line:
           ESC M   0
           1B 4D

                           43   CONTINUED ====>
```
```

```
--------------------------------------------------------------------------
     Manufacturer:                    Beehive International
     Terminal:                        ATL 083
--------------------------------------------------------------------------
```

41. Information provided by:
    MANUFACTURER

42. PROGRAM FUNCTION KEYS   NOTES
    1.   42. Programmable function keys.

    2.

    3.

    4.

    5.

    6.

    7.

    8.

    9.

    10.

    11.

    12.

    13.

    14.

    15.

    16.

```
--------------------------------------------------------------------------------
   1. Manufacturer:                    Beehive International
   2. Terminal:                        ATL-004
--------------------------------------------------------------------------------


SCREEN LAYOUT                          VIDEO ATTRIBUTES
   3. Number of rows:         24            ON                    OFF
   4. Number of columns:      80       24. Blinking:
   5. Top Row:                 0        ESC  d    B          ESC  d    @
   6. Left Column:             0        1B   64   42          1B   64   40
   7. Printing in bottom right         25. Reverse video:
      cause scroll?          PROG       ESC  d    P          ESC  d    @
                                        1B   64   50          1B   64   40
CURSOR ADDRESSING                       26. Underline:
   8. Lead-in sequence:                 ESC  d    `          ESC  d    @
               ESC  F                   1B   64   60          1B   64   40
               1B   46                  27. High intensity:
   9. Row or column first:    ROW
  10. Numeric form of row and column:
      BINARY                            28. Half intensity:
  11. Add offset to:      Row:  20       ESC  d    A          ESC  d    @
                          Col:  20       1B   64   41          1B   64   40
  12. Separator sequence:               29. Attributes occupy position: NO
                                        30. Attributes cumulative:       NO
                                        31. All attributes off:
  13. End sequence:                              ESC  d    @
                                                 1B   64   40


  14. Cursor to top row, left column:  CURSOR CONTROL KEYS
  ESC  F    SP   SP                     32. Cursor up:
  1B   46   20   20                              ESC  A
  15. 10th Row, 50th Column:                     1B   41
  ESC  F    )    Q                      33. Cursor down:
  1B   46   29   51                              ESC  B
  16. Delay after positioning:    0              1B   42
  17. Cursor home:                      34. Cursor right:
               ESC  H                            ESC  C
               1B   48                           1B   43
                                        35. Cursor left:
ERASURE                       DELAY              ESC  D
  18. Entire screen:                             1B   44
         ESC  E
         1B   45                  0     CHARACTER SET
  19. Cursor to end of screen:          36. Full upper and lower ASCII: YES
         ESC  J                  0      37. Generate all control codes: YES
         1B   4A                        38. Bell or tone sequence:
  20. Beginning of screen to cursor:             ^G
                                                 07

  21. Cursor to end of line:           EMULATION
         ESC  K                  0      39. Conform to ANSI X3.64?      NO
         1B   4B                        40. Terminals Emulated:
  22. Beginning of line to cursor:          DEC VT100


  23. Entire cursor line:
```

41. Information provided by:
    MANUFACTURER

42. PROGRAM FUNCTION KEYS
    1. ^B   ESC p
       02   1B   70

    2. ^B   ESC q
       02   1B   71

    3. ^B   ESC r
       02   1B   72

    4. ^B   ESC s
       02   1B   73

    5. ^B   ESC t
       02   1B   74

    6. ^B   ESC u
       02   1B   75

    7. ^B   ESC v
       02   1B   76

    8. ^B   ESC w
       02   1B   77

    9. ^B   ESC x
       02   1B   78

   10. ^B   ESC y
       02   1B   79

   11. ^B   ESC z
       02   1B   7A

   12. ^B   ESC {
       02   1B   7B

   13. ^B   ESC |
       02   1B   7C

   14. ^B   ESC }
       02   1B   7D

   15. ^B   ESC ~
       02   1B   7E

   16. ^B   ESC DEL
       02   1B   7F

NOTES
2. Dependent upon destructive scroll
   setting.
30. Alternate sequences provide
    combinations.
31. 512 characters including line
    graphics, foreign characters,
    icons, and math symbols.
42. STX sequence is programmable up to
    16 characters.
    Termination sequence is program-
    mable up to 16 characters OR
    Entire key is programmable up to
    16 characters.

```
--------------------------------------------------------------------------
1. Manufacturer:                    Beehive International
2. Terminal:                        ATL-078
--------------------------------------------------------------------------
```

SCREEN LAYOUT
3. Number of rows: 24
4. Number of columns: 80
5. Top Row: 1
6. Left Column: 1
7. Printing in bottom right
   cause scroll?   NO

CURSOR ADDRESSING
8. Lead-in sequence:
        ESC F
        1B   46
9. Row or column first: ROW
10. Numeric form of row and column:
    BINARY
11. Add offset to: Row: 1F
                         Col: 1F
12. Separator sequence:

13. End sequence:

14. Cursor to top row, left column:
ESC F   SP   SP
1B   46   20   20
15. 10th Row, 50th Column:
ESC F   )   Q
1B   46   29   51
16. Delay after positioning: 0
17. Cursor home:
        ESC H
        1B   48

ERASURE   DELAY
18. Entire screen:
        ESC E   0
        1B   45
19. Cursor to end of screen:
        ESC J   0
        1B   4A
20. Beginning of screen to cursor:

21. Cursor to end of line:
        ESC K   0
        1B   4B
22. Beginning of line to cursor:

23. Entire cursor line:

VIDEO ATTRIBUTES
        ON   OFF
24. Blinking:
    ESC d   B   ESC d   @
    1B   64   42   1B   64   40
25. Reverse video:
    ESC d   P   ESC d   @
    1B   64   50   1B   64   40
26. Underline:
    ESC d   `   ESC d   @
    1B   64   60   1B   64   40
27. High intensity:

28. Half intensity:
    ESC d   A   ESC d   @
    1B   64   41   1B   64   40
29. Attributes occupy position: NO
30. Attributes cumulative: NO
31. All attributes off:
                ESC d   @
                1B   64   40

CURSOR CONTROL KEYS
32. Cursor up:
                ESC A
                1B   41
33. Cursor down:
                ESC B
                1B   42
34. Cursor right:
                ESC C
                1B   43
35. Cursor left:
                ESC D
                1B   44

CHARACTER SET
36. Full upper and lower ASCII: YES
37. Generate all control codes: YES
38. Bell or tone sequence:
                ^G
                07

EMULATION
39. Conform to ANSI X3.64?   NO
40. Terminals Emulated:

CONTINUED ====>

41. Information provided by:
    MANUFACTURER

42. PROGRAM FUNCTION KEYS

			NOTES
1. ^B ESC p			2. Dependent upon destructive scroll
02 1B 70			setting.
			30. Alternate sequences provide
2. ^B ESC q			combinations.
02 1B 71			42. All function keys require termina-
			tion sequence, which is switch
3. ^B ESC r			selectable between CR; CRLF; EOT;
02 1B 72			and ETX.

4. ^B ESC s
   02 1B 73

5. ^B ESC t
   02 1B 74

6. ^B ESC u
   02 1B 75

7. ^B ESC v
   02 1B 76

8. ^B ESC w
   02 1B 77

9. ^B ESC x
   02 1B 78

10. ^B ESC y
   02 1B 79

11. ^B ESC z
   02 1B 7A

12. ^B ESC {
   02 1B 7B

13. ^B ESC |
   02 1B 7C

14. ^B ESC }
   02 1B 7D

15. ^B ESC ~
   02 1B 7E

16. ^B ESC DEL
   02 1B 7F

```
-------------------------------------------------------------------------
  1. Manufacturer:                    Beehive International
  2. Terminal:                        DMSB (Standard)
-------------------------------------------------------------------------


SCREEN LAYOUT                         VIDEO ATTRIBUTES
  3. Number of rows:         24          ON                      OFF
  4. Number of columns:      80       24. Blinking:
  5. Top Row:                 0        ESC d    B          ESC d    @
  6. Left Column:             0        1B  64   42         1B  64   40
  7. Printing in bottom right         25. Reverse video:
     cause scroll?          PROG       ESC d    P          ESC d    @
                                       1B  64   50         1B  64   40
CURSOR ADDRESSING                     26. Underline:
  8. Lead-in sequence:                  ESC d    `          ESC d    @
            ESC F                       1B  64   60         1B  64   40
            1B   46                    27. High intensity:
  9. Row or column first:     ROW
 10. Numeric form of row and column:
     BINARY                           28. Half intensity:
 11. Add offset to:     Row:   20      ESC d    A          ESC d    @
                        Col:   20      1B  64   41         1B  64   40
 12. Separator sequence:              29. Attributes occupy position: NO
                                      30. Attributes cumulative:      NO
                                      31. All attributes off:
 13. End sequence:                              ESC d    @
                                                1B  64   40


 14. Cursor to top row, left column:  CURSOR CONTROL KEYS
 ESC F    SP  SP                      32. Cursor up:
 1B  46   20  20                                ESC A
 15. 10th Row, 50th Column:                     1B   41
 ESC F    )   Q                       33. Cursor down:
 1B  46   29  51                                ESC B
 16. Delay after positioning:    0              1B   42
 17. Cursor home:                     34. Cursor right:
            ESC H                               ESC C
            1B   48                             1B   43
                                      35. Cursor left:
ERASURE                      DELAY              ESC D
 18. Entire screen:                             1B   44
       ESC E                     0
       1B   45                        CHARACTER SET
 19. Cursor to end of screen:         36. Full upper and lower ASCII: YES
       ESC J                     0    37. Generate all control codes: YES
       1B   4A                        38. Bell or tone sequence:
 20. Beginning of screen to cursor:             ^G
                                                07

 21. Cursor to end of line:           EMULATION
       ESC K                     0    39. Conform to ANSI X3.64?      NO
       1B   4B                        40. Terminals Emulated:
 22. Beginning of line to cursor:


 23. Entire cursor line:
```

41. Information provided by:
    MANUFACTURER

42. PROGRAM FUNCTION KEYS   NOTES
 1. ^B ESC p   2. Dependent upon destructive scroll
    02   1B   70   setting.
                                     30. Alternate sequences provide
 2. ^B ESC q   combinations.
    02   1B   71   42. All function keys require termina-
                                         tion sequence, which is switch
 3. ^B ESC r   selectable between CR; CRLF; EOT;
    02   1B   72   and ETX.

 4. ^B ESC s
    02   1B   73

 5. ^B ESC t
    02   1B   74

 6. ^B ESC u
    02   1B   75

 7. ^B ESC v
    02   1B   76

 8. ^B ESC w
    02   1B   77

 9. ^B ESC x
    02   1B   78

10. ^B ESC y
    02   1B   79

11. ^B ESC z
    02   1B   7A

12. ^B ESC {
    02   1B   7B

13. ^B ESC |
    02   1B   7C

14. ^B ESC }
    02   1B   7D

15. ^B ESC ~
    02   1B   7E

16. ^B ESC DEL
    02   1B   7F

```
--------------------------------------------------------------------------------
 1. Manufacturer:                    Beehive International
 2. Terminal:                        DMSC (Basic)
--------------------------------------------------------------------------------


SCREEN LAYOUT                        VIDEO ATTRIBUTES
 3. Number of rows:          24          ON                      OFF
 4. Number of columns:       80     24. Blinking:
 5. Top Row:                  0       ESC d    B           ESC d    @
 6. Left Column:              0       1B  64   42          1B  64   40
 7. Printing in bottom right        25. Reverse video:
    cause scroll?           PROG      ESC d    P           ESC d    @
                                      1B  64   50          1B  64   40
CURSOR ADDRESSING                   26. Underline:
 8. Lead-in sequence:                 ESC d    `           ESC d    @
            ESC F                     1B  64   60          1B  64   40
            1B   46                 27. High intensity:
 9. Row or column first:     ROW
10. Numeric form of row and column:
    BINARY                          28. Half intensity:
11. Add offset to:     Row:  20       ESC d    A           ESC d    @
                       Col:  20       1B  64   41          1B  64   40
12. Separator sequence:             29. Attributes occupy position: NO
                                    30. Attributes cumulative:      NO
                                    31. All attributes off:
13. End sequence:                             ESC d    @
                                              1B   64   40


14. Cursor to top row, left column: CURSOR CONTROL KEYS
ESC F    SP   SP                    32. Cursor up:
1B   46   20   20                             ESC A
15. 10th Row, 50th Column:                    1B   41
ESC F    )    Q                     33. Cursor down:
1B   46   29   51                             ESC B
16. Delay after positioning:     0            1B   42
17. Cursor home:                    34. Cursor right:
            ESC H                             ESC C
            1B   48                           1B   43
                                    35. Cursor left:
ERASURE                     DELAY             ESC D
18. Entire screen:                            1B   44
            ESC E               0
            1B   45                 CHARACTER SET
19. Cursor to end of screen:        36. Full upper and lower ASCII: YES
            ESC J               0   37. Generate all control codes: YES
            1B   4A                 38. Bell or tone sequence:
20. Beginning of screen to cursor:            ^G
                                              07

21. Cursor to end of line:          EMULATION
            ESC K               0   39. Conform to ANSI X3.64?      NO
            1B   4B                 40. Terminals Emulated:
22. Beginning of line to cursor:


23. Entire cursor line:
```

Manufacturer:	Beehive International
Terminal:	DMSC (Basic)

41. Information provided by:
    MANUFACTURER

42. PROGRAM FUNCTION KEYS

1. ^B ESC p
   02   1B   70

2. ^B ESC q
   02   1B   71

3. ^B ESC r
   02   1B   72

4. ^B ESC s
   02   1B   73

5. ^B ESC t
   02   1B   74

6. ^B ESC u
   02   1B   75

7. ^B ESC v
   02   1B   76

8. ^B ESC w
   02   1B   77

9. ^B ESC x
   02   1B   78

10. ^B ESC y
    02   1B   79

11. ^B ESC z
    02   1B   7A

12. ^B ESC {
    02   1B   7B

13. ^B ESC |
    02   1B   7C

14. ^B ESC }
    02   1B   7D

15. ^B ESC ~
    02   1B   7E

16. ^B ESC DEL
    02   1B   7F

NOTES

2. Dependent upon destructive scroll setting.

30. Alternate sequences provide combinations.

42. All function keys require termination sequence, which is switch selectable between CR; CRLF; EOT; and ETX.

```
--------------------------------------------------------------------------
  1. Manufacturer:                    Beehive International
  2. Terminal:                        DMSD (Plus)
--------------------------------------------------------------------------

SCREEN LAYOUT                         VIDEO ATTRIBUTES
  3. Number of rows:        24            ON                    OFF
  4. Number of columns:     80        24. Blinking:
  5. Top Row:                0         ESC d    B          ESC d    @
  6. Left Column:            0         1B  64  42          1B  64  40
  7. Printing in bottom right         25. Reverse video:
     cause scroll?         PROG        ESC d    P          ESC d    @
                                       1B  64  50          1B  64  40
CURSOR ADDRESSING                     26. Underline:
  8. Lead-in sequence:                 ESC d               ESC d    @
            ESC F                      1B  64  60          1B  64  40
            1B  46                    27. High intensity:
  9. Row or column first:     ROW
 10. Numeric form of row and column:
     BINARY                           28. Half intensity:
 11. Add offset to:    Row:  20        ESC d    A          ESC d    @
                       Col:  20        1B  64  41          1B  64  40
 12. Separator sequence:              29. Attributes occupy position: NO
                                      30. Attributes cumulative:       NO
                                      31. All attributes off:
 13. End sequence:                              ESC d    @
                                                1B  64  40

 14. Cursor to top row, left column:  CURSOR CONTROL KEYS
 ESC F    SP  SP                      32. Cursor up:
 1B  46   20  20                                ESC A
 15. 10th Row, 50th Column:                     1B  41
 ESC F    )   Q                       33. Cursor down:
 1B  46   29  51                                ESC B
 16. Delay after positioning:    0              1B  42
 17. Cursor home:                     34. Cursor right:
            ESC H                               ESC C
            1B  48                              1B  43
                                      35. Cursor left:
ERASURE                    DELAY                ESC D
 18. Entire screen:                             1B  44
            ESC E            0
            1B  45                    CHARACTER SET
 19. Cursor to end of screen:         36. Full upper and lower ASCII: YES
            ESC J            0        37. Generate all control codes: YES
            1B  4A                    38. Bell or tone sequence:
 20. Beginning of screen to cursor:             ^G
                                                07

 21. Cursor to end of line:           EMULATION
            ESC K            0        39. Conform to ANSI X3.64?      NO
            1B  4B                    40. Terminals Emulated:
 22. Beginning of line to cursor:


 23. Entire cursor line:
```

41. Information provided by:
    MANUFACTURER

42. PROGRAM FUNCTION KEYS   NOTES
    1. ^B   ESC p   2. Dependent upon destructive scroll
       02   1B   70   setting.
                                     30. Alternate sequences provide
    2. ^B   ESC q   combinations.
       02   1B   71   42. All function keys require termina-
                                          tion sequence, which is switch
    3. ^B   ESC r   selectable between CR; CRLF; EOT;
       02   1B   72   and ETX.

    4. ^B   ESC s
       02   1B   73

    5. ^B   ESC t
       02   1B   74

    6. ^B   ESC u
       02   1B   75

    7. ^B   ESC v
       02   1B   76

    8. ^B   ESC w
       02   1B   77

    9. ^B   ESC x
       02   1B   78

   10. ^B   ESC y
       02   1B   79

   11. ^B   ESC z
       02   1B   7A

   12. ^B   ESC {
       02   1B   7B

   13. ^B   ESC |
       02   1B   7C

   14. ^B   ESC }
       02   1B   7D

   15. ^B   ESC ~
       02   1B   7E

   16. ^B   ESC DEL
       02   1B   7F

```
--------------------------------------------------------------------------------
  1. Manufacturer:                    Beehive International
  2. Terminal:                        Topper (in DM78 mode)
--------------------------------------------------------------------------------
```

SCREEN LAYOUT   VIDEO ATTRIBUTES
  3. Number of rows: 24   ON   OFF
  4. Number of columns: 80   24. Blinking:
  5. Top Row: 1   ESC d   B   ESC d   @
  6. Left Column: 1   1B   64   42   1B   64   40
  7. Printing in bottom right   25. Reverse video:
     cause scroll?   NO   ESC d   P   ESC d   @
                                        1B   64   50   1B   64   40
CURSOR ADDRESSING   26. Underline:
  8. Lead-in sequence: ESC d   `   ESC d   @
          ESC F   1B   64   60   1B   64   40
          1B   46   27. High intensity:
  9. Row or column first: ROW
 10. Numeric form of row and column:
     BINARY   28. Half intensity:
 11. Add offset to: Row: 1F   ESC d   A   ESC d   @
                         Col: 1F   1B   64   41   1B   64   40
 12. Separator sequence: 29. Attributes occupy position: NO
                                        30. Attributes cumulative: NO
                                        31. All attributes off:
 13. End sequence: ESC d   @
                                                 1B   64   40

 14. Cursor to top row, left column: CURSOR CONTROL KEYS
 ESC F   SP   SP   32. Cursor up:
 1B   46   20   20   ESC A
 15. 10th Row, 50th Column: 1B   41
 ESC F   )   Q   33. Cursor down:
 1B   46   29   51   ESC B
 16. Delay after positioning: 0   1B   42
 17. Cursor home: 34. Cursor right:
          ESC H   ESC C
          1B   48   1B   43
                                        35. Cursor left:
ERASURE   DELAY   ESC D
 18. Entire screen: 1B   44
          ESC E   0
          1B   45   CHARACTER SET
 19. Cursor to end of screen: 36. Full upper and lower ASCII: YES
          ESC J   0   37. Generate all control codes: YES
          1B   4A   38. Bell or tone sequence:
 20. Beginning of screen to cursor: ^G
                                                 07

 21. Cursor to end of line: EMULATION
          ESC K   0   39. Conform to ANSI X3.64?   NO
          1B   4B   40. Terminals Emulated:
 22. Beginning of line to cursor:

 23. Entire cursor line:

                               55   CONTINUED ====>
```
```

41. Information provided by:
    MANUFACTURER

42. PROGRAM FUNCTION KEYS   NOTES
   1. ^B   ESC p   2. Dependent upon destructive scroll
      02   1B   70   setting.
                                        30. Alternate sequences provide
   2. ^B   ESC q   combinations.
      02   1B   71   42. All function keys require termina-
                                            tion sequence, which is switch
   3. ^B   ESC r   selectable between CR; CRLF; EOT;
      02   1B   72   and ETX.

   4. ^B   ESC s
      02   1B   73

   5. ^B   ESC t
      02   1B   74

   6. ^B   ESC u
      02   1B   75

   7. ^B   ESC v
      02   1B   76

   8. ^B   ESC w
      02   1B   77

   9. ^B   ESC x
      02   1B   78

  10. ^B   ESC y
      02   1B   79

  11. ^B   ESC z
      02   1B   7A

  12. ^B   ESC {
      02   1B   7B

  13. ^B   ESC |
      02   1B   7C

  14. ^B   ESC }
      02   1B   7D

  15. ^B   ESC ~
      02   1B   7E

  16. ^B   ESC DEL
      02   1B   7F

```
--------------------------------------------------------------------------
1. Manufacturer:                    CIE Terminals
2. Terminal:                        CIT-101 and CIT-101e (ANSI mode)
--------------------------------------------------------------------------
```

SCREEN LAYOUT
3. Number of rows: 24
4. Number of columns: 80
5. Top Row: 1
6. Left Column: 1
7. Printing in bottom right
   cause scroll?   PROG

CURSOR ADDRESSING
8. Lead-in sequence:
            ESC [
            1B 5B
9. Row or column first: ROW
10. Numeric form of row and column:
    VARIABLE-LENGTH ASCII
11. Add offset to: Row: 0
                          Col: 0
12. Separator sequence:
            ;
            3B
13. End sequence:
            H
            48
14. Cursor to top row, left column:
ESC [1   ;   1   H
1B 5B 31 3B 31 48
15. 10th Row, 50th Column:
ESC [1   0   ;   5   0   H
1B 5B 31 30 3B 35 30 48
16. Delay after positioning: 0
17. Cursor home:
            ESC [H
            1B 5B 48

ERASURE   DELAY
18. Entire screen:
        ESC [2   J   0
        1B 5B 32 4A
19. Cursor to end of screen:
        ESC [J   0
        1B 5B 4A
20. Beginning of screen to cursor:
        ESC [1   J   0
        1B 5B 31 4A
21. Cursor to end of line:
        ESC [K   0
        1B 5B 4B
22. Beginning of line to cursor:
        ESC [1   K   0
        1B 5B 31 4B
23. Entire cursor line:
        ESC [2   K   0
        1B 5B 32 4B

VIDEO ATTRIBUTES
        ON   OFF
24. Blinking:
ESC [5   m   ESC [m
1B 5B 35 6D   1B 5B   6D
25. Reverse video:
ESC [7   m   ESC [m
1B 5B 37 6D   1B 5B   6D
26. Underline:
ESC [4   m   ESC [m
1B 5B 34 6D   1B 5B   6D
27. High intensity:
ESC [1   m   ESC [m
1B 5B 31 6D   1B 5B   6D
28. Half intensity:

29. Attributes occupy position: NO
30. Attributes cumulative: YES
31. All attributes off:
            ESC [m
            1B 5B   6D

CURSOR CONTROL KEYS
32. Cursor up:
            ESC [A
            1B 5B 41
33. Cursor down:
            ESC [B
            1B 5B 42
34. Cursor right:
            ESC [C
            1B 5B 43
35. Cursor left:
            ESC [D
            1B 5B 44

CHARACTER SET
36. Full upper and lower ASCII: YES
37. Generate all control codes: YES
38. Bell or tone sequence:
            ^G
            07

EMULATION
39. Conform to ANSI X3.64?   YES
40. Terminals Emulated:
    DEC VT100

            CONTINUED ====>

41. Information provided by:
    MANUFACTURER

42. PROGRAM FUNCTION KEYS   NOTES
    1. ESC O   P   4. Optionally 132.
       1B 4F 50   30. See ANSI video attribute
                                       discussion.
    2. ESC O   Q   36. Plus 32 standard graphics
       1B 4F 51   characters, 32 alternate graphics
                                       characters, 96 alternate characters
    3. ESC O   R
       1B 4F 52

    4. ESC O   S
       1B 4F 53

    5.

    6.

    7.

    8.

    9.

   10.

   11.

   12.

   13.

   14.

   15.

   16.

```
--------------------------------------------------------------------
  1. Manufacturer:                   CIE Terminals
  2. Terminal:                       CIT-101 and CIT-101e (VT52 mode)
--------------------------------------------------------------------
```

SCREEN LAYOUT   VIDEO ATTRIBUTES
  3. Number of rows: 24   ON   OFF
  4. Number of columns: 80   24. Blinking:
  5. Top Row: 1
  6. Left Column: 1
  7. Printing in bottom right   25. Reverse video:
     cause scroll?   PROG

CURSOR ADDRESSING   26. Underline:
  8. Lead-in sequence:
           ESC Y
           1B 59   27. High intensity:
  9. Row or column first: ROW
 10. Numeric form of row and column:
     BINARY   28. Half intensity:
 11. Add offset to: Row: 1F
                          Col: 1F
 12. Separator sequence: 29. Attributes occupy position: NO
                                      30. Attributes cumulative: NO
                                      31. All attributes off:
 13. End sequence:

 14. Cursor to top row, left column: CURSOR CONTROL KEYS
 ESC Y   SP SP   32. Cursor up:
 1B 59   20 20   ESC A
 15. 10th Row, 50th Column: 1B   41
 ESC Y   )   Q   33. Cursor down:
 1B 59   29 51   ESC B
 16. Delay after positioning: 0   1B   42
 17. Cursor home: 34. Cursor right:
           ESC H   ESC C
           1B 48   1B   43
                                      35. Cursor left:
ERASURE   DELAY   ESC D
 18. Entire screen: 1B   44
       ESC H   ESC J   0
       1B 48 1B 4A   CHARACTER SET
 19. Cursor to end of screen: 36. Full upper and lower ASCII: YES
       ESC J   0   37. Generate all control codes: YES
       1B 4A   38. Bell or tone sequence:
 20. Beginning of screen to cursor: ^G
                                                07
 21. Cursor to end of line: EMULATION
       ESC K   0   39. Conform to ANSI X3.64?   NO
       1B 4B   40. Terminals Emulated:
 22. Beginning of line to cursor: DEC VT52

 23. Entire cursor line:
```

                      CONTINUED ====>
```

41. Information provided by:
    MANUFACTURER

42. PROGRAM FUNCTION KEYS   NOTES
    1. ESC P   36. Plus 32 stardard graphics
       1B   50   characters, 32 alternate
                                      graphics characters, 96 alternate
    2. ESC Q   characters.
       1B   51

    3. ESC R
       1B   52

    4. ESC S
       1B   53

    5.

    6.

    7.

    8.

    9.

   10.

   11.

   12.

   13.

   14.

   15.

   16.

---

1. Manufacturer: CIE Terminals
2. Terminal: CIT-161 (ANSI mode)

SCREEN LAYOUT
3. Number of rows: 24
4. Number of columns: 80
5. Top Row: 1
6. Left Column: 1
7. Printing in bottom right
   cause scroll?   PROG

CURSOR ADDRESSING
8. Lead-in sequence:
                ESC [
                1B 5B
9. Row or column first: ROW
10. Numeric form of row and column:
    VARIABLE-LENGTH ASCII
11. Add offset to: Row: 0
                          Col: 0
12. Separator sequence:
                ;
                3B
13. End sequence:
                H
                48
14. Cursor to top row, left column:
ESC [1   ;   1   H
1B 5B 31 3B 31 48
15. 10th Row, 50th Column:
ESC [1   0   ;   5   0   H
1B 5B 31 30 3B 35 30 48
16. Delay after positioning: 0
17. Cursor home:
                ESC [H
                1B 5B 48

ERASURE   DELAY
18. Entire screen:
        ESC [2   J   0
        1B 5B 32 4A
19. Cursor to end of screen:
        ESC [J   0
        1B 5B 4A
20. Beginning of screen to cursor:
        ESC [1   J   0
        1B 5B 31 4A
21. Cursor to end of line:
        ESC [K   0
        1B 5B 4B
22. Beginning of line to cursor:
        ESC [1   K   0
        1B 5B 31 4B
23. Entire cursor line:
        ESC [2   K   0
        1B 5B 32 4B

VIDEO ATTRIBUTES
          ON   OFF
24. Blinking:
ESC [5   m   ESC [m
1B 5B 35 6D   1B 5B 6D
25. Reverse video:
ESC [7   m   ESC [m
1B 5B 37 6D   1B 5B 6D
26. Underline:
ESC [4   m   ESC [m
1B 5B 34 6D   1B 5B 6D
27. High intensity:
ESC [1   m   ESC [m
1B 5B 31 6D   1B 5B 6D
28. Half intensity:

29. Attributes occupy position: NO
30. Attributes cumulative: YES
31. All attributes off:
                ESC [m
                1B 5B 6D

CURSOR CONTROL KEYS
32. Cursor up:
                ESC [A
                1B 5B 41
33. Cursor down:
                ESC [B
                1B 5B 42
34. Cursor right:
                ESC [C
                1B 5B 43
35. Cursor left:
                ESC [D
                1B 5B 44

CHARACTER SET
36. Full upper and lower ASCII: YES
37. Generate all control codes: YES
38. Bell or tone sequence:
                ^G
                07

EMULATION
39. Conform to ANSI X3.64?   YES
40. Terminals Emulated:
    DEC VT100

CONTINUED ====>

```
--------------------------------------------------------------------------
         Manufacturer:                    CIE Terminals
         Terminal:                        CIT-161 (ANSI mode)
--------------------------------------------------------------------------
```

41. Information provided by:
    MANUFACTURER

42. PROGRAM FUNCTION KEYS   NOTES
    1. ESC O   P   4. Optionally 132.
       1B   4F   50   30. See ANSI video attribute
                                        discussion.
    2. ESC O   Q   36. Plus 32 standard graphics
       1B   4F   51   characters, 32 alternate graphics
                                       characters, 96 alternate characters
    3. ESC O   R
       1B   4F   52   This terminal allows color video

    4. ESC O   S
       1B   4F   53

    5.

    6.

    7.

    8.

    9.

   10.

   11.

   12.

   13.

   14.

   15.

   16.

```
--------------------------------------------------------------------------------
     1. Manufacturer:                    CIE Terminals
     2. Terminal:                        CIT-161 (VT52 mode)
--------------------------------------------------------------------------------

SCREEN LAYOUT                          VIDEO ATTRIBUTES
 3. Number of rows:          24              ON                   OFF
 4. Number of columns:       80        24. Blinking:
 5. Top Row:                  1
 6. Left Column:              1
 7. Printing in bottom right           25. Reverse video:
    cause scroll?           PROG

CURSOR ADDRESSING                      26. Underline:
 8. Lead-in sequence:
          ESC Y
          1B  59                       27. High intensity:
 9. Row or column first:      ROW
10. Numeric form of row and column:
    BINARY                             28. Half intensity:
11. Add offset to:       Row:   1F
                         Col:   1F
12. Separator sequence:                29. Attributes occupy position: NO
                                       30. Attributes cumulative:      NO
                                       31. All attributes off:
13. End sequence:


14. Cursor to top row, left column:    CURSOR CONTROL KEYS
ESC Y    SP  SP                        32. Cursor up:
1B  59   20  20                                  ESC  A
15. 10th Row, 50th Column:                       1B   41
ESC Y    )   Q                         33. Cursor down:
1B  59   29  51                                  ESC  B
16. Delay after positioning:     0               1B   42
17. Cursor home:                       34. Cursor right:
          ESC H                                  ESC  C
          1B  48                                 1B   43
                                       35. Cursor left:
ERASURE                      DELAY               ESC  D
18. Entire screen:                               1B   44
      ESC H   ESC J           0
      1B  48  1B  4A                   CHARACTER SET
19. Cursor to end of screen:           36. Full upper and lower ASCII: YES
      ESC J                   0        37. Generate all control codes: YES
      1B  4A                           38. Bell or tone sequence:
20. Beginning of screen to cursor:               ^G
                                                 07

21. Cursor to end of line:             EMULATION
      ESC K                   0        39. Conform to ANSI X3.64?      NO
      1B  4B                           40. Terminals Emulated:
22. Beginning of line to cursor:           DEC VT52


23. Entire cursor line:
```

CONTINUED ====>

```
--------------------------------------------------------------------------
       Manufacturer:                    CIE Terminals
       Terminal:                        CIT-161 (VT52 mode)
--------------------------------------------------------------------------
```

41. Information provided by:
    MANUFACTURER

42. PROGRAM FUNCTION KEYS   NOTES
    1. ESC P   36. Plus 32 stardard graphics
       1B   50   characters, 32 alternate
                                       graphics characters, 96 alternate
    2. ESC Q   characters.
       1B   51

    3. ESC R
       1B   52

    4. ESC S
       1B   53

    5.

    6.

    7.

    8.

    9.

   10.

   11.

   12.

   13.

   14.

   15.

   16.

```
-------------------------------------------------------------------------
  1. Manufacturer:                  CIE Terminals
  2. Terminal:                      CIT-467 (ANSI mode)
-------------------------------------------------------------------------
```

SCREEN LAYOUT
  3. Number of rows: 24
  4. Number of columns: 80
  5. Top Row: 1
  6. Left Column: 1
  7. Printing in bottom right
     cause scroll?   PROG

CURSOR ADDRESSING
  8. Lead-in sequence:
                 ESC [
                 1B   5B
  9. Row or column first: ROW
 10. Numeric form of row and column:
     VARIABLE-LENGTH ASCII
 11. Add offset to: Row: 0
                            Col: 0
 12. Separator sequence:
                 ;
                 3B
 13. End sequence:
                 H
                 48
 14. Cursor to top row, left column:
     ESC [1   ;   1   H
     1B   5B 31 3B 31 48
 15. 10th Row, 50th Column:
     ESC [1   0   ;   5   0   H
     1B   5B 31 30 3B 35 30 48
 16. Delay after positioning: 0
 17. Cursor home:
                 ESC [H
                 1B   5B 48

ERASURE   DELAY
 18. Entire screen:
           ESC [2   J   0
           1B   5B 32 4A
 19. Cursor to end of screen:
           ESC [J   0
           1B   5B 4A
 20. Beginning of screen to cursor:
           ESC [1   J   0
           1B   5B 31 4A
 21. Cursor to end of line:
           ESC [K   0
           1B   5B 4B
 22. Beginning of line to cursor:
           ESC [1   K   0
           1B   5B 31 4B
 23. Entire cursor line:
           ESC [2   K   0
           1B   5B 32 4B

VIDEO ATTRIBUTES
                ON   OFF
 24. Blinking:
     ESC [5   m   ESC [m
     1B   5B 35 6D   1B   5B   6D
 25. Reverse video:
     ESC [7   m   ESC [m
     1B   5B 37 6D   1B   5B   6D
 26. Underline:
     ESC [4   m   ESC [m
     1B   5B 34 6D   1B   5B   6D
 27. High intensity:
     ESC [1   m   ESC [m
     1B   5B 31 6D   1B   5B   6D
 28. Half intensity:

 29. Attributes occupy position: NO
 30. Attributes cumulative: YES
 31. All attributes off:
                 ESC [m
                 1B   5B   6D

CURSOR CONTROL KEYS
 32. Cursor up:
                 ESC [A
                 1B   5B 41
 33. Cursor down:
                 ESC [B
                 1B   5B 42
 34. Cursor right:
                 ESC [C
                 1B   5B 43
 35. Cursor left:
                 ESC [D
                 1B   5B 44

CHARACTER SET
 36. Full upper and lower ASCII: YES
 37. Generate all control codes: YES
 38. Bell or tone sequence:
                 ^G
                 07

EMULATION
 39. Conform to ANSI X3.64?   YES
 40. Terminals Emulated:
     Compatible with DEC VT100
     and TEK 4010/4014, 4027
     Software compatible with
     DEC VT52

| Manufacturer: | CIE Terminals |
| Terminal: | CIT-467 (ANSI mode) |

41. Information provided by:
    MANUFACTURER

42. PROGRAM FUNCTION KEYS   NOTES

1. ESC O   P
      1B   4F   50

2. ESC O   Q
      1B   4F   51

3. ESC O   R
      1B   4F   52

4. ESC O   S
      1B   4F   53

5.

6.

7.

8.

9.

10.

11.

12.

13.

14.

15.

16.

NOTES

4. Optionally 132.

30. See ANSI video attribute
    discussion.

36. Plus 32 standard graphics
    characters, 32 alternate graphics
    characters, 96 alternate characters

```
-------------------------------------------------------------------------------
1. Manufacturer:                         CIE Terminals
2. Terminal:                             CIT-467 (VT52 mode)
-------------------------------------------------------------------------------

SCREEN LAYOUT                            VIDEO ATTRIBUTES
  3. Number of rows:             24          ON                    OFF
  4. Number of columns:          80      24. Blinking:
  5. Top Row:                     1
  6. Left Column:                 1
  7. Printing in bottom right            25. Reverse video:
     cause scroll?             PROG

CURSOR ADDRESSING                        26. Underline:
  8. Lead-in sequence:
           ESC Y
           1B  59                         27. High intensity:
  9. Row or column first:      ROW
 10. Numeric form of row and column:
     BINARY                               28. Half intensity:
 11. Add offset to:        Row:  1F
                           Col:  1F
 12. Separator sequence:                  29. Attributes occupy position: NO
                                          30. Attributes cumulative:      NO
                                          31. All attributes off:
 13. End sequence:


 14. Cursor to top row, left column:     CURSOR CONTROL KEYS
 ESC Y   SP  SP                          32. Cursor up:
 1B  59  20  20                                      ESC A
 15. 10th Row, 50th Column:                          1B  41
 ESC Y   )   Q                           33. Cursor down:
 1B  59  29  51                                      ESC B
 16. Delay after positioning:    0                   1B  42
 17. Cursor home:                        34. Cursor right:
           ESC H                                     ESC C
           1B  48                                    1B  43
                                         35. Cursor left:
ERASURE                        DELAY                 ESC D
 18. Entire screen:                                  1B  44
       ESC H    ESC J             0
       1B  48   1B  4A                   CHARACTER SET
 19. Cursor to end of screen:            36. Full upper and lower ASCII: YES
       ESC J                      0      37. Generate all control codes: YES
       1B  4A                            38. Bell or tone sequence:
 20. Beginning of screen to cursor:                  ^G
                                                     07

 21. Cursor to end of line:              EMULATION
       ESC K                      0      39. Conform to ANSI X3.64?      NO
       1B  4B                            40. Terminals Emulated:
 22. Beginning of line to cursor:            Software compatible with
                                             DEC VT52

 23. Entire cursor line:
```

| Manufacturer: | CIE Terminals |
| Terminal: | CIT-467 (VT52 mode) |

41. Information provided by:
    MANUFACTURER

42. PROGRAM FUNCTION KEYS   NOTES
    1. ESC P   36. Plus 32 stardard graphics
       1B   50   characters, 32 alternate
                                        graphics characters, 96 alternate
    2. ESC Q   characters.
       1B   51

    3. ESC R
       1B   52

    4. ESC S
       1B   53

    5.

    6.

    7.

    8.

    9.

   10.

   11.

   12.

   13.

   14.

   15.

   16.

```
--------------------------------------------------------------------------------
1. Manufacturer:                    CIE Terminals
2. Terminal:                        CIT-500 (ANSI mode)
--------------------------------------------------------------------------------
```

SCREEN LAYOUT
3. Number of rows: 24
4. Number of columns: 80
5. Top Row: 1
6. Left Column: 1
7. Printing in bottom right
   cause scroll?   PROG

CURSOR ADDRESSING
8. Lead-in sequence:
        ESC [
        1B 5B
9. Row or column first: ROW
10. Numeric form of row and column:
    VARIABLE-LENGTH ASCII
11. Add offset to: Row: 0
                         Col: 0
12. Separator sequence:
        ;
        3B
13. End sequence:
        H
        48
14. Cursor to top row, left column:
ESC [1   ;   1   H
1B 5B 31 3B 31 48
15. 10th Row, 50th Column:
ESC [1   0   ;   5   0   H
1B 5B 31 30 3B 35 30 48
16. Delay after positioning: 0
17. Cursor home:
        ESC [H
        1B 5B 48

ERASURE   DELAY
18. Entire screen:
        ESC [2   J   0
        1B 5B 32 4A
19. Cursor to end of screen:
        ESC [J   0
        1B 5B 4A
20. Beginning of screen to cursor:
        ESC [1   J   0
        1B 5B 31 4A
21. Cursor to end of line:
        ESC [K   0
        1B 5B 4B
22. Beginning of line to cursor:
        ESC [1   K   0
        1B 5B 31 4B
23. Entire cursor line:
        ESC [2   K   0
        1B 5B 32 4B

VIDEO ATTRIBUTES
              ON   OFF
24. Blinking:
    ESC [5   m   ESC [m
    1B 5B 35 6D   1B 5B   6D
25. Reverse video:
    ESC [7   m   ESC [m
    1B 5B 37 6D   1B 5B   6D
26. Underline:
    ESC [4   m   ESC [m
    1B 5B 34 6D   1B 5B   6D
27. High intensity:
    ESC [1   m   ESC [m
    1B 5B 31 6D   1B 5B   6D
28. Half intensity:

29. Attributes occupy position: NO
30. Attributes cumulative: YES
31. All attributes off:
              ESC [m
              1B 5B   6D

CURSOR CONTROL KEYS
32. Cursor up:
              ESC [A
              1B 5B 41
33. Cursor down:
              ESC [B
              1B 5B 42
34. Cursor right:
              ESC [C
              1B 5B 43
35. Cursor left:
              ESC [D
              1B 5B 44

CHARACTER SET
36. Full upper and lower ASCII: YES
37. Generate all control codes: YES
38. Bell or tone sequence:
              ^G
              07

EMULATION
39. Conform to ANSI X3.64?   YES
40. Terminals Emulated:
    DEC VT100

69   CONTINUED ====>

| Manufacturer: | CIE Terminals |
| Terminal: | CIT-500 (ANSI mode) |

41. Information provided by:
    MANUFACTURER

42. PROGRAM FUNCTION KEYS
    1. ESC O   P
       1B 4F 50

    2. ESC O   Q
       1B 4F 51

    3. ESC O   R
       1B 4F 52

    4. ESC O   S
       1B 4F 53

    5.

    6.

    7.

    8.

    9.

    10.

    11.

    12.

    13.

    14.

    15.

    16.

NOTES
 3. Optionally 64.
 4. Optionally 120.
30. See ANSI video attribute
    discussion.
36. Plus 32 standard graphics
    characters, RAM loadable and down-
    line loadable 128 character set.

----
1. Manufacturer: CIE Terminals
2. Terminal: CIT-500 (VT52 mode)

SCREEN LAYOUT   VIDEO ATTRIBUTES
  3. Number of rows: 24   ON   OFF
  4. Number of columns: 80   24. Blinking:
  5. Top Row: 1
  6. Left Column: 1
  7. Printing in bottom right   25. Reverse video:
     cause scroll?   PROG

CURSOR ADDRESSING   26. Underline:
  8. Lead-in sequence:
           ESC Y
           1B 59   27. High intensity:
  9. Row or column first: ROW
 10. Numeric form of row and column:
     BINARY   28. Half intensity:
 11. Add offset to: Row: 1F
                         Col: 1F
 12. Separator sequence: 29. Attributes occupy position: NO
                                    30. Attributes cumulative: NO
                                    31. All attributes off:

 13. End sequence:

 14. Cursor to top row, left column: CURSOR CONTROL KEYS
 ESC Y   SP SP   32. Cursor up:
 1B 59 20 20   ESC A
 15. 10th Row, 50th Column: 1B 41
 ESC Y   )   Q   33. Cursor down:
 1B 59 29 51   ESC B
 16. Delay after positioning: 0   1B 42
 17. Cursor home: 34. Cursor right:
           ESC H   ESC C
           1B 48   1B 43
                                    35. Cursor left:
ERASURE   DELAY   ESC D
 18. Entire screen: 1B 44
        ESC H   ESC J   0
        1B 48 1B 4A   CHARACTER SET
 19. Cursor to end of screen: 36. Full upper and lower ASCII: YES
        ESC J   0   37. Generate all control codes: YES
        1B 4A   38. Bell or tone sequence:
 20. Beginning of screen to cursor: ^G
                                            07

 21. Cursor to end of line: EMULATION
        ESC K   0   39. Conform to ANSI X3.64?   NO
        1B 4B   40. Terminals Emulated:
 22. Beginning of line to cursor: DEC VT52

 23. Entire cursor line:

41. Information provided by:
    MANUFACTURER

42. PROGRAM FUNCTION KEYS   NOTES
  1. ESC P   36. Plus 32 stardard graphics
     1B 50   characters, RAM loadable and down-
                                       line loadable 128 character set.
  2. ESC Q
     1B 51

  3. ESC R
     1B 52

  4. ESC S
     1B 53

  5.

  6.

  7.

  8.

  9.

 10.

 11.

 12.

 13.

 14.

 15.

 16.

---

1. Manufacturer: CIE Terminals
2. Terminal: CIT-80 (ANSI mode)

SCREEN LAYOUT
3. Number of rows: 24
4. Number of columns: 80
5. Top Row: 1
6. Left Column: 1
7. Printing in bottom right
   cause scroll?   PROG

CURSOR ADDRESSING
8. Lead-in sequence:
              ESC [
              1B 5B
9. Row or column first: ROW
10. Numeric form of row and column:
    VARIABLE-LENGTH ASCII
11. Add offset to: Row: 0
                         Col: 0
12. Separator sequence:
              ;
              3B
13. End sequence:
              H
              48
14. Cursor to top row, left column:
ESC [1   ;   1   H
1B 5B 31 3B 31 48
15. 10th Row, 50th Column:
ESC [1   0   ;   5   0   H
1B 5B 31 30 3B 35 30 48
16. Delay after positioning: 0
17. Cursor home:
              ESC [H
              1B 5B 48

ERASURE   DELAY
18. Entire screen:
        ESC [2   J   0
        1B 5B 32 4A
19. Cursor to end of screen:
        ESC [J   0
        1B 5B 4A
20. Beginning of screen to cursor:
        ESC [1   J   0
        1B 5B 31 4A
21. Cursor to end of line:
        ESC [K   0
        1B 5B 4B
22. Beginning of line to cursor:
        ESC [1   K   0
        1B 5B 31 4B
23. Entire cursor line:
        ESC [2   K   0
        1B 5B 32 4B

VIDEO ATTRIBUTES
       ON   OFF
24. Blinking:
    ESC [5   m   ESC [m
    1B 5B 35 6D   1B 5B 6D
25. Reverse video:
    ESC [7   m   ESC [m
    1B 5B 37 6D   1B 5B 6D
26. Underline:
    ESC [4   m   ESC [m
    1B 5B 34 6D   1B 5B 6D
27. High intensity:
    ESC [1   m   ESC [m
    1B 5B 31 6D   1B 5B 6D
28. Half intensity:

29. Attributes occupy position: NO
30. Attributes cumulative: YES
31. All attributes off:
              ESC [m
              1B 5B 6D

CURSOR CONTROL KEYS
32. Cursor up:
              ESC [A
              1B 5B 41
33. Cursor down:
              ESC [B
              1B 5B 42
34. Cursor right:
              ESC [C
              1B 5B 43
35. Cursor left:
              ESC [D
              1B 5B 44

CHARACTER SET
36. Full upper and lower ASCII: YES
37. Generate all control codes: YES
38. Bell or tone sequence:
              ^G
              07

EMULATION
39. Conform to ANSI X3.64?   YES
40. Terminals Emulated:

                        CONTINUED ====>

| Manufacturer: | CIE Terminals |
| Terminal: | CIT-80 (ANSI mode) |

41. Information provided by:
    MANUFACTURER

42. PROGRAM FUNCTION KEYS   NOTES
    1. ESC O   P   30. See ANSI video attribute
       1B   4F 50   discussion.
                                     36. Plus 32 standard graphics
    2. ESC O   Q   characters.
       1B   4F 51

    3. ESC O   R
       1B   4F 52

    4. ESC O   S
       1B   4F 53

    5.

    6.

    7.

    8.

    9.

   10.

   11.

   12.

   13.

   14.

   15.

   16.

----
1. Manufacturer: CIE Terminals
2. Terminal: CIT-80 (VT52 mode)

SCREEN LAYOUT   VIDEO ATTRIBUTES
3. Number of rows: 24   ON   OFF
4. Number of columns: 80   24. Blinking:
5. Top Row: 1   ESC d   B   ESC d   @
6. Left Column: 1   1B   64 42   1B   64 40
7. Printing in bottom right   25. Reverse video:
   cause scroll?   PROG   ESC d   P   ESC d   @
                                     1B   64 50   1B   64 40
CURSOR ADDRESSING   26. Underline:
8. Lead-in sequence: ESC d   \   ESC d   @
            ESC Y   1B   64 5C   1B   64 40
            1B   59   27. High intensity:
9. Row or column first: ROW   ESC d   A   ESC d   @
10. Numeric form of row and column: 1B   64 41   1B   64 40
    BINARY   28. Half intensity:
11. Add offset to: Row: 1F
                         Col: 1F
12. Separator sequence: 29. Attributes occupy position: NO
                                    30. Attributes cumulative: NO
                                    31. All attributes off:
13. End sequence: ESC d   @
                                              1B   64 40

14. Cursor to top row, left column: CURSOR CONTROL KEYS
ESC Y   SP SP   32. Cursor up:
1B   59 20 20   ESC A
15. 10th Row, 50th Column: 1B   41
ESC Y   )   Q   33. Cursor down:
1B   59 29 51   ESC B
16. Delay after positioning: 0   1B   42
17. Cursor home: 34. Cursor right:
            ESC H   ESC C
            1B   48   1B   43
                                    35. Cursor left:
ERASURE   DELAY   ESC D
18. Entire screen: 1B   44
        ESC H   ESC J   0
        1B   48 1B   4A   CHARACTER SET
19. Cursor to end of screen: 36. Full upper and lower ASCII: YES
        ESC J   0   37. Generate all control codes: YES
        1B   4A   38. Bell or tone sequence:
20. Beginning of screen to cursor: ^G
                                              07

21. Cursor to end of line: EMULATION
        ESC K   0   39. Conform to ANSI X3.64?   NO
        1B   4B   40. Terminals Emulated:
22. Beginning of line to cursor: DEC VT52

23. Entire cursor line:

41. Information provided by:
    MANUFACTURER

42. PROGRAM FUNCTION KEYS   NOTES
    1. ESC P   30. Half intensity-blinking
       1B   50   ESC d C
                                       Reverse video-high intensity
    2. ESC Q   ESC d Q
       1B   51   Reverse video-blinking
                                       ESC d R
    3. ESC R   Reverse video-high intensity-blink
       1B   52   ESC d S
                                       Underline-half intensity
    4. ESC S   ESC d a
       1B   53   Underline-blink-high intensity
                                       ESC d c
    5.   Underline-reverse-high intensity
                                       ESC d q
                                       Underline-reverse-blink
    6.   ESC d r
                                       Underline-reverse video
                                       ESC d p
    7.

    8.

    9.

   10.

   11.

   12.

   13.

   14.

   15.

   16.

```
--------------------------------------------------------------------------------
1. Manufacturer:                    Cobar
2. Terminal:                        Cobar 3100, Cobar 3132
--------------------------------------------------------------------------------
```

SCREEN LAYOUT
3. Number of rows: 24
4. Number of columns: 80
5. Top Row: 1
6. Left Column: 1
7. Printing in bottom right
   cause scroll?   PROG

CURSOR ADDRESSING
8. Lead-in sequence:
               ESC [
               1B 5B
9. Row or column first: ROW
10. Numeric form of row and column:
   VARIABLE-LENGTH ASCII
11. Add offset to: Row: 0
                          Col: 0
12. Separator sequence:
               ;
               3B
13. End sequence:
               H
               48
14. Cursor to top row, left column:
   ESC [1   ;   1   H
   1B 5B 31 3B 31 48
15. 10th Row, 50th Column:
   ESC [1   0   ;   5   0   H
   1B 5B 31 30 3B 35 30 48
16. Delay after positioning: 0
17. Cursor home:
               ESC [H
               1B 5B 48

ERASURE   DELAY
18. Entire screen:
       ESC [2   J   0
       1B 5B 32 4A
19. Cursor to end of screen:
       ESC [J   0
       1B 5B 4A
20. Beginning of screen to cursor:
       ESC [1   J   0
       1B 5B 31 4A
21. Cursor to end of line:
       ESC [K   0
       1B 5B 4B
22. Beginning of line to cursor:
       ESC [1   K   0
       1B 5B 31 4B
23. Entire cursor line:
       ESC [2   K   0
       1B 5B 32 4B

VIDEO ATTRIBUTES
                ON   OFF
24. Blinking:
   ESC [5   m   ESC [m
   1B 5B 35 6D   1B 5B   6D
25. Reverse video:
   ESC [7   m   ESC [m
   1B 5B 37 6D   1B 5B   6D
26. Underline:
   ESC [4   m   ESC [m
   1B 5B 34 6D   1B 5B   6D
27. High intensity:
   ESC [1   m   ESC [m
   1B 5B 31 6D   1B 5B   6D
28. Half intensity:

29. Attributes occupy position: NO
30. Attributes cumulative: YES
31. All attributes off:
               ESC [m
               1B 5B 6D

CURSOR CONTROL KEYS
32. Cursor up:
               ESC [A
               1B 5B 41
33. Cursor down:
               ESC [B
               1B 5B 42
34. Cursor right:
               ESC [C
               1B 5B 43
35. Cursor left:
               ESC [D
               1B 5B 44

CHARACTER SET
36. Full upper and lower ASCII: YES
37. Generate all control codes: YES
38. Bell or tone sequence:
               ^G
               07

EMULATION
39. Conform to ANSI X3.64?   YES
40. Terminals Emulated:
   DEC VT100/102
   DEC VT52
   Cobar 3132 emulates DEC VT132

CONTINUED ====>

Manufacturer:	Cobar
Terminal:	Cobar 3100, Cobar 3132

41. Information provided by:
    MANUFACTURER

42. PROGRAM FUNCTION KEYS

1. ESC O   P
   1B   4F   50

2. ESC O   Q
   1B   4F   51

3. ESC O   R
   1B   4F   52

4. ESC O   S
   1B   4F   53

5. ESC O   w
   1B   4F   77

6. ESC O   x
   1B   4F   78

7. ESC O   y
   1B   4F   79

8. ESC O   m
   1B   4F   6D

9. ESC O   t
   1B   4F   74

10. ESC O   u
    1B   4F   75

11. ESC O   v
    1B   4F   76

12. ESC O   q
    1B   4F   71

13. ESC O   l
    1B   4F   6C

14. ESC O   s
    1B   4F   73

15. ESC O   t
    1B   4F   74

16. ESC O   M
    1B   4F   4D

NOTES

4. Optionally 132.
7. Set-up feature.
13. Or f (66H).
14. Or ESC [1 ; 1 f
15. Or ESC [1 0 ; 5 0 f
17. Or ESC [f
30. Blinking and reverse video:
    ESC [5 ; 7 m
42. PF17   ESC O n
    PF18   ESC O p

```
--------------------------------------------------------------------------------
1. Manufacturer:                    Colorgraphic Communications Corp.
2. Terminal:                        MVI-100 Model 100, 489, 119, 113
--------------------------------------------------------------------------------
```

SCREEN LAYOUT
3. Number of rows: 48
4. Number of columns: 80
5. Top Row: 1
6. Left Column: 1
7. Printing in bottom right
   cause scroll?   PROG

CURSOR ADDRESSING
8. Lead-in sequence:
            ESC [
            1B 5B
9. Row or column first: ROW
10. Numeric form of row and column:
    VARIABLE-LENGTH ASCII
11. Add offset to: Row: 0
                          Col: 0
12. Separator sequence:
            ;
            3B
13. End sequence:
            H
            48
14. Cursor to top row, left column:
ESC [1   ;   1   H
1B 5B 31 3B 31 48
15. 10th Row, 50th Column:
ESC [1   0   ;   5   0   H
1B 5B 31 30 3B 35 30 48
16. Delay after positioning: 0
17. Cursor home:
            ESC [H
            1B 5B 48

ERASURE   DELAY
18. Entire screen:
            ESC [2   J   0
            1B 5B 32 4A
19. Cursor to end of screen:
            ESC [0   J   0
            1B 5B 30 4A
20. Beginning of screen to cursor:
            ESC [1   J   0
            1B 5B 31 4A
21. Cursor to end of line:
            ESC [0   K   0
            1B 5B 30 4B
22. Beginning of line to cursor:
            ESC [1   K   0
            1B 5B 31 4B
23. Entire cursor line:
            ESC [2   K   0
            1B 5B 32 4B

VIDEO ATTRIBUTES
                ON   OFF
24. Blinking:
ESC [5   m   ESC [2   2   m
1B 5B 35 6D   1B 5B 32 32 6D
25. Reverse video:
ESC [7   m   ESC [2   3   m
1B 5B 37 6D   1B 5B 32 33 6D
26. Underline:
ESC [4   m   ESC [2   1   m
1B 5B 34 6D   1B 5B 32 31 6D
27. High intensity:
ESC [1   m   ESC [2   m
1B 5B 31 6D   1B 5B 32 6D
28. Half intensity:

29. Attributes occupy position: NO
30. Attributes cumulative: YES
31. All attributes off:
            ESC [0   m
            1B 5B 30 6D

CURSOR CONTROL KEYS
32. Cursor up:
            ESC [A
            1B 5B 41
33. Cursor down:
            ESC [B
            1B 5B 42
34. Cursor right:
            ESC [C
            1B 5B 43
35. Cursor left:
            ESC [D
            1B 5B 44

CHARACTER SET
36. Full upper and lower ASCII: YES
37. Generate all control codes: YES
38. Bell or tone sequence:
            ^G
            07

EMULATION
39. Conform to ANSI X3.64?   YES
40. Terminals Emulated:
    DEC VT100, DEC VT52, ADDS, ADM3
    HAZELTINE 1500, IBM 3101

CONTINUED ====>

Manufacturer: Colorgraphic Communications Corp.
Terminal: MVI-100 Model 100, 489, 119, 113

41. Information provided by:
    MANUFACTURER

42. PROGRAM FUNCTION KEYS   NOTES
    1.   30. See ANSI cumulative attribute
                                           discussion.
                                 36. Also process control set.
    2.   42. PF1-PF12 programmable.

    3.

    4.

    5.

    6.

    7.

    8.

    9.

    10.

    11.

    12.

    13. ESC O   w
        1B 4F 77

    14. ESC O   x
        1B 4F 78

    15. ESC O   y
        1B 4F 79

    16. ESC O   t
        1B 4F 74

```
--------------------------------------------------------------------------
1. Manufacturer:                    Colorgraphic Communications Corp.
2. Terminal:                        MVI-100 Model 813/819 VT100 mode
--------------------------------------------------------------------------
```

SCREEN LAYOUT   VIDEO ATTRIBUTES
3. Number of rows: 48   ON   OFF
4. Number of columns: 80   24. Blinking:
5. Top Row: 1   ESC [5   m   ESC [2   2   m
6. Left Column: 1   1B 5B 35 6D   1B 5B 32 32 6D
7. Printing in bottom right   25. Reverse video:
   cause scroll?   PROG   ESC [7   m   ESC [2   3   m
                                      1B 5B 37 6D   1B 5B 32 33 6D
CURSOR ADDRESSING   26. Underline:
8. Lead-in sequence: ESC [4   m   ESC [2   1   m
           ESC [1B 5B 34 6D   1B 5B 32 31 6D
           1B 5B   27. High intensity:
9. Row or column first: ROW   ESC [1   m   ESC [2   m
10. Numeric form of row and column: 1B 5B 31 6D   1B 5B 32 6D
    VARIABLE-LENGTH ASCII   28. Half intensity:
11. Add offset to: Row: 0
                          Col: 0
12. Separator sequence: 29. Attributes occupy position: NO
           ;   30. Attributes cumulative: YES
           3B   31. All attributes off:
13. End sequence: ESC [0   m
           H   1B 5B 30 6D
           48
14. Cursor to top row, left column: CURSOR CONTROL KEYS
ESC [1   ;   1   H   32. Cursor up:
1B 5B 31 3B 31 48   ESC [A
15. 10th Row, 50th Column: 1B 5B 41
ESC [1   0   ;   5   0   H   33. Cursor down:
1B 5B 31 30 3B 35 30 48   ESC [B
16. Delay after positioning: 0   1B 5B 42
17. Cursor home: 34. Cursor right:
           ESC [H   ESC [C
           1B 5B 48   1B 5B 43
                                      35. Cursor left:
ERASURE   DELAY   ESC [D
18. Entire screen: 1B 5B 44
           ESC [2   J   0
           1B 5B 32 4A   CHARACTER SET
19. Cursor to end of screen: 36. Full upper and lower ASCII: YES
           ESC [0   J   0   37. Generate all control codes: YES
           1B 5B 30 4A   38. Bell or tone sequence:
20. Beginning of screen to cursor: ^G
           ESC [1   J   0   07
           1B 5B 31 4A
21. Cursor to end of line: EMULATION
           ESC [0   K   0   39. Conform to ANSI X3.64?   YES
           1B 5B 30 4B   40. Terminals Emulated:
22. Beginning of line to cursor: ISC8001G
           ESC [1   K   0   MVI-100-8
           1B 5B 31 4B   VT100
23. Entire cursor line: VT52
           ESC [2   K   0
           1B 5B 32 4B

                            81   CONTINUED ====>
```
```

41. Information provided by:
    MANUFACTURER

42. PROGRAM FUNCTION KEYS
    1.

    2.

    3.

    4.

    5.

    6.

    7.

    8.

    9.

    10.

    11.

    12.

    13. ESC O   w
        1B   4F   77

    14. ESC O   x
        1B   4F   78

    15. ESC O   y
        1B   4F   79

    16. ESC O   t
        1B   4F   74

NOTES
30. See ANSI cumulative attribute
    discussion.
36. Also process control set.
42. PF1-PF12 programmable.
    PF13-PF24 fixed sequence.

```
--------------------------------------------------------------------------
  1. Manufacturer:                    Colorgraphic Communications Corp.
  2. Terminal:                        MVI-100 Model 813/819 ISC8001G mode
--------------------------------------------------------------------------

SCREEN LAYOUT                         VIDEO ATTRIBUTES
  3. Number of rows:         48              ON                    OFF
  4. Number of columns:      80       24. Blinking:
  5. Top Row:                 0       ^_                    ^O
  6. Left Column:             0       1F                    OF
  7. Printing in bottom right         25. Reverse video:
     cause scroll?         PROG

CURSOR ADDRESSING                     26. Underline:
  8. Lead-in sequence:
               ^C
               03                     27. High intensity:
  9. Row or column first:     COL
 10. Numeric form of row and column:
     BINARY                           28. Half intensity:
 11. Add offset to:     Row:   0
                        Col:   0
 12. Separator sequence:              29. Attributes occupy position: NO
                                      30. Attributes cumulative:     YES
                                      31. All attributes off:
 13. End sequence:                               ^F  ^B
                                                 06  02

 14. Cursor to top row, left column:  CURSOR CONTROL KEYS
 ^C  NUL NUL                          32. Cursor up:
 03  00  00                                      ^\
 15. 10th Row, 50th Column:                      1C
 ^C   2   ^J                          33. Cursor down:
 03  32  0A                                      ^J
 16. Delay after positioning:     0              0A
 17. Cursor home:                     34. Cursor right:
               ^H                                ^Z
               08                                1A
                                      35. Cursor left:
                                                 ^Y
ERASURE                      DELAY               19
 18. Entire screen:
               ^L                 0
               0C                     CHARACTER SET
 19. Cursor to end of screen:         36. Full upper and lower ASCII: YES
                                  0   37. Generate all control codes: YES
                                      38. Bell or tone sequence:
 20. Beginning of screen to cursor:              ^G
                                  0              07

 21. Cursor to end of line:           EMULATION
                                  0   39. Conform to ANSI X3.64?     YES
                                      40. Terminals Emulated:
 22. Beginning of line to cursor:         ISC8001G
                                  0       MVI-100-8
                                          VT100
 23. Entire cursor line:                  VT52
               ^K                 0
               0B
```

                    CONTINUED ====>

Manufacturer: Colorgraphic Communications Corp.
Terminal: MVI-100 Model 813/819 ISC8001G mode

41. Information provided by:
    MANUFACTURER

42. PROGRAM FUNCTION KEYS   NOTES
  1.   36. Also process control set.
                                 42. PF1-PF12 programmable.
                                     PF13-PF24 fixed sequences.

  2.

  3.

  4.

  5.

  6.

  7.

  8.

  9.

 10.

 11.

 12.

 13. ESC O   w
     1B   4F   77

 14. ESC O   x
     1B   4F   78

 15. ESC O   y
     1B   4F   79

 16. ESC O   t
     1B   4F   74

```
--------------------------------------------------------------------------------
 1. Manufacturer:                    Colorgraphic Communications Corp.
 2. Terminal:                        MVI-7 Models 7, 719
--------------------------------------------------------------------------------
```

SCREEN LAYOUT
3. Number of rows: 24
4. Number of columns: 80
5. Top Row: 1
6. Left Column: 1
7. Printing in bottom right
   cause scroll?   PROG

CURSOR ADDRESSING
8. Lead-in sequence:
            ESC [
            1B 5B
9. Row or column first: ROW
10. Numeric form of row and column:
    VARIABLE-LENGTH ASCII
11. Add offset to: Row: 0
                          Col: 0
12. Separator sequence:
            ;
            3B
13. End sequence:
            H
            48
14. Cursor to top row, left column:
ESC [1   ;   1   H
1B 5B 31 3B 31 48
15. 10th Row, 50th Column:
ESC [1   0   ;   5   0   H
1B 5B 31 30 3B 35 30 48
16. Delay after positioning: 0
17. Cursor home:
            ESC [H
            1B 5B 48

ERASURE   DELAY
18. Entire screen:
      ESC [2   J   0
      1B 5B 32 4A
19. Cursor to end of screen:
      ESC [0   J   0
      1B 5B 30 4A
20. Beginning of screen to cursor:
      ESC [1   J   0
      1B 5B 31 4A
21. Cursor to end of line:
      ESC [0   K   0
      1B 5B 30 4B
22. Beginning of line to cursor:
      ESC [1   K   0
      1B 5B 31 4B
23. Entire cursor line:
      ESC [2   K   0
      1B 5B 32 4B

VIDEO ATTRIBUTES
     ON   OFF
24. Blinking:
ESC [5   m   ESC [2   2   m
1B 5B 35 6D   1B 5B 32 32 6D
25. Reverse video:
ESC [7   m   ESC [2   3   m
1B 5B 37 6D   1B 5B 32 33 6D
26. Underline:
ESC [4   m   ESC [2   1   m
1B 5B 34 6D   1B 5B 32 31 6D
27. High intensity:
ESC [1   m   ESC [2   m
1B 5B 31 6D   1B 5B 32 6D
28. Half intensity:

29. Attributes occupy position: NO
30. Attributes cumulative: YES
31. All attributes off:
            ESC [0   m
            1B 5B 30 6D

CURSOR CONTROL KEYS
32. Cursor up:
            ESC [A
            1B 5B 41
33. Cursor down:
            ESC [B
            1B 5B 42
34. Cursor right:
            ESC [C
            1B 5B 43
35. Cursor left:
            ESC [D
            1B 5B 44

CHARACTER SET
36. Full upper and lower ASCII: YES
37. Generate all control codes: YES
38. Bell or tone sequence:
            ^G
            07

EMULATION
39. Conform to ANSI X3.64?   YES
40. Terminals Emulated:
    DEC VT100, DEC VT52, ADDS, ADM3
    HAZELTINE 1500, IBM 3101

41. Information provided by:
    MANUFACTURER

42. PROGRAM FUNCTION KEYS   NOTES
    1.   30. See ANSI cumulative attribute
                                       discussion.
                                   36. Also process control set.
    2.   42. PF1-PF12 programmable.

    3.

    4.

    5.

    6.

    7.

    8.

    9.

   10.

   11.

   12.

   13. ESC O   w
        1B   4F 77

   14. ESC O   x
        1B   4F 78

   15. ESC O   y
        1B   4F 79

   16. ESC O   t
        1B   4F 74

---
1. Manufacturer: Corona Data Systems Inc.
2. Terminal: Personal Computer

SCREEN LAYOUT
3. Number of rows: 25
4. Number of columns: 80
5. Top Row: 0
6. Left Column: 0
7. Printing in bottom right
   cause scroll?   YES

CURSOR ADDRESSING
8. Lead-in sequence:
              ESC [
              1B   5B
9. Row or column first: ROW
10. Numeric form of row and column:
    VARIABLE-LENGTH ASCII
11. Add offset to: Row: 0
                          Col: 0
12. Separator sequence:
              ;
              3B
13. End sequence:
              H
              48
14. Cursor to top row, left column:
ESC [0   ;   0   H
1B 5B 30   3B   30   48
15. 10th Row, 50th Column:
ESC [1   0   ;   5   0   H
1B 5B 31   30   3B   35   30   48
16. Delay after positioning: 0
17. Cursor home:
              ESC [H
              1B   5B   48

ERASURE   DELAY
18. Entire screen:
       ESC [2   J
       1B   5B 32   4A   0
19. Cursor to end of screen:
       ESC [J
       1B   5B 4A   0
20. Beginning of screen to cursor:
       ESC [1   J
       1B   5B 31   4A   0
21. Cursor to end of line:
       ESC [K
       1B   5B 4B   0
22. Beginning of line to cursor:
       ESC [1   K
       1B   5B 31   4B   0
23. Entire cursor line:
       ESC [2   K
       1B   5B 32   4B   0

VIDEO ATTRIBUTES
      ON   OFF
24. Blinking:
   ESC [5   m   ESC [m
   1B 5B 35   6D   1B 5B   6D
25. Reverse video:
   ESC [7   m   ESC [m
   1B 5B 37   6D   1B 5B   6D
26. Underline:
   ESC [4   m   ESC [m
   1B 5B 34   6D   1B 5B   6D
27. High intensity:
   ESC [1   m   ESC [m
   1B 5B 31   6D   1B 5B   6D
28. Half intensity:

29. Attributes occupy position: NO
30. Attributes cumulative: YES
31. All attributes off:
              ESC [m
              1B   5B   6D

CURSOR CONTROL KEYS
32. Cursor up:
              ESC [A
              1B   5B   41
33. Cursor down:
              ESC [B
              1B   5B   42
34. Cursor right:
              ESC [C
              1B   5B   43
35. Cursor left:
              ESC [D
              1B   5B   44

CHARACTER SET
36. Full upper and lower ASCII: YES
37. Generate all control codes: YES
38. Bell or tone sequence:
              ^G
              07

EMULATION
39. Conform to ANSI X3.64?   YES
40. Terminals Emulated:
    Runs "IBM PC" compatible progra

                   CONTINUED ====>

41. Information provided by:
    MANUFACTURER

42. PROGRAM FUNCTION KEYS   NOTES
    1. NUL ;
       00 3B

    2. NUL <
       00 3C

    3. NUL =
       00 3D

    4. NUL >
       00 3E

    5. NUL ?
       00 3F

    6. NUL @
       00 40

    7. NUL A
       00 41

    8. NUL B
       00 42

    9. NUL C
       00 43

    10. NUL D
        00 44

    11.

    12.

    13.

    14.

    15.

    16.

```
--------------------------------------------------------------------------
1. Manufacturer:                        Cromemco, Inc.
2. Terminal:                            C-10
--------------------------------------------------------------------------
```

SCREEN LAYOUT   VIDEO ATTRIBUTES
3. Number of rows: 24   ON   OFF
4. Number of columns: 80   24. Blinking:
5. Top Row: 1   ESC d   B   ESC d   @
6. Left Column: 1   1B 64   42   1B 64   40
7. Printing in bottom right   25. Reverse video:
   cause scroll?   YES   ESC d   P   ESC d   @
                                       1B 64   50   1B 64   40
CURSOR ADDRESSING   26. Underline:
8. Lead-in sequence: ESC d   `   ESC d   @
          ESC Y   1B 64   60   1B 64   40
          1B 59   27. High intensity:
9. Row or column first: ROW   ESC d   H   ESC d   @
10. Numeric form of row and column: 1B 64   48   1B 64   40
    BINARY   28. Half intensity:
11. Add offset to: Row: 1F   ESC d   A   ESC d   @
                          Col: 1F   1B 64   41   1B 64   40
12. Separator sequence: 29. Attributes occupy position: NO
                                       30. Attributes cumulative: NO
                                       31. All attributes off:
13. End sequence: ESC d   @
                                                 1B 64   40

14. Cursor to top row, left column: CURSOR CONTROL KEYS
ESC Y   SP   SP   32. Cursor up:
1B 59   20   20   ESC A
15. 10th Row, 50th Column: 1B   41
ESC Y   )   Q   33. Cursor down:
1B 59   29   51   ESC B
16. Delay after positioning: 0   1B   42
17. Cursor home: 34. Cursor right:
          ESC H   ESC C
          1B 48   1B   43
                                       35. Cursor left:
ERASURE   DELAY   ESC D
18. Entire screen: 1B   44
          ESC E   0
          1B 45   CHARACTER SET
19. Cursor to end of screen: 36. Full upper and lower ASCII: YES
          ESC J   0   37. Generate all control codes: YES
          1B 4A   38. Bell or tone sequence:
20. Beginning of screen to cursor: ^G
                                                 07

21. Cursor to end of line: EMULATION
          ESC K   0   39. Conform to ANSI X3.64?   NO
          1B 4B   40. Terminals Emulated:
22. Beginning of line to cursor:

23. Entire cursor line:

                              89   CONTINUED ====>
```
CONTINUED ====>
```

Manufacturer:	Cromemco, Inc.
Terminal:	C-10

41. Information provided by:
    MANUFACTURER

42. PROGRAM FUNCTION KEYS

1.	^B	p
	02	70

2.	^B	q
	02	71

3.	^B	r
	02	72

4.	^B	s
	02	73

5.	^B	t
	02	74

6.	^B	u
	02	75

7.	^B	v
	02	76

8.	^B	w
	02	77

9.	^B	x
	02	78

10.	^B	y
	02	79

11.	^B	z
	02	7A

12.	^B	{
	02	7B

13.	^B		
	02	7C

14.	^B	}
	02	7D

15.	^B	~
	02	7E

16.	^B	DEL
	02	7F

NOTES

1. 25th status line.
8. Or ESC F.
14. Or ESC F SP SP.
15. Or ESC F) Q.
27. This sequence selects bold set.
30. All attributes preceeded by ESC d:

std	gra	bold	misc	
@	D	H	L	normal
A	E	I	M	half
B	F	J	N	blink
C	G	K	O	half-blink
P	T	X	\	reverse
Q	U	Y	]	half-reverse
R	V	Z	^	blink-reverse
S	W	[	_	half-blink-rev
`	d	h	l	underline
a	e	i	m	half-under
b	f	j	n	blink-under
c	g	k	o	half-blink-und
p	t	x	|	rev-underlined
q	u	y	}	half-rev-under
r	v	z	~	blink-rev-und
s	w	{	DEL	half-blink-rev-underline

31. All attributes off returns to
    normal character set.
36. Four character sets standard:
    normal, graphics, bold, misc.
42. Additional program function keys:
    PF17 STX o
    PF18 STX n
    PF19 STX m
    PF20 STX l

----
1. Manufacturer: CTi DATA Corporation
2. Terminal: CTi 3078

SCREEN LAYOUT   VIDEO ATTRIBUTES
3. Number of rows: 24   ON   OFF
4. Number of columns: 80   24. Blinking:
5. Top Row: 1   ESC 0   B   ESC 0   @
6. Left Column: 1   1B   30   42   1B   30   40
7. Printing in bottom right   25. Reverse video:
   cause scroll?   NO   ESC 0   P   ESC 0   @
                                          1B   30   50   1B   30   40
CURSOR ADDRESSING   26. Underline:
8. Lead-in sequence: ESC 0   `   ESC 0   @
         ESC Y   1B   30   60   1B   30   40
         1B   59   27. High intensity:
9. Row or column first: ROW   ESC 0   0   ESC 0   @
10. Numeric form of row and column: 1B   30   30   1B   30   40
    BINARY   28. Half intensity:
11. Add offset to: Row: 1F   ESC 0   A   ESC 0   @
                         Col: 1F   1B   30   41   1B   30   40
12. Separator sequence: 29. Attributes occupy position: YES
                                          30. Attributes cumulative: NO
                                          31. All attributes off:
13. End sequence: ESC 0   @
                                                    1B   30   40

14. Cursor to top row, left column: CURSOR CONTROL KEYS
ESC Y   SP   SP   32. Cursor up:
1B   59   20   20   ^Z
15. 10th Row, 50th Column: 1A
ESC Y   )   Q   33. Cursor down:
1B   59   29   51   ^J
16. Delay after positioning: 0   0A
17. Cursor home: 34. Cursor right:
         ^A   ^F
         01   06
                                          35. Cursor left:
ERASURE   DELAY   ^H
18. Entire screen: 08
         ^L   0
         0C   CHARACTER SET
19. Cursor to end of screen: 36. Full upper and lower ASCII: YES
         ESC k   0   37. Generate all control codes: NO
         1B   6B   38. Bell or tone sequence:
20. Beginning of screen to cursor: ^G
                                                    07
21. Cursor to end of line:
         ESC K   0   EMULATION
         1B   4B   39. Conform to ANSI X3.64?   NO
22. Beginning of line to cursor: 40. Terminals Emulated:
                                              ADDS VP60
                                              ADDS VP78
23. Entire cursor line:
         ESC l   20
         1B   6C

                                91   CONTINUED ====>

Manufacturer: CTi DATA Corporation
Terminal: CTi 3078

---

41. Information provided by:
    MANUFACTURER

42. PROGRAM FUNCTION KEYS   NOTES
    1. ESC SP   42. Additional PF keys:
       1B   20   17. ESC   0
                                         1B   30
    2. ESC !   18. ESC   1
       1B   21   1B   31
                                     19. ESC   2
    3. ESC "   1B   32
       1B   22   20. ESC   3
                                         1B   33
    4. ESC #   21. ESC   4
       1B   23   1B   34
                                     22. ESC   5
    5. ESC $ 1B   35
       1B   24   23. ESC   6
                                         1B   36
    6. ESC %   24. ESC   7
       1B   25   1B   37

    7. ESC &
       1B   26

    8. ESC ´
       1B   27

    9. ESC (
       1B   28

   10. ESC)
       1B   29

   11. ESC *
       1B   2A

   12. ESC +
       1B   2B

   13. ESC ,
       1B   2C

   14. ESC -
       1B   2D

   15. ESC .
       1B   2E

   16. ESC /
       1B   2F

```
--------------------------------------------------------------------------------
   1. Manufacturer:                    Digital Equipment Corporation
   2. Terminal:                        VT100, 101, 102, 131, 125
--------------------------------------------------------------------------------
```

SCREEN LAYOUT   VIDEO ATTRIBUTES
 3. Number of rows: 24   ON   OFF
 4. Number of columns: 80   24. Blinking:
 5. Top Row: 1   ESC [5   m   ESC [m
 6. Left Column: 1   1B   5B 35   6D   1B   5B   6D
 7. Printing in bottom right   25. Reverse video:
    cause scroll?   PROG   ESC [7   m   ESC [m
                                       1B   5B 37   6D   1B   5B   6D
CURSOR ADDRESSING   26. Underline:
 8. Lead-in sequence: ESC [4   m   ESC [m
            ESC [1B   5B 34   6D   1B   5B   6D
            1B   5B   27. High intensity:
 9. Row or column first: ROW   ESC [1   m   ESC [m
10. Numeric form of row and column: 1B   5B 31   6D   1B   5B   6D
    VARIABLE-LENGTH ASCII   28. Half intensity:
11. Add offset to: Row: 0
                          Col: 0
12. Separator sequence: 29. Attributes occupy position: NO
            ;   30. Attributes cumulative: YES
            3B   31. All attributes off:
13. End sequence: ESC [m
            H   1B   5B   6D
            48
14. Cursor to top row, left column: CURSOR CONTROL KEYS
ESC [1   ;   1   H   32. Cursor up:
1B   5B 31   3B   31   48   ESC [A
15. 10th Row, 50th Column: 1B   5B   41
ESC [1   0   ;   5   0   H   33. Cursor down:
1B   5B 31   30   3B   35   30   48   ESC [B
16. Delay after positioning: 0   1B   5B   42
17. Cursor home: 34. Cursor right:
            ESC [H   ESC [C
            1B   5B 48   1B   5B   43
                                       35. Cursor left:
ERASURE   DELAY   ESC [D
18. Entire screen: 1B   5B   44
            ESC [2   J   0
            1B   5B 32   4A   CHARACTER SET
19. Cursor to end of screen: 36. Full upper and lower ASCII: YES
            ESC [J   0 37. Generate all control codes: YES
            1B   5B 4A   38. Bell or tone sequence:
20. Beginning of screen to cursor: ^G
            ESC [1   J   0   07
            1B   5B 31   4A
21. Cursor to end of line: EMULATION
            ESC [K   0 39. Conform to ANSI X3.64?   YES
            1B   5B 4B   40. Terminals Emulated:
22. Beginning of line to cursor: DEC VT52
            ESC [1   K   0
            1B   5B 31   4B
23. Entire cursor line:
            ESC [2   K   0
            1B   5B 32   4B

                                    93   CONTINUED ====>

Manufacturer: Digital Equipment Corporation
Terminal: VT100, 101, 102, 131, 125

41. Information provided by:
    MANUFACTURER

42. PROGRAM FUNCTION KEYS   NOTES
    1. ESC O   P   3. Optionally 14x132.
       1B 4F   50   4. Optionally 14x132.
                                       VT102 allows 24x132.
    2. ESC O   Q   36. Includes 32 line drawing and
       1B 4F   51   other graphic characters.
                                       National Replacement character
    3. ESC O   R   sets optional.
       1B 4F   52
                                       VT125 includes 240x768 bit-
    4. ESC O   S   mapped graphics.
       1B 4F   53

    5.

    6.

    7.

    8.

    9.

   10.

   11.

   12.

   13.

   14.

   15.

   16.

---
1. Manufacturer: Digital Equipment Corporation
2. Terminal: VT220, 240, 241

SCREEN LAYOUT
3. Number of rows: 24
4. Number of columns: 80
5. Top Row: 1
6. Left Column: 1
7. Printing in bottom right
   cause scroll?   PROG

CURSOR ADDRESSING
8. Lead-in sequence:
            ESC [
            1B 5B
9. Row or column first: ROW
10. Numeric form of row and column:
    VARIABLE-LENGTH ASCII
11. Add offset to: Row: 0
                          Col: 0
12. Separator sequence:
            ;
            3B
13. End sequence:
            H
            48
14. Cursor to top row, left column:
ESC [1   ;   1   H
1B 5B 31 3B 31 48
15. 10th Row, 50th Column:
ESC [1   0   ;   5   0   H
1B 5B 31 30 3B 35 30 48
16. Delay after positioning: 0
17. Cursor home:
            ESC [H
            1B 5B 48

ERASURE   DELAY
18. Entire screen:
      ESC [2   J   0
      1B 5B 32 4A
19. Cursor to end of screen:
      ESC [J   0
      1B 5B 4A
20. Beginning of screen to cursor:
      ESC [1   J   0
      1B 5B 31 4A
21. Cursor to end of line:
      ESC [K   0
      1B 5B 4B
22. Beginning of line to cursor:
      ESC [1   K   0
      1B 5B 31 4B
23. Entire cursor line:
      ESC [2   K   0
      1B 5B 32 4B

VIDEO ATTRIBUTES
            ON   OFF
24. Blinking:
ESC [5   m   ESC [m
1B 5B 35 6D   1B 5B   6D
25. Reverse video:
ESC [7   m   ESC [m
1B 5B 37 6D   1B 5B   6D
26. Underline:
ESC [4   m   ESC [m
1B 5B 34 6D   1B 5B   6D
27. High intensity:
ESC [1   m   ESC [m
1B 5B 31 6D   1B 5B   6D
28. Half intensity:

29. Attributes occupy position: NO
30. Attributes cumulative: YES
31. All attributes off:
            ESC [m
            1B 5B   6D

CURSOR CONTROL KEYS
32. Cursor up:
            ESC [A
            1B 5B 41
33. Cursor down:
            ESC [B
            1B 5B 42
34. Cursor right:
            ESC [C
            1B 5B 43
35. Cursor left:
            ESC [D
            1B 5B 44

CHARACTER SET
36. Full upper and lower ASCII: YES
37. Generate all control codes: YES
38. Bell or tone sequence:
            ^G
            07

EMULATION
39. Conform to ANSI X3.64?   YES
40. Terminals Emulated:
    DEC VT52

95   CONTINUED ====>

Manufacturer:	Digital Equipment Corporation
Terminal:	VT220, 240, 241

41. Information provided by:
    MANUFACTURER

42. PROGRAM FUNCTION KEYS

1. ESC O   P
   1B   4F   50

2. ESC O   Q
   1B   4F   51

3. ESC O   R
   1B   4F   52

4. ESC O   S
   1B   4F   53

5.

6.

7.

8.

9.

10.

11.

12.

13.

14.

15.

16.

NOTES

4. Optionally 132.

36. Includes 32 line drawing and
    other graphic characters.
    Multinational character sets.
    Downline loadable character
    sets.

    VT240 and VT241 include
    240x800 bit-mapped graphics.

```
--------------------------------------------------------------------------
  1. Manufacturer:                    Digital Equipment Corporation
  2. Terminal:                        VT52, VT55
--------------------------------------------------------------------------
```

SCREEN LAYOUT   VIDEO ATTRIBUTES
3. Number of rows: 24   ON   OFF
4. Number of columns: 80   24. Blinking:
5. Top Row: 1
6. Left Column: 1
7. Printing in bottom right   25. Reverse video:
   cause scroll?   PROG

CURSOR ADDRESSING   26. Underline:
8. Lead-in sequence:
        ESC Y
        1B 59   27. High intensity:
9. Row or column first: ROW
10. Numeric form of row and column:
    BINARY   28. Half intensity:
11. Add offset to: Row: 1F
                        Col: 1F
12. Separator sequence: 29. Attributes occupy position: NO
                                      30. Attributes cumulative: NO
                                      31. All attributes off:
13. End sequence:

14. Cursor to top row, left column: CURSOR CONTROL KEYS
ESC Y   SP   SP   32. Cursor up:
1B 59   20   20   ESC A
15. 10th Row, 50th Column: 1B   41
ESC Y   )   Q   33. Cursor down:
1B 59   29   51   ESC B
16. Delay after positioning: 0   1B   42
17. Cursor home: 34. Cursor right:
        ESC H   ESC C
        1B 48   1B   43
                                      35. Cursor left:
ERASURE   DELAY   ESC D
18. Entire screen: 1B   44
        ESC H   ESC J   0
        1B 48 1B 4A   CHARACTER SET
19. Cursor to end of screen: 36. Full upper and lower ASCII: YES
        ESC J   0   37. Generate all control codes: YES
        1B 4A   38. Bell or tone sequence:
20. Beginning of screen to cursor: ^G
                                              07
21. Cursor to end of line: EMULATION
        ESC K   0   39. Conform to ANSI X3.64?   NO
        1B 4B   40. Terminals Emulated:
22. Beginning of line to cursor:

23. Entire cursor line:

                         97   CONTINUED ====>
```

CONTINUED ====>
```

41. Information provided by:
    MANUFACTURER

42. PROGRAM FUNCTION KEYS   NOTES
 1. ESC O   P
    1B   4F   50

 2. ESC O   Q
    1B   4F   51

 3. ESC O   R
    1B   4F   52

 4. ESC O   S
    1B   4F   53

 5.

 6.

 7.

 8.

 9.

10.

11.

12.

13.

14.

15.

16.

```
--------------------------------------------------------------------------------
  1. Manufacturer:                      Digital Microsystems
  2. Terminal:                          DMS-3/F, DMS-15, DMS-501
--------------------------------------------------------------------------------
```

SCREEN LAYOUT   VIDEO ATTRIBUTES
 3. Number of rows: 24   ON   OFF
 4. Number of columns: 80   24. Blinking:
 5. Top Row: 1   ESC B   ESC N
 6. Left Column: 1   1B 42   1B 4E
 7. Printing in bottom right   25. Reverse video:
    cause scroll?   YES   ESC R   ESC N
                                       1B 52   1B 4E
CURSOR ADDRESSING   26. Underline:
 8. Lead-in sequence: ESC U   ESC N
            ESC Y   1B 55   1B 4E
            1B 59   27. High intensity:
 9. Row or column first: ROW
10. Numeric form of row and column:
    BINARY   28. Half intensity:
11. Add offset to: Row: 1F   ESC H   ESC N
                        Col: 1F   1B 48   1B 4E
12. Separator sequence: 29. Attributes occupy position: NO
                                       30. Attributes cumulative: YES
                                       31. All attributes off:
13. End sequence: ESC N
                                                   1B 4E

14. Cursor to top row, left column: CURSOR CONTROL KEYS
ESC Y   SP SP   32. Cursor up:
1B 59 20 20   ^Z
15. 10th Row, 50th Column: 1A
ESC Y   )   Q   33. Cursor down:
1B 59 29 51   ^J
16. Delay after positioning: 0A
17. Cursor home: 34. Cursor right:
            ^A   ^F
            01   06
                                       35. Cursor left:
ERASURE   DELAY   ^H
18. Entire screen: 08
            ^L   0
            0C   CHARACTER SET
19. Cursor to end of screen: 36. Full upper and lower ASCII: YES
            ESC k   0   37. Generate all control codes: YES
            1B 6B   38. Bell or tone sequence:
20. Beginning of screen to cursor: ^G
                                                   07

21. Cursor to end of line: EMULATION
            ESC K   0   39. Conform to ANSI X3.64?   NO
            1B 4B   40. Terminals Emulated:
22. Beginning of line to cursor: ADDS Regent 20/25
                                           ADDS Viewpoint
                                           Hazeltine 1500
23. Entire cursor line:

                          99   CONTINUED ====>

Manufacturer: Digital Microsystems
Terminal: DMS-3/F, DMS-15, DMS-501

41. Information provided by:
    MANUFACTURER

42. PROGRAM FUNCTION KEYS   NOTES
  1.   36. Foreign character sets.
                                       42. Programmable function keys.
                                           90 programmable keys.
  2.

  3.

  4.

  5.

  6.

  7.

  8.

  9.

 10.

 11.

 12.

 13.

 14.

 15.

 16.

```
--------------------------------------------------------------------------------
1. Manufacturer:                    Digital Microsystems
2. Terminal:                        DMS-5080, DMS-5086
--------------------------------------------------------------------------------
```

SCREEN LAYOUT   VIDEO ATTRIBUTES
3. Number of rows: 24   ON   OFF
4. Number of columns: 80   24. Blinking:
5. Top Row: 1   ESC B   ESC N
6. Left Column: 1   1B 42   1B 4E
7. Printing in bottom right   25. Reverse video:
   cause scroll?   YES   ESC R   ESC N
                                          1B 52   1B 4E
CURSOR ADDRESSING   26. Underline:
8. Lead-in sequence: ESC U   ESC N
      ESC Y   1B 55   1B 4E
      1B 59   27. High intensity:
9. Row or column first: ROW
10. Numeric form of row and column:
    BINARY   28. Half intensity:
11. Add offset to: Row: 1F   ESC H   ESC N
                       Col: 1F   1B 48   1B 4E
12. Separator sequence: 29. Attributes occupy position: NO
                                       30. Attributes cumulative: YES
                                       31. All attributes off:
13. End sequence: ESC N
                                              1B 4E

14. Cursor to top row, left column: CURSOR CONTROL KEYS
ESC Y   SP SP   32. Cursor up:
1B 59   20 20   ^Z
15. 10th Row, 50th Column: 1A
ESC Y   )   Q   33. Cursor down:
1B 59   29 51   ^J
16. Delay after positioning: 0A
17. Cursor home: 34. Cursor right:
         ^A   ^F
         01   06
                                       35. Cursor left:
ERASURE   DELAY   ^H
18. Entire screen: 08
      ^L   0
      0C   CHARACTER SET
19. Cursor to end of screen: 36. Full upper and lower ASCII: YES
      ESC k   0   37. Generate all control codes: YES
      1B 6B   38. Bell or tone sequence:
20. Beginning of screen to cursor: ^G
                                                07

21. Cursor to end of line: EMULATION
      ESC K   0   39. Conform to ANSI X3.64?   NO
      1B 4B   40. Terminals Emulated:
22. Beginning of line to cursor: Tektronix 4010 compatible
                                             graphics.

23. Entire cursor line:

                              101   CONTINUED ====>

41. Information provided by:
    MANUFACTURER

42. PROGRAM FUNCTION KEYS
    1.

    2.

    3.

    4.

    5.

    6.

  · 7.

    8.

    9.

   10.

   11.

   12.

   13.

   14.

   15.

   16.

NOTES
  3. Optionally 24 or 50.
  4. Optionally 132.
 36. Foreign character sets, user-
     definable characters.
 42. Programmable function keys.
     90 programmable keys.

```
------------------------------------------------------------------------
  1. Manufacturer:                    Direct Incorporated
  2. Terminal:                        825-(HP)
------------------------------------------------------------------------
```

SCREEN LAYOUT   VIDEO ATTRIBUTES
3. Number of rows: 24   ON   OFF
4. Number of columns: 80   24. Blinking:
5. Top Row: 1   ESC &   d   A   ESC &   d   @
6. Left Column: 1   1B 26 64 41   1B 26 64 40
7. Printing in bottom right   25. Reverse video:
   cause scroll?   PROG   ESC &   d   B   ESC &   d   @
                                        1B 26 64 42   1B 26 64 40
CURSOR ADDRESSING   26. Underline:
8. Lead-in sequence: ESC &   d   D   ESC &   d   @
          ESC &   a   1B 26 64 44   1B 26 64 40
          1B 26 61   27. High intensity:
9. Row or column first: COL   ESC &   d   @
10. Numeric form of row and column: 1B 26 64 40
    VARIABLE-LENGTH ASCII   28. Half intensity:
11. Add offset to: Row: 0   ESC &   d   H   ESC &   d   @
                        Col: 0   1B 26 64 48   1B 26 64 40
12. Separator sequence: 29. Attributes occupy position: NO
                                    30. Attributes cumulative: YES
                                    31. All attributes off:
13. End sequence: ESC &   d   @
          R   1B 26 64 40
          52
14. Cursor to top row, left column: CURSOR CONTROL KEYS
ESC &   a   0   R   0   c   32. Cursor up:
1B 26 61 30 52 30 63   ESC A
15. 10th Row, 50th Column: 1B 41
ESC &   a   9   R   4   9   c   33. Cursor down:
1B 26 61 39 52 34 39 63   ESC B
16. Delay after positioning: 0   1B 42
17. Cursor home: 34. Cursor right:
          ESC H   ESC C
          1B 48   1B 43
                                    35. Cursor left:
ERASURE   DELAY   ESC D
18. Entire screen: 1B 44
                             0
                                    CHARACTER SET
19. Cursor to end of screen: 36. Full upper and lower ASCII: YES
          ESC J   0   37. Generate all control codes: YES
          1B 4A   38. Bell or tone sequence:
20. Beginning of screen to cursor: ^G
                             0   07
21. Cursor to end of line: EMULATION
          ESC K   0   39. Conform to ANSI X3.64?   YES
          1B 4B   40. Terminals Emulated:
22. Beginning of line to cursor: HP2640, HP2645A
                             0   HP2622
23. Entire cursor line:
          ESC K   0
          1B 4B

                              103   CONTINUED ====>
```
```

```
Manufacturer:                    Direct Incorporated
Terminal:                        825-(HP)
```
---

41. Information provided by:
    MANUFACTURER

42. PROGRAM FUNCTION KEYS   NOTES
    1.   4. Optionally 132.
                                   42. All function keys programmable.

    2.

    3.

    4.

    5.

    6.

    7.

    8.

    9.

    10.

    11.

    12.

    13.

    14.

    15.

    16.

```
--------------------------------------------------------------------------
1. Manufacturer:                    Direct Incorporated
2. Terminal:                        828/1 (ANSI mode)
--------------------------------------------------------------------------


SCREEN LAYOUT                       VIDEO ATTRIBUTES
3. Number of rows:          24          ON                  OFF
4. Number of columns:       80      24. Blinking:
5. Top Row:                  1      ESC [    5    m       ESC [    m
6. Left Column:              1      1B  5B  35   6D       1B  5B  6D
7. Printing in bottom right         25. Reverse video:
   cause scroll?          PROG      ESC [    7    m       ESC [    m
                                    1B  5B  37   6D       1B  5B  6D
CURSOR ADDRESSING                   26. Underline:
8. Lead-in sequence:                ESC [    4    m       ESC [    m
          ESC [                     1B  5B  34   6D       1B  5B  6D
          1B  5B                    27. High intensity:
9. Row or column first:     ROW     ESC [    1    m       ESC [    m
10. Numeric form of row and column: 1B  5B  31   6D       1B  5B  6D
    VARIABLE-LENGTH ASCII           28. Half intensity:
11. Add offset to:        Row:   0
                          Col:   0
12. Separator sequence:             29. Attributes occupy position: NO
          ;                         30. Attributes cumulative:      YES
          3B                        31. All attributes off:
13. End sequence:                             ESC [    m
          H                                   1B  5B  6D
          48
14. Cursor to top row, left column: CURSOR CONTROL KEYS
ESC [    1    ;    1    H            32. Cursor up:
1B  5B  31  3B  31   48                        ESC [    A
15. 10th Row, 50th Column:                     1B  5B  41
ESC [    1    0    ;    5    0    H  33. Cursor down:
1B  5B  31  30  3B  35  30   48                ESC [    B
16. Delay after positioning:    0              1B  5B  42
17. Cursor home:                    34. Cursor right:
          ESC [    H                           ESC [    C
          1B  5B  48                           1B  5B  43
                                    35. Cursor left:
ERASURE                    DELAY              ESC [    D
18. Entire screen:                            1B  5B  44
      ESC [    2    J          0
      1B  5B  32   4A               CHARACTER SET
19. Cursor to end of screen:        36. Full upper and lower ASCII: YES
      ESC [    J              0      37. Generate all control codes: YES
      1B  5B  4A                     38. Bell or tone sequence:
20. Beginning of screen to cursor:            ^G
      ESC [    1    J          0               07
      1B  5B  31   4A
21. Cursor to end of line:          EMULATION
      ESC [    K              0      39. Conform to ANSI X3.64?      YES
      1B  5B  4B                     40. Terminals Emulated:
22. Beginning of line to cursor:        DEC VT100, VT102, VT131, VT52
      ESC [    1    K          0
      1B  5B  31   4B
23. Entire cursor line:
      ESC [    2    K          0
      1B  5B  32   4B
```

                    CONTINUED ====>

```
----------------------------------------------------------------------
        Manufacturer:                    Direct Incorporated
        Terminal:                        828/1 (ANSI mode)
----------------------------------------------------------------------
```

41. Information provided by:
    MANUFACTURER

42. PROGRAM FUNCTION KEYS   NOTES
    1. ESC O   P   3. Optionally 28.
       1B   4F   50   4. Optionally 132.
                                    42. All function keys programmable.
    2. ESC O   Q
       1B   4F   51

    3. ESC O   R
       1B   4F   52

    4. ESC O   S
       1B   4F   53

    5. ESC O   T
       1B   4F   54

    6. ESC O   U
       1B   4F   55

    7. ESC O   V
       1B   4F   56

    8. ESC O   W
       1B   4F   57

    9. ESC O   X
       1B   4F   58

   10. ESC O   Y
       1B   4F   59

   11. ESC O   Z
       1B   4F   5A

   12. ESC O   [
       1B   4F   5B

   13. ESC O   \
       1B   4F   5C

   14. ESC O   ]
       1B   4F   5D

   15. ESC O   ^
       1B   4F   5E

   16. ESC O   _
       1B   4F   5F

```
------------------------------------------------------------------------
  1. Manufacturer:                    Direct Incorporated
  2. Terminal:                        828/1 (HP2622 mode)
------------------------------------------------------------------------
```

SCREEN LAYOUT   VIDEO ATTRIBUTES
  3. Number of rows: 24   ON   OFF
  4. Number of columns: 80   24. Blinking:
  5. Top Row: 1   ESC &   d   A   ESC &   d   @
  6. Left Column: 1   1B   26   64   41   1B   26   64   40
  7. Printing in bottom right   25. Reverse video:
     cause scroll?   PROG   ESC &   d   B   ESC &   d   @
                                      1B   26   64   42   1B   26   64   40
CURSOR ADDRESSING   26. Underline:
  8. Lead-in sequence: ESC &   d   D   ESC &   d   @
           ESC &   a   1B   26   64   44   1B   26   64   40
           1B   26   61   27. High intensity:
  9. Row or column first: COL   ESC &   d   @
 10. Numeric form of row and column: 1B   26   64   40
     VARIABLE-LENGTH ASCII   28. Half intensity:
 11. Add offset to: Row: 0   ESC &   d   H   ESC &   d   @
                        Col: 0   1B   26   64   48   1B   26   64   40
 12. Separator sequence: 29. Attributes occupy position: NO
                                     30. Attributes cumulative: YES
                                     31. All attributes off:
 13. End sequence: ESC &   d   @
            R   1B   26   64   40
            52
 14. Cursor to top row, left column: CURSOR CONTROL KEYS
 ESC &   a   0   R   0   c   32. Cursor up:
 1B   26   61   30   52   30   63   ESC A
 15. 10th Row, 50th Column: 1B   41
 ESC &   a   9   R   4   9   c 33. Cursor down:
 1B   26   61   39   52   34   39   63   ESC B
 16. Delay after positioning: 0   1B   42
 17. Cursor home: 34. Cursor right:
            ESC H   ESC C
            1B   48   1B   43
                                     35. Cursor left:
ERASURE   DELAY   ESC D
 18. Entire screen: 1B   44
                             0
                                     CHARACTER SET
 19. Cursor to end of screen: 36. Full upper and lower ASCII: YES
            ESC J   0   37. Generate all control codes: YES
            1B   4A   38. Bell or tone sequence:
 20. Beginning of screen to cursor: ^G
                             0   07
 21. Cursor to end of line: EMULATION
            ESC K   0   39. Conform to ANSI X3.64?   YES
            1B   4B   40. Terminals Emulated:
 22. Beginning of line to cursor: HP2640, HP2645A
                             0   HP2622
 23. Entire cursor line:
            ESC K   0
            1B   4B
```

CONTINUED ====>
```

41. Information provided by:
    MANUFACTURER

42. PROGRAM FUNCTION KEYS   NOTES
 1.   4. Optionally 132.
                                  42. All function keys programmable.

 2.

 3.

 4.

 5.

 6.

 7.

 8.

 9.

10.

11.

12.

13.

14.

15.

16.

```
--------------------------------------------------------------------------
  1. Manufacturer:               Direct Incorporated
  2. Terminal:                   831
--------------------------------------------------------------------------
```

SCREEN LAYOUT
3. Number of rows: 24
4. Number of columns: 80
5. Top Row: 1
6. Left Column: 1
7. Printing in bottom right
   cause scroll?   PROG

CURSOR ADDRESSING
8. Lead-in sequence:
              ESC [
              1B 5B
9. Row or column first: ROW
10. Numeric form of row and column:
    VARIABLE-LENGTH ASCII
11. Add offset to: Row: 0
                        Col: 0
12. Separator sequence:
              ;
              3B
13. End sequence:
              H
              48
14. Cursor to top row, left column:
ESC [1   ;   1   H
1B 5B 31   3B   31   48
15. 10th Row, 50th Column:
ESC [1   0   ;   5   0   H
1B 5B 31   30   3B   35   30   48
16. Delay after positioning: 0
17. Cursor home:
              ESC [H
              1B 5B   48

ERASURE   DELAY
18. Entire screen:
       ESC [2   J   0
       1B 5B   32   4A
19. Cursor to end of screen:
       ESC [J   0
       1B 5B   4A
20. Beginning of screen to cursor:
       ESC [1   J   0
       1B 5B   31   4A
21. Cursor to end of line:
       ESC [K   0
       1B 5B   4B
22. Beginning of line to cursor:
       ESC [1   K   0
       1B 5B   31   4B
23. Entire cursor line:
       ESC [2   K   0
       1B 5B   32   4B

VIDEO ATTRIBUTES
        ON   OFF
24. Blinking:
ESC [5   m   ESC [m
1B 5B   35   6D   1B 5B   6D
25. Reverse video:
ESC [7   m   ESC [m
1B 5B   37   6D   1B 5B   6D
26. Underline:
ESC [4   m   ESC [m
1B 5B   34   6D   1B 5B   6D
27. High intensity:
ESC [1   m   ESC [m
1B 5B   31   6D   1B 5B   6D
28. Half intensity:

29. Attributes occupy position: NO
30. Attributes cumulative: YES
31. All attributes off:
              ESC [m
              1B 5B   6D

CURSOR CONTROL KEYS
32. Cursor up:
              ESC [A
              1B 5B   41
33. Cursor down:
              ESC [B
              1B 5B   42
34. Cursor right:
              ESC [C
              1B 5B   43
35. Cursor left:
              ESC [D
              1B 5B   44

CHARACTER SET
36. Full upper and lower ASCII: YES
37. Generate all control codes: YES
38. Bell or tone sequence:
              ^G
              07

EMULATION
39. Conform to ANSI X3.64?   YES
40. Terminals Emulated:
    DEC VT100, VT102, VT131, VT52

CONTINUED ====>

41. Information provided by:
    MANUFACTURER

42. PROGRAM FUNCTION KEYS   NOTES
 1. ESC O   P   3. Optionally 28.
    1B   4F   50   4. Optionally 132.
                                   42. All function keys programmable.

 2. ESC O   Q
    1B   4F   51

 3. ESC O   R
    1B   4F   52

 4. ESC O   S
    1B   4F   53

 5. ESC O   T
    1B   4F   54

 6. ESC O   U
    1B   4F   55

 7. ESC O   V
    1B   4F   56

 8. ESC O   W
    1B   4F   57

 9. ESC O   X
    1B   4F   58

10. ESC O   Y
    1B   4F   59

11. ESC O   Z
    1B   4F   5A

12. ESC O   [
    1B   4F   5B

13. ESC O   \
    1B   4F   5C

14. ESC O   ]
    1B   4F   5D

15. ESC O   ^
    1B   4F   5E

16. ESC O   _
    1B   4F   5F

---

1. Manufacturer: Esprit Systems Inc.
2. Terminal: 6310

SCREEN LAYOUT   VIDEO ATTRIBUTES
3. Number of rows: 23   ON   OFF
4. Number of columns: 79   24. Blinking:
5. Top Row: 0
6. Left Column: 0
7. Printing in bottom right   25. Reverse video:
   cause scroll?   PROG

CURSOR ADDRESSING   26. Underline:
8. Lead-in sequence:
         ESC ^Q
         1B   11   27. High intensity:
9. Row or column first: COL
10. Numeric form of row and column:
    BINARY   28. Half intensity:
11. Add offset to: Row: 0
                           Col: 0
12. Separator sequence: 29. Attributes occupy position: NO
                                        30. Attributes cumulative: NO
                                        31. All attributes off:
13. End sequence:

14. Cursor to top row, left column: CURSOR CONTROL KEYS
ESC ^Q   NUL NUL   32. Cursor up:
1B 11   00 00   ESC ^L
15. 10th Row, 50th Column: 1B   0C
ESC ^Q   1   ^I   33. Cursor down:
1B 11   31   09   ESC ^K
16. Delay after positioning: 0   1B   0B
17. Cursor home: 34. Cursor right:
         ESC ^R   ^P
         1B   12   10
                                        35. Cursor left:
ERASURE   DELAY   ^H
18. Entire screen: 08
         ESC ^\   0
         1B   1C   CHARACTER SET
19. Cursor to end of screen: 36. Full upper and lower ASCII: YES
         ESC ^X   0   37. Generate all control codes: YES
         1B   18   38. Bell or tone sequence:
20. Beginning of screen to cursor: ^G
                                                07

21. Cursor to end of line: EMULATION
         ESC ^O   0   39. Conform to ANSI X3.64?   NO
         1B   0F   40. Terminals Emulated:
22. Beginning of line to cursor: ADM 3A
                                            Regent 25
                                            Hazeltine 1500, Esprit I,
23. Entire cursor line: Esprit II, Esprit III,
                                            Televideo 925

41. Information provided by:
    MANUFACTURER

42. PROGRAM FUNCTION KEYS   NOTES
  1.

  2.

  3.

  4.

  5.

  6.

  7.

  8.

  9.

 10.

 11.

 12.

 13.

 14.

 15.

 16.

```
------------------------------------------------------------------------
  1. Manufacturer:                    Esprit Systems Inc.
  2. Terminal:                        Esprit
------------------------------------------------------------------------

SCREEN LAYOUT                         VIDEO ATTRIBUTES
  3. Number of rows:          23          ON                    OFF
  4. Number of columns:       79      24. Blinking:
  5. Top Row:                  0
  6. Left Column:              0
  7. Printing in bottom right          25. Reverse video:
     cause scroll?            NO

CURSOR ADDRESSING                      26. Underline:
  8. Lead-in sequence:
         ESC ^Q
         1B   11                       27. High intensity:
  9. Row or column first:     COL      ESC ^_                ESC ^Y
 10. Numeric form of row and column:   1B  1F                1B  19
     BINARY                            28. Half intensity:
 11. Add offset to:        Row:   0    ESC ^Y                ESC ^_
                           Col:   0    1B  19                1B  1F
 12. Separator sequence:               29. Attributes occupy position: NO
                                       30. Attributes cumulative:      NO
                                       31. All attributes off:
 13. End sequence:


 14. Cursor to top row, left column:   CURSOR CONTROL KEYS
 ESC ^Q  NUL NUL                       32. Cursor up:
 1B  11   00  00                                         ESC ^L
 15. 10th Row, 50th Column:                              1B  0C
 ESC ^Q  1    ^I                       33. Cursor down:
 1B  11   31  09                                         ESC ^K
 16. Delay after positioning:    0                       1B  0B
 17. Cursor home:                      34. Cursor right:
         ESC ^R                                          ^P
         1B  12                                          10
                                       35. Cursor left:
ERASURE                     DELAY                         ^H
 18. Entire screen:                                      08
         ESC ^\                   0
         1B  1C                        CHARACTER SET
 19. Cursor to end of screen:          36. Full upper and lower ASCII: YES
         ESC ^X                   0    37. Generate all control codes: YES
         1B  18                        38. Bell or tone sequence:
 20. Beginning of screen to cursor:                      ^G
                                                         07

 21. Cursor to end of line:            EMULATION
         ESC ^O                   0    39. Conform to ANSI X3.64?       NO
         1B  0F                        40. Terminals Emulated:
 22. Beginning of line to cursor:          ADM 3A
                                           Regent 25
                                           Hazeltine 1500
 23. Entire cursor line:
```

Manufacturer:	Esprit Systems Inc.
Terminal:	Esprit

41. Information provided by:
MANUFACTURER

42. PROGRAM FUNCTION KEYS   NOTES
    1.   11. Or 60H.
                                   14. Or 1BH 11H 60H 60H.
                                   15. Or 1BH 11H 91H 69H.
    2.   25. Switch selectable.
                                   26. Switch selectable.
                                   27. Switch selectable.
    3.

    4.

    5.

    6.

    7.

    8.

    9.

   10.

   11.

   12.

   13.

   14.

   15.

   16.

```
--------------------------------------------------------------------------------
  1. Manufacturer:                       Esprit Systems Inc.
  2. Terminal:                           Esprit II
--------------------------------------------------------------------------------
```

SCREEN LAYOUT   VIDEO ATTRIBUTES
  3. Number of rows: 23   ON   OFF
  4. Number of columns: 79   24. Blinking:
  5. Top Row: 0
  6. Left Column: 0
  7. Printing in bottom right   25. Reverse video:
     cause scroll?   PROG

CURSOR ADDRESSING   26. Underline:
  8. Lead-in sequence:
           ESC ^Q
           1B 11   27. High intensity:
  9. Row or column first: COL   ESC ^_   ESC ^Y
 10. Numeric form of row and column: 1B 1F   1B 19
     BINARY   28. Half intensity:
 11. Add offset to: Row: 0   ESC ^Y   ESC ^_
                           Col: 0   1B 19   1B 1F
 12. Separator sequence: 29. Attributes occupy position: NO
                                        30. Attributes cumulative: NO
                                        31. All attributes off:
 13. End sequence:

 14. Cursor to top row, left column: CURSOR CONTROL KEYS
 ESC ^Q NUL NUL   32. Cursor up:
 1B 11   00 00   ESC ^L
 15. 10th Row, 50th Column: 1B 0C
 ESC ^Q 1   ^I   33. Cursor down:
 1B 11   31   09   ESC ^K
 16. Delay after positioning: 0   1B 0B
 17. Cursor home: 34. Cursor right:
           ESC ^R   ^P
           1B 12   10
                                        35. Cursor left:
                                                         ^H
 ERASURE   DELAY   08
 18. Entire screen:
        ESC ^\   0   CHARACTER SET
        1B 1C   36. Full upper and lower ASCII: YES
 19. Cursor to end of screen: 37. Generate all control codes: YES
        ESC ^X   0   38. Bell or tone sequence:
        1B 18   ^G
 20. Beginning of screen to cursor: 07

 21. Cursor to end of line: EMULATION
        ESC ^O   0   39. Conform to ANSI X3.64?   NO
        1B 0F   40. Terminals Emulated:
 22. Beginning of line to cursor: ADM 3A
                                            Regent 25
                                            Hazeltine 1500
 23. Entire cursor line:

CONTINUED ====>

Manufacturer:	Esprit Systems Inc.
Terminal:	Esprit II

41. Information provided by:
    MANUFACTURER

42. PROGRAM FUNCTION KEYS   NOTES
    1.   25. Switch selectable.
                                  26. Switch selectable.
                                  27. Switch selectable.
    2.   31. Switch selectable.

    3.

    4.

    5.

    6.

    7.

    8.

    9.

   10.

   11.

   12.

   13.

   14.

   15.

   16.

```
---------------------------------------------------------------------
  1. Manufacturer:              Esprit Systems Inc.
  2. Terminal:                  Esprit III
---------------------------------------------------------------------

SCREEN LAYOUT                   VIDEO ATTRIBUTES
  3. Number of rows:      24        ON              OFF
  4. Number of columns:   80    24. Blinking:
  5. Top Row:              1    ESC G   2         ESC G   0
  6. Left Column:          1    1B  47  32        1B  47  30
  7. Printing in bottom right   25. Reverse video:
     cause scroll?      PROG     ESC G   4         ESC G   0
                                 1B  47  34        1B  47  30
CURSOR ADDRESSING               26. Underline:
  8. Lead-in sequence:          ESC G   8         ESC G   0
        ESC =                   1B  47  38        1B  47  30
        1B   3D                 27. High intensity:
  9. Row or column first:  COL  ESC (             ESC )
 10. Numeric form of row and column: 1B  28            1B  29
     BINARY                     28. Half intensity:
 11. Add offset to:    Row: 1F  ESC )             ESC (
                       Col: 1F  1B  29            1B  28
 12. Separator sequence:        29. Attributes occupy position: YES
                                30. Attributes cumulative:      NO
                                31. All attributes off:
 13. End sequence:                        ESC G   0
                                          1B  47  30

 14. Cursor to top row, left column:  CURSOR CONTROL KEYS
 ESC =    SP  SP                32. Cursor up:
 1B   3D  20  20                           ^K
 15. 10th Row, 50th Column:                0B
 ESC =    Q   )                 33. Cursor down:
 1B   3D  51  29                           ^V
 16. Delay after positioning:    0         16
 17. Cursor home:               34. Cursor right:
           ^^                              ^L
           1E                              0C
                                35. Cursor left:
ERASURE                DELAY               ^H
 18. Entire screen:                        08
        ESC *             0
        1B   2A                 CHARACTER SET
 19. Cursor to end of screen:   36. Full upper and lower ASCII: YES
        ESC Y             0     37. Generate all control codes: YES
        1B   59                 38. Bell or tone sequence:
 20. Beginning of screen to cursor:         ^G
                                            07
 21. Cursor to end of line:     EMULATION
        ESC T             0     39. Conform to ANSI X3.64?      NO
        1B   54                 40. Terminals Emulated:
 22. Beginning of line to cursor:   TVI 950

 23. Entire cursor line:
```

Manufacturer:	Esprit Systems Inc.
Terminal:	Esprit III

41. Information provided by:
MANUFACTURER

42. PROGRAM FUNCTION KEYS

1. ^A   @   ^M
   01   40 0D

2. ^A   A   ^M
   01   41 0D

3. ^A   B   ^M
   01   42 0D

4. ^A   C   ^M
   01   43 0D

5. ^A   D   ^M
   01   44 0D

6. ^A   E   ^M
   01   45 0D

7. ^A   F   ^M
   01   46 0D

8. ^A   G   ^M
   01   47 0D

9. ^A   H   ^M
   01   48 0D

10. ^A   I   ^M
    01   49 0D

11. ^A   J   ^M
    01   4A 0D

12.

13.

14.

15.

16.

NOTES
30. Binary add LSBs.
42. PF1-PF11 shown unshifted.
    PF1-PF11 shifted shown below:
    01 60 0d
    01 61 0d
    01 62 0d
    01 63 0d
    01 64 0d
    01 65 0d
    01 66 0d
    01 67 0d
    01 68 0d
    01 69 0d
    01 6a 0d

```
-----------------------------------------------------------------------
1. Manufacturer:                    Esprit Systems Inc.
2. Terminal:                        Esprit III Color
-----------------------------------------------------------------------
```

SCREEN LAYOUT   VIDEO ATTRIBUTES
3. Number of rows: 24   ON   OFF
4. Number of columns: 80   24. Blinking:
5. Top Row: 1
6. Left Column: 1
7. Printing in bottom right   25. Reverse video:
   cause scroll?   PROG   ESC G   4   ESC G   0
                                        1B 47 34   1B 47 30
CURSOR ADDRESSING   26. Underline:
8. Lead-in sequence:
         ESC =
         1B 3D   27. High intensity:
9. Row or column first: COL   ESC (ESC)
10. Numeric form of row and column: 1B 28   1B 29
    BINARY   28. Half intensity:
11. Add offset to: Row: 1F   ESC)   ESC (
                        Col: 1F   1B 29   1B 28
12. Separator sequence: 29. Attributes occupy position: YES
                                    30. Attributes cumulative: NO
                                    31. All attributes off:
13. End sequence: ESC c
                                             1B 63

14. Cursor to top row, left column: CURSOR CONTROL KEYS
ESC =   SP SP   32. Cursor up:
1B 3D   20 20   ^K
15. 10th Row, 50th Column: 0B
ESC =   Q   )   33. Cursor down:
1B 3D   51 29   ^V
16. Delay after positioning: 0   16
17. Cursor home: 34. Cursor right:
        ^^   ^L
        1E   0C
                                    35. Cursor left:
ERASURE   DELAY   ^H
18. Entire screen: 08
        ESC *   0
        1B 2A   CHARACTER SET
19. Cursor to end of screen: 36. Full upper and lower ASCII: YES
        ESC Y   0   37. Generate all control codes: YES
        1B 59   38. Bell or tone sequence:
20. Beginning of screen to cursor: ^G
                                             07

21. Cursor to end of line: EMULATION
        ESC T   0   39. Conform to ANSI X3.64?   NO
        1B 54   40. Terminals Emulated:
22. Beginning of line to cursor: TVI 950

23. Entire cursor line:

41. Information provided by:
    MANUFACTURER

42. PROGRAM FUNCTION KEYS   NOTES
    1. ^A @   ^M   42. PF1-PF11 shown unshifted.
       01 40 0D   PF1-PF11 shifted shown below:
                                        01 60 0d
    2. ^A A   ^M   01 61 0d
       01 41 0D   01 62 0d
                                        01 63 0d
    3. ^A B   ^M   01 64 0d
       01 42 0D   01 65 0d
                                        01 66 0d
    4. ^A C   ^M   01 67 0d
       01 43 0D   01 68 0d
                                        01 69 0d
    5. ^A D   ^M   01 6a 0d
       01 44 0D

    6. ^A E   ^M
       01 45 0D

    7. ^A F   ^M
       01 46 0D

    8. ^A G   ^M
       01 47 0D

    9. ^A H   ^M
       01 48 0D

   10. ^A I   ^M
       01 49 0D

   11. ^A J   ^M
       01 4A 0D

   12.

   13.

   14.

   15.

   16.

120

----
1. Manufacturer: Esprit Systems Inc.
2. Terminal: Exec 10

SCREEN LAYOUT   VIDEO ATTRIBUTES
3. Number of rows: 23   ON   OFF
4. Number of columns: 79   24. Blinking:
5. Top Row: 0   ESC SP   B   G   ESC SP   H   G
6. Left Column: 0   1B   20   42 47   1B   20   48 47
7. Printing in bottom right   25. Reverse video:
   cause scroll?   PROG   ESC SP   I   G   ESC SP   H   G
                                    1B   20   49 47   1B   20   48 47
CURSOR ADDRESSING   26. Underline:
8. Lead-in sequence: ESC SP   H   I   ESC SP   H   G
         ESC ^Q   1B   20   48 49   1B   20   48 47
         1B   11   27. High intensity:
9. Row or column first: COL   ESC SP   @   G   ESC SP   H   G
10. Numeric form of row and column: 1B   20   40 47   1B   20   48 47
    BINARY   28. Half intensity:
11. Add offset to: Row: 0   ESC SP   H   G   ESC SP   @   G
                        Col: 0   1B   20   48 47   1B   20   40 47
12. Separator sequence: 29. Attributes occupy position: NO
                                    30. Attributes cumulative: NO
                                    31. All attributes off:
13. End sequence: ESC SP   H   G
                                             1B   20   48   47

14. Cursor to top row, left column: CURSOR CONTROL KEYS
ESC ^Q   NUL NUL   32. Cursor up:
1B   11   00   00   ESC ^L
15. 10th Row, 50th Column: 1B   0C
ESC ^Q   1   ^I   33. Cursor down:
1B   11   31 09   ESC ^K
16. Delay after positioning: 0   1B   0B
17. Cursor home: 34. Cursor right:
         ESC ^R   ^P
         1B   12   10
                                    35. Cursor left:
                                             ^H
ERASURE   DELAY   08
18. Entire screen:
         ESC ^\   0   CHARACTER SET
         1B   1C   36. Full upper and lower ASCII: YES
19. Cursor to end of screen: 37. Generate all control codes: YES
         ESC ^X   0   38. Bell or tone sequence:
         1B   18   ^G
20. Beginning of screen to cursor: 07

21. Cursor to end of line: EMULATION
         ESC ^O   0   39. Conform to ANSI X3.64?   NO
         1B   0F   40. Terminals Emulated:
22. Beginning of line to cursor: Hazeltine 1500

23. Entire cursor line:

                                121   CONTINUED ====>

41. Information provided by:
    MANUFACTURER

42. PROGRAM FUNCTION KEYS   NOTES
   1. ESC O   O   O   ^Y   42. F1-F8 shown unshifted.
      1B   4F   30   30   19   F1-F8 shifted shown below:
                                            1b 4f 30 38 19
   2. ESC O   O   1   ^Y   1b 4f 30 39 19
      1B   4F   30   31   19   1b 4f 31 30 19
                                            1b 4f 31 31 19
   3. ESC O   O   2   ^Y   1b 4f 31 32 19
      1B   4F   30   32   19   1b 4f 31 33 19
                                            1b 4f 31 34 19
   4. ESC O   O   3   ^Y   1b 4f 31 35 19
      1B   4F   30   33   19

   5. ESC O   O   4   ^Y
      1B   4F   30   34   19

   6. ESC O   O   5   ^Y
      1B   4F   30   35   19

   7. ESC O   O   6   ^Y
      1B   4F   30   36   19

   8. ESC O   O   7   ^Y
      1B   4F   30   37   19

   9.

  10.

  11.

  12.

  13.

  14.

  15.

  16.

---

1. Manufacturer:	Esprit Systems Inc.
2. Terminal:	Exec 10/102

SCREEN LAYOUT
3. Number of rows: 24
4. Number of columns: 80
5. Top Row: 1
6. Left Column: 1
7. Printing in bottom right
   cause scroll? PROG

CURSOR ADDRESSING
8. Lead-in sequence:
   ESC Y
   1B 59
9. Row or column first: COL
10. Numeric form of row and column:
    BINARY
11. Add offset to: Row: 1F
    Col: 1F
12. Separator sequence:

13. End sequence:

14. Cursor to top row, left column:
ESC Y SP SP
1B 59 20 20
15. 10th Row, 50th Column:
ESC Y Q)
1B 59 51 29
16. Delay after positioning: 0
17. Cursor home:
    ESC H
    1B 48

ERASURE   DELAY
18. Entire screen:
    ESC J 2   0
    1B 4A 32
19. Cursor to end of screen:
    ESC J 0   0
    1B 4A 30
20. Beginning of screen to cursor:
    ESC J 1   0
    1B 4A 31
21. Cursor to end of line:
    ESC K 0   0
    1B 4B 30
22. Beginning of line to cursor:
    ESC K 1   0
    1B 4B 31
23. Entire cursor line:
    ESC K 2   0
    1B 4B 32

VIDEO ATTRIBUTES
                    ON   OFF
24. Blinking:
    ESC m 5   ESC m 0
    1B 6D 35   1B 6D 30
25. Reverse video:
    ESC m 7   ESC m 0
    1B 6D 37   1B 6D 30
26. Underline:
    ESC m 4   ESC m 0
    1B 6D 34   1B 6D 30
27. High intensity:
    ESC m 1   ESC m 0
    1B 6D 31   1B 6D 30
28. Half intensity:
    ESC m 0   ESC m 1
    1B 6D 30   1B 6D 31
29. Attributes occupy position: NO
30. Attributes cumulative: YES
31. All attributes off:
            ESC m 0
            1B 6D 30

CURSOR CONTROL KEYS
32. Cursor up:
            ESC A
            1B 41
33. Cursor down:
            ESC B
            1B 42
34. Cursor right:
            ESC C
            1B 43
35. Cursor left:
            ESC D
            1B 44

CHARACTER SET
36. Full upper and lower ASCII: YES
37. Generate all control codes: YES
38. Bell or tone sequence:
            ^G
            07

EMULATION
39. Conform to ANSI X3.64?   NO
40. Terminals Emulated:
    DEC VT52
    DEC VT100, 101, 102, 131

      CONTINUED ====>

Manufacturer:	Esprit Systems Inc.
Terminal:	Exec 10/102

41. Information provided by:
    MANUFACTURER

42. PROGRAM FUNCTION KEYS   NOTES
  1.

  2.

  3.

  4.

  5.

  6.

  7.

  8.

  9.

 10.

 11.

 12.

 13.

 14.

 15.

 16.

```
-------------------------------------------------------------------
1. Manufacturer:                    Esprit Systems Inc.
2. Terminal:                        Exec 10/102 (ANSI mode)
-------------------------------------------------------------------
```

SCREEN LAYOUT   VIDEO ATTRIBUTES
3. Number of rows: 24   ON   OFF
4. Number of columns: 80   24. Blinking:
5. Top Row: 1   ESC [5   m   ESC [m
6. Left Column: 1   1B   5B 35   6D   1B   5B 6D
7. Printing in bottom right   25. Reverse video:
   cause scroll?   PROG   ESC [7   m   ESC [m
                                    1B   5B 37   6D   1B   5B 6D
CURSOR ADDRESSING   26. Underline:
8. Lead-in sequence: ESC [4   m   ESC [m
            ESC [1B   5B 34   6D   1B   5B 6D
            1B   5B   27. High intensity:
9. Row or column first: ROW   ESC [1   m   ESC [m
10. Numeric form of row and column: 1B   5B 31   6D   1B   5B 6D
    VARIABLE-LENGTH ASCII   28. Half intensity:
11. Add offset to: Row: 0
                          Col: 0
12. Separator sequence: 29. Attributes occupy position: NO
            ;   30. Attributes cumulative: YES
            3B   31. All attributes off:
13. End sequence: ESC [m
            H   1B   5B 6D
            48
14. Cursor to top row, left column: CURSOR CONTROL KEYS
ESC [1   ;   1   H   32. Cursor up:
1B   5B 31   3B   31   48   ESC [A
15. 10th Row, 50th Column: 1B   5B 41
ESC [1   0   ;   5   0   H 33. Cursor down:
1B   5B 31   30   3B   35   30   48   ESC [B
16. Delay after positioning: 0   1B   5B 42
17. Cursor home: 34. Cursor right:
            ESC [H   ESC [C
            1B   5B 48   1B   5B 43
                                    35. Cursor left:
ERASURE   DELAY   ESC [D
18. Entire screen: 1B   5B 44
            ESC [2   J   0
            1B   5B 32   4A   CHARACTER SET
19. Cursor to end of screen: 36. Full upper and lower ASCII: YES
            ESC [J   0 37. Generate all control codes: YES
            1B   5B 4A   38. Bell or tone sequence:
20. Beginning of screen to cursor: ^G
            ESC [1   J   0   07
            1B   5B 31   4A
21. Cursor to end of line: EMULATION
            ESC [K   0 39. Conform to ANSI X3.64?   YES
            1B   5B 4B   40. Terminals Emulated:
22. Beginning of line to cursor:
            ESC [1   K   0
            1B   5B 31   4B
23. Entire cursor line:
            ESC [2   K   0
            1B   5B 32   4B

                              125   CONTINUED ====>
```
```

41. Information provided by:
    MANUFACTURER

42. PROGRAM FUNCTION KEYS   NOTES
 1.

 2.

 3.

 4.

 5.

 6.

 7.

 8.

 9.

10.

11.

12.

13.

14.

15.

16.

```
---------------------------------------------------------------------
  1. Manufacturer:                    Esprit Systems Inc.
  2. Terminal:                        Exec 10/25
---------------------------------------------------------------------

SCREEN LAYOUT                         VIDEO ATTRIBUTES
  3. Number of rows:          23           ON               OFF
  4. Number of columns:       79      24. Blinking:
  5. Top Row:                  0       ESC SP  B   G     ESC SP  H   G
  6. Left Column:              0       1B  20  42  47    1B  20  48  47
  7. Printing in bottom right          25. Reverse video:
     cause scroll?          PROG       ESC SP  I   G     ESC SP  H   G
                                       1B  20  49  47    1B  20  48  47
CURSOR ADDRESSING                      26. Underline:
  8. Lead-in sequence:                 ESC SP  H   I     ESC SP  H   G
              ESC ^Q                   1B  20  48  49    1B  20  48  47
              1B  11                   27. High intensity:
  9. Row or column first:     COL      ESC SP  @   G     ESC SP  H   G
 10. Numeric form of row and column:   1B  20  40  47    1B  20  48  47
     BINARY                            28. Half intensity:
 11. Add offset to:     Row:    0      ESC SP  H   G     ESC SP  @   G
                        Col:    0      1B  20  48  47    1B  20  40  47
 12. Separator sequence:               29. Attributes occupy position: NO
                                       30. Attributes cumulative:      NO
                                       31. All attributes off:
 13. End sequence:                                ESC SP  H   G
                                                  1B  20  48  47


 14. Cursor to top row, left column:  CURSOR CONTROL KEYS
 ESC ^Q  NUL NUL                       32. Cursor up:
 1B  11  00  00                                   ESC ^L
 15. 10th Row, 50th Column:                        1B  0C
 ESC ^Q  1   ^I                        33. Cursor down:
 1B  11  31  09                                   ESC ^K
 16. Delay after positioning:    0                 1B  0B
 17. Cursor home:                      34. Cursor right:
              ESC ^R                               ^P
              1B  12                               10
                                       35. Cursor left:
ERASURE                     DELAY                  ^H
 18. Entire screen:                                08
         ESC ^\                 0
         1B  1C                       CHARACTER SET
 19. Cursor to end of screen:          36. Full upper and lower ASCII: YES
         ESC ^X                0       37. Generate all control codes: YES
         1B  18                        38. Bell or tone sequence:
 20. Beginning of screen to cursor:               ^G
                                                  07

 21. Cursor to end of line:           EMULATION
         ESC ^O                0       39. Conform to ANSI X3.64?      NO
         1B  0F                        40. Terminals Emulated:
 22. Beginning of line to cursor:          Hazeltine EXEC 80/30
                                           Hazeltine EXEC 80/20

 23. Entire cursor line:
```

                      CONTINUED ====>

Manufacturer: Esprit Systems Inc.
Terminal: Exec 10/25

41. Information provided by:
    MANUFACTURER

42. PROGRAM FUNCTION KEYS   NOTES
    1. ESC O   0   0   ^Y   27. Also ESC US
       1B   4F   30   30   19   42. F1-F8 shown unshifted.
                                           F1-F8 shifted shown below:
    2. ESC O   0   1   ^Y   1b 4f 30 38 19
       1B   4F   30   31   19   1b 4f 30 39 19
                                           1b 4f 31 30 19
    3. ESC O   0   2   ^Y   1b 4f 31 31 19
       1B   4F   30   32   19   1b 4f 31 32 19
                                           1b 4f 31 33 19
    4. ESC O   0   3   ^Y   1b 4f 31 34 19
       1B   4F   30   33   19   1b 4f 31 35 19

    5. ESC O   0   4   ^Y
       1B   4F   30   34   19

    6. ESC O   0   5   ^Y
       1B   4F   30   35   19

    7. ESC O   0   6   ^Y
       1B   4F   30   36   19

    8. ESC O   0   7   ^Y
       1B   4F   30   37   19

    9.

   10.

   11.

   12.

   13.

   14.

   15.

   16.

---

1. Manufacturer:	Falco Data Products
2. Terminal:	Fame 100

SCREEN LAYOUT
3. Number of rows: 24
4. Number of columns: 80
5. Top Row: 1
6. Left Column: 1
7. Printing in bottom right
   cause scroll?   PROG

CURSOR ADDRESSING
8. Lead-in sequence:
                    ESC [
                    1B   5B
9. Row or column first: ROW
10. Numeric form of row and column:
    VARIABLE-LENGTH ASCII
11. Add offset to: Row: 0
                          Col: 0
12. Separator sequence:
                    ;
                    3B
13. End sequence:
                    H
                    48
14. Cursor to top row, left column:
ESC [1   ;   1   H
1B 5B 31 3B 31 48
15. 10th Row, 50th Column:
ESC [1   0   ;   5   0   H
1B 5B 31 30 3B 35 30 48
16. Delay after positioning: 0
17. Cursor home:
                    ESC [H
                    1B   5B 48

ERASURE   DELAY
18. Entire screen:
      ESC [2   J   0
      1B 5B 32 4A
19. Cursor to end of screen:
      ESC [J   0
      1B 5B 4A
20. Beginning of screen to cursor:
      ESC [1   J   0
      1B 5B 31 4A
21. Cursor to end of line:
      ESC [K   0
      1B 5B 4B
22. Beginning of line to cursor:
      ESC [1   K   0
      1B 5B 31 4B
23. Entire cursor line:
      ESC [2   K   0
      1B 5B 32 4B

VIDEO ATTRIBUTES
         ON   OFF
24. Blinking:
ESC [5   m   ESC [m
1B 5B 35 6D   1B 5B 6D
25. Reverse video:
ESC [7   m   ESC [m
1B 5B 37 6D   1B 5B 6D
26. Underline:
ESC [4   m   ESC [m
1B 5B 34 6D   1B 5B 6D
27. High intensity:
ESC [1   m   ESC [m
1B 5B 31 6D   1B 5B 6D
28. Half intensity:

29. Attributes occupy position: NO
30. Attributes cumulative: YES
31. All attributes off:
                    ESC [m
                    1B   5B 6D

CURSOR CONTROL KEYS
32. Cursor up:
                    ESC [A
                    1B   5B 41
33. Cursor down:
                    ESC [B
                    1B   5B 42
34. Cursor right:
                    ESC [C
                    1B   5B 43
35. Cursor left:
                    ESC [D
                    1B   5B 44

CHARACTER SET
36. Full upper and lower ASCII: YES
37. Generate all control codes: YES
38. Bell or tone sequence:
                    ^G
                    07

EMULATION
39. Conform to ANSI X3.64?   YES
40. Terminals Emulated:
    DEC VT100, VT102
    DEC VT52

CONTINUED ====>

41. Information provided by:
    MANUFACTURER

42. PROGRAM FUNCTION KEYS   NOTES
 1. ESC O   P
    1B   4F   50

 2. ESC O   Q
    1B   4F   51

 3. ESC O   R
    1B   4F   52

 4. ESC O   S
    1B   4F   53

 5.

 6.

 7.

 8.

 9.

10.

11.

12.

13.

14.

15.

16.

----
1. Manufacturer: Falco Data Products
2. Terminal: Fame 78

SCREEN LAYOUT   VIDEO ATTRIBUTES
  3. Number of rows: 24   ON   OFF
  4. Number of columns: 80   24. Blinking:
  5. Top Row: 1
  6. Left Column: 1
  7. Printing in bottom right   25. Reverse video:
     cause scroll?   NO

CURSOR ADDRESSING   26. Underline:
  8. Lead-in sequence:
          ESC F
          1B 46   27. High intensity:
  9. Row or column first: ROW
 10. Numeric form of row and column:
     BINARY   28. Half intensity:
 11. Add offset to: Row: 1F   ESC d   @   ESC d   A
                         Col: 1F   1B 64   40   1B   64   41
 12. Separator sequence: 29. Attributes occupy position: YES
                                    30. Attributes cumulative: NO
                                    31. All attributes off:
 13. End sequence:

 14. Cursor to top row, left column: CURSOR CONTROL KEYS
 ESC F   SP SP   32. Cursor up:
 1B 46 20 20   ESC A
 15. 10th Row, 50th Column: 1B 41
 ESC F   )   Q   33. Cursor down:
 1B 46 29 51   ESC B
 16. Delay after positioning: 0   1B 42
 17. Cursor home: 34. Cursor right:
          ESC H   ESC C
          1B 48   1B 43
                                    35. Cursor left:
ERASURE   DELAY   ESC D
 18. Entire screen: 1B 44
          ESC E   0
          1B 45   CHARACTER SET
 19. Cursor to end of screen: 36. Full upper and lower ASCII: YES
          ESC J   0   37. Generate all control codes: YES
          1B 4A   38. Bell or tone sequence:
 20. Beginning of screen to cursor: ^G
                                            07

 21. Cursor to end of line: EMULATION
          ESC K   0   39. Conform to ANSI X3.64?   YES
          1B 4B   40. Terminals Emulated:
 22. Beginning of line to cursor: Beehive DM78
                                        DEC VT100

 23. Entire cursor line:

41. Information provided by:
    MANUFACTURER

42. PROGRAM FUNCTION KEYS   NOTES
    1. ^B   ESC p   42. 24 function keys.
       02   1B   70

    2. ^B   ESC q
       02   1B   71

    3. ^B   ESC r
       02   1B   72

    4. ^B   ESC s
       02   1B   73

    5. ^B   ESC t
       02   1B   74

    6. ^B   ESC u
       02   1B   75

    7. ^B   ESC v
       02   1B   76

    8. ^B   ESC w
       02   1B   77

    9. ^B   ESC x
       02   1B   78

   10. ^B   ESC y
       02   1B   79

   11. ^B   ESC z
       02   1B   7A

   12. ^B   ESC {
       02   1B   7B

   13. ^B   ESC |
       02   1B   7C

   14. ^B   ESC }
       02   1B   7D

   15. ^B   ESC ~
       02   1B   7E

   16. ^B   ESC DEL
       02   1B   7F

---
1. Manufacturer: Falco Data Products
2. Terminal: Fame III

SCREEN LAYOUT   VIDEO ATTRIBUTES
3. Number of rows: 24   ON   OFF
4. Number of columns: 80   24. Blinking:
5. Top Row: 1
6. Left Column: 1
7. Printing in bottom right   25. Reverse video:
   cause scroll?   PROG

CURSOR ADDRESSING   26. Underline:
8. Lead-in sequence:
        ESC [
        1B 5B   27. High intensity:
9. Row or column first: ROW   ESC (ESC)
10. Numeric form of row and column: 1B 28   1B 29
    VARIABLE-LENGTH ASCII   28. Half intensity:
11. Add offset to: Row: 0   ESC)   ESC (
                         Col: 0   1B 29   1B 28
12. Separator sequence: 29. Attributes occupy position: NO
        ;   30. Attributes cumulative: YES
        3B   31. All attributes off:
13. End sequence:
        H
        48
14. Cursor to top row, left column: CURSOR CONTROL KEYS
ESC [1   ;   1   H   32. Cursor up:
1B 5B 31 3B 31 48   ESC [A
15. 10th Row, 50th Column: 1B 5B 41
ESC [1   0   ;   5   0   H   33. Cursor down:
1B 5B 31 30 3B 35 30 48   ESC [B
16. Delay after positioning: 0   1B 5B 42
17. Cursor home: 34. Cursor right:
        ESC [H   ESC [C
        1B 5B 48   1B 5B 43
                                    35. Cursor left:
ERASURE   DELAY   ESC [D
18. Entire screen: 1B 5B 44
        ESC [2   J   0
        1B 5B 32 4A   CHARACTER SET
19. Cursor to end of screen: 36. Full upper and lower ASCII: YES
        ESC [J   0   37. Generate all control codes: YES
        1B 5B 4A   38. Bell or tone sequence:
20. Beginning of screen to cursor: ^G
        ESC [1   J   0   07
        1B 5B 31 4A
21. Cursor to end of line: EMULATION
        ESC [K   0   39. Conform to ANSI X3.64?   YES
        1B 5B 4B   40. Terminals Emulated:
22. Beginning of line to cursor:
        ESC [1   K   0
        1B 5B 31 4B
23. Entire cursor line:
        ESC [2   K   0
        1B 5B 32 4B

41. Information provided by:
    MANUFACTURER

42. PROGRAM FUNCTION KEYS   NOTES
   1. ESC a
      1B   61

   2. ESC b
      1B   62

   3. ESC c
      1B   63

   4. ESC d
      1B   64

   5. ESC e
      1B   65

   6. ESC f
      1B   66

   7. ESC g
      1B   67

   8. ESC h
      1B   68

   9. ESC i
      1B   69

  10. ESC j
      1B   6A

  11. ESC k
      1B   6B

  12. ESC l
      1B   6C

  13.

  14.

  15.

  16.

```
--------------------------------------------------------------------------
1. Manufacturer:                    Falco Data Products
2. Terminal:                        TS 2624-B
--------------------------------------------------------------------------
```

SCREEN LAYOUT   VIDEO ATTRIBUTES
3. Number of rows: 24   ON   OFF
4. Number of columns: 80   24. Blinking:
5. Top Row: 0   ESC &   d   A   ESC &   d   @
6. Left Column: 0   1B 26 64 41   1B 26 64 40
7. Printing in bottom right   25. Reverse video:
   cause scroll?   YES   ESC &   d   B   ESC &   d   @
                                    1B 26 64 42   1B 26 64 40
CURSOR ADDRESSING   26. Underline:
8. Lead-in sequence: ESC &   d   D   ESC &   d   @
          ESC &   a   1B 26 64 44   1B 26 64 40
          1B 26 61   27. High intensity:
9. Row or column first: COL
10. Numeric form of row and column:
    VARIABLE-LENGTH ASCII   28. Half intensity:
11. Add offset to: Row: 0 ESC &   d   H   ESC &   d   @
                          Col: 0 1B 26 64 48   1B 26 64 40
12. Separator sequence: 29. Attributes occupy position: NO
                                    30. Attributes cumulative: NO
                                    31. All attributes off:
13. End sequence: ESC &   d   @
                                              1B 26 64 40

14. Cursor to top row, left column: CURSOR CONTROL KEYS
ESC &   a   0   c   0   R   32. Cursor up:
1B 26 61 30 63 30 52   ESC A
15. 10th Row, 50th Column: 1B 41
ESC &   a   4   9   c   9   R   33. Cursor down:
1B 26 61 34 39 63 39 52   ESC B
16. Delay after positioning: 0   1B 42
17. Cursor home: 34. Cursor right:
          ESC h   ESC C
          1B 68   1B 43
                                    35. Cursor left:
ERASURE   DELAY   ESC D
18. Entire screen: 1B 44
          ESC h   ESC J   0
          1B 68 1B 4A   CHARACTER SET
19. Cursor to end of screen: 36. Full upper and lower ASCII: YES
          ESC J   0   37. Generate all control codes: YES
          1B 4A   38. Bell or tone sequence:
20. Beginning of screen to cursor: ^G
                                              07

21. Cursor to end of line: EMULATION
          ESC K   0   39. Conform to ANSI X3.64?   NO
          1B 4B   40. Terminals Emulated:
22. Beginning of line to cursor:

23. Entire cursor line:

                          135   CONTINUED ====>
```
```

41. Information provided by:
    MANUFACTURER

42. PROGRAM FUNCTION KEYS   NOTES

1. ESC p   9. Either row or column first is
   1B 70   acceptable, depending on sequence
                                       sent. See notes 12, 13, 14, and 15.
2. ESC q   12. To send row first, use r (72H).
   1B 71   13. To send row first, use C (43H).
                                   14. To send row first:
3. ESC r   ESC &   a   0   r   0   C
   1B 72   1B 26 61 30 72 30 43
                                   15. To send row first:
4. ESC s   ESC &   a   9   r   4   9   C
   1B 73   1B 26 61 39 72 34 39 43
                                   23. To delete entire cursor line:
5. ESC t   ESC &   a   0   C   ESC K
   1B 74   1B 26 61 30 43 1B 4B
                                   30. Combinations preceeded by ESC & d:
6. ESC u   @ABCDEFGHIJKLMNOS
   1B 75   Half-intensity   XXXXXXXX
                                       Underline   XXXX   XXXX
7. ESC v   Reverse   XX XX XX XX
   1B 76   Blinking   X X X X X X X X
                                       Security   X
8. ESC w   End enhancement X
   1B 77   Example: Reverse, blinking and
                                                underline:
9.   ESC &   d   G
                                                1B 26 64 47
                                   36. Three complete 128-character sets
10.   (base, line drawing and mathematics)
                                       are available standard. The 8-bit
                                       extended ASCII code is used to
11.   generate an additional 128-charac-
                                       ter foreign set.
                                       ESC) @ selects base set
12.   ESC) A selects math set
                                       ESC) B selects line drawing set
                                   42. Sequences shown are default. All 8
13.   function keys are programmable.

14.

15.

16.

```
--------------------------------------------------------------------------
  1. Manufacturer:                    Falco Data Products
  2. Terminal:                        TS-1
--------------------------------------------------------------------------
```

SCREEN LAYOUT   VIDEO ATTRIBUTES
  3. Number of rows: 24   ON   OFF
  4. Number of columns: 80   24. Blinking:
  5. Top Row: 1   ESC g   2   ESC g   0
  6. Left Column: 1   1B   67   32   1B   67   30
  7. Printing in bottom right   25. Reverse video:
     cause scroll?   YES   ESC g   4   ESC g   0
                               1B   67   34   1B   67   30
CURSOR ADDRESSING   26. Underline:
  8. Lead-in sequence: ESC g   1   ESC g   0
            ESC =   1B   67   31   1B   67   30
            1B   3D   27. High intensity:
  9. Row or column first: ROW
10. Numeric form of row and column:
     BINARY   28. Half intensity:
11. Add offset to: Row: 1F   ESC (ESC)
                 Col: 1F   1B   28   1B   29
12. Separator sequence: 29. Attributes occupy position: NO
                              30. Attributes cumulative: NO
                              31. All attributes off:
13. End sequence:

14. Cursor to top row, left column: CURSOR CONTROL KEYS
  ESC =   SP SP   32. Cursor up:
  1B   3D   20   20   ESC [A
15. 10th Row, 50th Column: 1B   5B   41
  ESC =   )   Q   33. Cursor down:
  1B   3D   29   51   ESC [B
16. Delay after positioning: 0   1B   5B   42
17. Cursor home: 34. Cursor right:
        ESC [H   ESC [C
        1B   5B   48   1B   5B   43
                         35. Cursor left:
ERASURE   DELAY   ESC [D
18. Entire screen: 1B   5B   44
     ESC *   0
     1B   2A   CHARACTER SET
19. Cursor to end of screen: 36. Full upper and lower ASCII: YES
     ESC Y   0   37. Generate all control codes: YES
     1B   59   38. Bell or tone sequence:
20. Beginning of screen to cursor: ^G
                                  07

21. Cursor to end of line: EMULATION
     ESC t   0   39. Conform to ANSI X3.64?   YES
     1B   74   40. Terminals Emulated:
22. Beginning of line to cursor: DEC VT100
                                Lear Diegler ADM-31

23. Entire cursor line:

Manufacturer: Falco Data Products
Terminal: TS-1

41. Information provided by:
    MANUFACTURER

42. PROGRAM FUNCTION KEYS   NOTES
    1.   30. See manual for combination
                                       attributes.
                                   42. 12 programmable function keys.
    2.

    3.

    4.

    5.

    6.

    7.

    8.

    9.

    10.

    11.

    12.

    13.

    14.

    15.

    16.

```
--------------------------------------------------------------------------------
  1. Manufacturer:                    Falco Data Products
  2. Terminal:                        TS-100/132
--------------------------------------------------------------------------------
```

SCREEN LAYOUT   VIDEO ATTRIBUTES
  3. Number of rows: 24   ON   OFF
  4. Number of columns: 80   24. Blinking:
  5. Top Row: 1   ESC [5   m   ESC [m
  6. Left Column: 1   1B 5B 35 6D   1B 5B 6D
  7. Printing in bottom right   25. Reverse video:
     cause scroll?   PROG   ESC [7   m   ESC [m
                                      1B 5B 37 6D   1B 5B 6D
CURSOR ADDRESSING   26. Underline:
  8. Lead-in sequence: ESC [4   m   ESC [m
           ESC [1B 5B 34 6D   1B 5B 6D
           1B 5B   27. High intensity:
  9. Row or column first: ROW   ESC [1   m   ESC [m
 10. Numeric form of row and column: 1B 5B 31 6D   1B 5B 6D
     VARIABLE-LENGTH ASCII   28. Half intensity:
 11. Add offset to: Row: 0
                          Col: 0
 12. Separator sequence: 29. Attributes occupy position: NO
           ;   30. Attributes cumulative: YES
           3B   31. All attributes off:
 13. End sequence: ESC [m
           H   1B 5B 6D
           48
 14. Cursor to top row, left column: CURSOR CONTROL KEYS
 ESC [1   ;   1   H   32. Cursor up:
 1B 5B 31 3B 31 48   ESC [A
 15. 10th Row, 50th Column: 1B 5B 41
 ESC [1   0   ;   5   0   H   33. Cursor down:
 1B 5B 31 30 3B 35 30 48   ESC [B
 16. Delay after positioning: 0   1B 5B 42
 17. Cursor home: 34. Cursor right:
           ESC [H   ESC [C
           1B 5B 48   1B 5B 43
                                      35. Cursor left:
ERASURE   DELAY   ESC [D
 18. Entire screen: 1B 5B 44
           ESC [2   J   0
           1B 5B 32 4A   CHARACTER SET
 19. Cursor to end of screen: 36. Full upper and lower ASCII: YES
           ESC [J   0   37. Generate all control codes: YES
           1B 5B 4A   38. Bell or tone sequence:
 20. Beginning of screen to cursor: ^G
           ESC [1   J   0   07
           1B 5B 31 4A
 21. Cursor to end of line: EMULATION
           ESC [K   0   39. Conform to ANSI X3.64?   YES
           1B 5B 4B   40. Terminals Emulated:
 22. Beginning of line to cursor: DEC VT100, VT102
           ESC [1   K   0   DEC VT52
           1B 5B 31 4B
 23. Entire cursor line:
           ESC [2   K   0
           1B 5B 32 4B

                            139   CONTINUED ====>
```
```

41. Information provided by:
    MANUFACTURER

42. PROGRAM FUNCTION KEYS   NOTES
 1. ESC O   P
    1B   4F 50

 2. ESC O   Q
    1B   4F 51

 3. ESC O   R
    1B   4F 52

 4. ESC O   S
    1B   4F 53

 5.

 6.

 7.

 8.

 9.

10.

11.

12.

13.

14.

15.

16.

----
1. Manufacturer: Falco Data Products
2. Terminal: TS-42

SCREEN LAYOUT   VIDEO ATTRIBUTES
3. Number of rows: 24   ON   OFF
4. Number of columns: 80   24. Blinking:
5. Top Row: 1   ESC G   2   ESC G   0
6. Left Column: 1   1B 47 32   1B 47 30
7. Printing in bottom right   25. Reverse video:
   cause scroll?   YES   ESC G   4   ESC G   0
                                     1B 47 34   1B 47 30
CURSOR ADDRESSING   26. Underline:
8. Lead-in sequence: ESC G   1   ESC G   0
            ESC =   1B 47 31   1B 47 30
            1B 3D   27. High intensity:
9. Row or column first: ROW
10. Numeric form of row and column:
    BINARY   28. Half intensity:
11. Add offset to: Row: 1F
                          Col: 1F
12. Separator sequence: 29. Attributes occupy position: YES
                                     30. Attributes cumulative: NO
                                     31. All attributes off:
13. End sequence: ESC G   0
                                                1B 47 30

14. Cursor to top row, left column: CURSOR CONTROL KEYS
ESC =   SP SP   32. Cursor up:
1B 3D 20 20   ^K
15. 10th Row, 50th Column: OB
ESC =   )   Q   33. Cursor down:
1B 3D 29 51   ^J
16. Delay after positioning: 0   OA
17. Cursor home: 34. Cursor right:
                                                ^L
                                                OC
                                     35. Cursor left:
ERASURE   DELAY   ^H
18. Entire screen: 08
        ESC *   0
        1B 2A   CHARACTER SET
19. Cursor to end of screen: 36. Full upper and lower ASCII: YES
        ESC y   0   37. Generate all control codes: YES
        1B 79   38. Bell or tone sequence:
20. Beginning of screen to cursor: ^G
                                                07
21. Cursor to end of line: EMULATION
        ESC t   0   39. Conform to ANSI X3.64?   NO
        1B 74   40. Terminals Emulated:
22. Beginning of line to cursor: Lear Siegler ADM-42

23. Entire cursor line:

CONTINUED ====>

41. Information provided by:
    MANUFACTURER

42. PROGRAM FUNCTION KEYS   NOTES
  1. ^A @   ^M   42. Function keys are programmable.
     01 40 0D

  2. ^A A   ^M
     01 41 0D

  3. ^A B   ^M
     01 42 0D

  4. ^A C   ^M
     01 43 0D

  5. ^A D   ^M
     01 44 0D

  6. ^A E   ^M
     01 45 0D

  7. ^A F   ^M
     01 46 0D

  8. ^A G   ^M
     01 47 0D

  9. ^A H   ^M
     01 48 0D

 10. ^A I   ^M
     01 49 0D

 11. ^A J   ^M
     01 4A 0D

 12. ^A K   ^M
     01 4B 0D

 13. ^A L   ^M
     01 4C 0D

 14. ^A M   ^M
     01 4D 0D

 15. ^A N   ^M
     01 4E 0D

 16. ^A O   ^M
     01 4F 0D

```
----------------------------------------------------------------------
  1. Manufacturer:               FMG Corporation
  2. Terminal:                   FMG CP/M for TRS80 Model II
----------------------------------------------------------------------
```

SCREEN LAYOUT   VIDEO ATTRIBUTES
  3. Number of rows: 24   ON   OFF
  4. Number of columns: 80   24. Blinking:
  5. Top Row: 1
  6. Left Column: 1
  7. Printing in bottom right   25. Reverse video:
    cause scroll?   YES   ESC ^W   ESC ^X
                      1B   17   1B   18
CURSOR ADDRESSING   26. Underline:
  8. Lead-in sequence:
         ESC ^Q
         1B   11   27. High intensity:
  9. Row or column first: COL
10. Numeric form of row and column:
    BINARY   28. Half intensity:
11. Add offset to: Row: 27
              Col: 27
12. Separator sequence: 29. Attributes occupy position: NO
                       30. Attributes cumulative: NO
                       31. All attributes off:
13. End sequence: ESC ^X
                         1B   18

14. Cursor to top row, left column: CURSOR CONTROL KEYS
ESC ^Q ((32. Cursor up:
1B   11   28   28   ^^
15. 10th Row, 50th Column: 1E
ESC ^Q 1   Y   33. Cursor down:
1B   11   31   59   ^
16. Delay after positioning: 0   1F
17. Cursor home: 34. Cursor right:
        ESC ^R   ^]
        1B   12   1D
                       35. Cursor left:
ERASURE   DELAY   ^\
18. Entire screen: 1C
      ESC ^S   0
      1B   13   CHARACTER SET
19. Cursor to end of screen: 36. Full upper and lower ASCII: YES
                       37. Generate all control codes: YES
                       38. Bell or tone sequence:
20. Beginning of screen to cursor:

21. Cursor to end of line: EMULATION
      ESC ^O   0   39. Conform to ANSI X3.64?   NO
      1B   OF   40. Terminals Emulated:
22. Beginning of line to cursor:

23. Entire cursor line:

CONTINUED ====>

41. Information provided by:
    PUBLISHER

42. PROGRAM FUNCTION KEYS   NOTES
    1.   This is an implementation of CP/M for
                                   the Radio Shack TRS-80 Model II. FMG
                                   Corporation is not the manufacturer of
    2.   the hardware.

                                   At publication FMG Corporation was no
    3.   longer in operation. Data was obtained
                                   by the publisher from documentation.

    4.

    5.

    6.

    7.

    8.

    9.

   10.

   11.

   12.

   13.

   14.

   15.

   16.

```
--------------------------------------------------------------------------
  1. Manufacturer:                    Franklin Computer Corp.
  2. Terminal:                        Ace Display
--------------------------------------------------------------------------

SCREEN LAYOUT                         VIDEO ATTRIBUTES
  3. Number of rows:          24          ON                    OFF
  4. Number of columns:       80      24. Blinking:
  5. Top Row:                  1
  6. Left Column:              1
  7. Printing in bottom right         25. Reverse video:
     cause scroll?           YES        ^O                      ^N
                                        OF                      OE
CURSOR ADDRESSING                     26. Underline:
  8. Lead-in sequence:
            ^^
            1E                         27. High intensity:
  9. Row or column first:    COL
 10. Numeric form of row and column:
     BINARY                            28. Half intensity:
 11. Add offset to:       Row:  1F
                          Col:  1F
 12. Separator sequence:              29. Attributes occupy position: NO
                                      30. Attributes cumulative:      NO
                                      31. All attributes off:
 13. End sequence:                              ^Z   0
                                                1A   30

 14. Cursor to top row, left column:  CURSOR CONTROL KEYS
     ^^   SP  SP                      32. Cursor up:
     1E   20  20
 15. 10th Row, 50th Column:
     ^^   Q   )                       33. Cursor down:
     1E   51  29                                ^J
 16. Delay after positioning:    0              0A
 17. Cursor home:                     34. Cursor right:
            ^Y                                  ^U
            19                                  15
                                      35. Cursor left:
ERASURE                     DELAY               ^H
 18. Entire screen:                             08
        ^L                   0
        0C                             CHARACTER SET
 19. Cursor to end of screen:         36. Full upper and lower ASCII: YES
        ^K                   0        37. Generate all control codes: YES
        0B                            38. Bell or tone sequence:
 20. Beginning of screen to cursor:             ^G
                                                07

 21. Cursor to end of line:           EMULATION
        ^]                   0        39. Conform to ANSI X3.64?      NO
        1D                            40. Terminals Emulated:
 22. Beginning of line to cursor:


 23. Entire cursor line:
```

Manufacturer: Franklin Computer Corp.
Terminal: Ace Display

41. Information provided by:
    MANUFACTURER

42. PROGRAM FUNCTION KEYS   NOTES
  1.

  2.

  3.

  4.

  5.

  6.

  7.

  8.

  9.

 10.

 11.

 12.

 13.

 14.

 15.

 16.

```
--------------------------------------------------------------------------
1. Manufacturer:                        General Terminal Corporation
2. Terminal:                            SW 10 (ANSI mode)
--------------------------------------------------------------------------
```

SCREEN LAYOUT
3. Number of rows: 24
4. Number of columns: 80
5. Top Row: 1
6. Left Column: 1
7. Printing in bottom right
   cause scroll?   PROG

CURSOR ADDRESSING
8. Lead-in sequence:
            ESC [
            1B 5B
9. Row or column first: ROW
10. Numeric form of row and column:
    VARIABLE-LENGTH ASCII
11. Add offset to: Row: 0
                          Col: 0
12. Separator sequence:
            ;
            3B
13. End sequence:
            H
            48
14. Cursor to top row, left column:
ESC [1   ;   1   H
1B 5B 31 3B 31 48
15. 10th Row, 50th Column:
ESC [1   0   ;   5   0   H
1B 5B 31 30 3B 35 30 48
16. Delay after positioning: 0
17. Cursor home:
            ESC [H
            1B 5B 48

ERASURE   DELAY
18. Entire screen:
      ESC [2   J   0
      1B 5B 32 4A
19. Cursor to end of screen:
      ESC [J   0
      1B 5B 4A
20. Beginning of screen to cursor:
      ESC [1   J   0
      1B 5B 31 4A
21. Cursor to end of line:
      ESC [K   0
      1B 5B 4B
22. Beginning of line to cursor:
      ESC [1   K   0
      1B 5B 31 4B
23. Entire cursor line:
      ESC [2   K   0
      1B 5B 32 4B

VIDEO ATTRIBUTES
          ON   OFF
24. Blinking:
ESC [5   m   ESC [m
1B 5B 35 6D   1B 5B   6D
25. Reverse video:
ESC [7   m   ESC [m
1B 5B 37 6D   1B 5B   6D
26. Underline:
ESC [4   m   ESC [m
1B 5B 34 6D   1B 5B   6D
27. High intensity:
ESC [1   m   ESC [m
1B 5B 31 6D   1B 5B   6D
28. Half intensity:

29. Attributes occupy position: NO
30. Attributes cumulative: YES
31. All attributes off:
            ESC [m
            1B 5B   6D

CURSOR CONTROL KEYS
32. Cursor up:
            ESC [A
            1B 5B 41
33. Cursor down:
            ESC [B
            1B 5B 42
34. Cursor right:
            ESC [C
            1B 5B 43
35. Cursor left:
            ESC [D
            1B 5B 44

CHARACTER SET
36. Full upper and lower ASCII: YES
37. Generate all control codes: YES
38. Bell or tone sequence:
            ^G
            07

EMULATION
39. Conform to ANSI X3.64?   YES
40. Terminals Emulated:
    DEC VT100

CONTINUED ====>

41. Information provided by:
    MANUFACTURER

42. PROGRAM FUNCTION KEYS   NOTES
    1.   42. 12 programmable function keys,
                                     each capable of holding up to 20
                                     user-defined characters.
    2.

    3.

    4.

    5.

    6.

    7.

    8.

    9.

    10.

    11.

    12.

    13.

    14.

    15.

    16.

```
-------------------------------------------------------------------------
  1. Manufacturer:              General Terminal Corporation
  2. Terminal:                  SW 10 (VT52 mode)
-------------------------------------------------------------------------
```

SCREEN LAYOUT   VIDEO ATTRIBUTES
  3. Number of rows: 24   ON   OFF
  4. Number of columns: 80   24. Blinking:
  5. Top Row: 1
  6. Left Column: 1
  7. Printing in bottom right   25. Reverse video:
     cause scroll?   PROG

CURSOR ADDRESSING   26. Underline:
  8. Lead-in sequence:
         ESC Y
         1B 59   27. High intensity:
  9. Row or column first: ROW
 10. Numeric form of row and column:
     BINARY   28. Half intensity:
 11. Add offset to: Row: 1F
                         Col: 1F
 12. Separator sequence: 29. Attributes occupy position: NO
                                30. Attributes cumulative: NO
                                31. All attributes off:
 13. End sequence:

 14. Cursor to top row, left column: CURSOR CONTROL KEYS
 ESC Y   SP SP   32. Cursor up:
 1B 59   20 20   ESC A
 15. 10th Row, 50th Column: 1B   41
 ESC Y   )   Q   33. Cursor down:
 1B 59   29 51   ESC B
 16. Delay after positioning: 0   1B   42
 17. Cursor home: 34. Cursor right:
         ESC H   ESC C
         1B   48   1B   43
                                35. Cursor left:
ERASURE   DELAY   ESC D
 18. Entire screen: 1B   44
         ESC H   ESC J   0
         1B 48 1B 4A   CHARACTER SET
 19. Cursor to end of screen: 36. Full upper and lower ASCII: YES
         ESC J   0   37. Generate all control codes: YES
         1B 4A   38. Bell or tone sequence:
 20. Beginning of screen to cursor: ^G
                                          07

 21. Cursor to end of line: EMULATION
         ESC K   0   39. Conform to ANSI X3.64?   NO
         1B 4B   40. Terminals Emulated:
 22. Beginning of line to cursor: DEC VT52

 23. Entire cursor line:

CONTINUED ====>

Manufacturer: General Terminal Corporation
Terminal: SW 10 (VT52 mode)

41. Information provided by:
    MANUFACTURER

42. PROGRAM FUNCTION KEYS   NOTES
    1.   42. 12 programmable function keys,
                                     each capable of holding up to
                                     20 user-defined characters.
    2.

    3.

    4.

    5.

    6.

    7.

    8.

    9.

   10.

   11.

   12.

   13.

   14.

   15.

   16.

1. Manufacturer:	General Terminal Corporation
2. Terminal:	SW 80

SCREEN LAYOUT
3. Number of rows: 24
4. Number of columns: 80
5. Top Row: 1
6. Left Column: 1
7. Printing in bottom right
   cause scroll?   YES

CURSOR ADDRESSING
8. Lead-in sequence:
             ESC =
             1B 3D
9. Row or column first: ROW
10. Numeric form of row and column:
    BINARY
11. Add offset to: Row: 1F
                        Col: 1F
12. Separator sequence:

13. End sequence:

14. Cursor to top row, left column:
ESC =   SP SP
1B 3D   20 20
15. 10th Row, 50th Column:
ESC =   )   Q
1B 3D   29 51
16. Delay after positioning: 0
17. Cursor home:
             ESC H
             1B 48

ERASURE   DELAY
18. Entire screen:
       ESC H   ESC J   0
       1B 48 1B 4A
19. Cursor to end of screen:
       ESC J   0
       1B 4A
20. Beginning of screen to cursor:

21. Cursor to end of line:
       ESC K   0
       1B 4B
22. Beginning of line to cursor:

23. Entire cursor line:

VIDEO ATTRIBUTES
          ON   OFF
24. Blinking:
ESC k   ^D   ESC a
1B 6B   04   1B   61
25. Reverse video:
ESC k   ^B   ESC a
1B 6B   02   1B   61
26. Underline:
ESC k   ^P   ESC a
1B 6B   10   1B   61
27. High intensity:

28. Half intensity:
ESC k   ^A   ESC a
1B 6B   01   1B   61
29. Attributes occupy position: NO
30. Attributes cumulative: NO
31. All attributes off:
             ESC a
             1B   61

CURSOR CONTROL KEYS
32. Cursor up:
             ESC A
             1B 41
33. Cursor down:
             ESC B
             1B 42
34. Cursor right:
             ESC C
             1B 43
35. Cursor left:
             ESC D
             1B 44

CHARACTER SET
36. Full upper and lower ASCII: YES
37. Generate all control codes: YES
38. Bell or tone sequence:
             ^G
             07

EMULATION
39. Conform to ANSI X3.64?   NO
40. Terminals Emulated:

CONTINUED ====>

```
-------------------------------------------------------------------------
    Manufacturer:                      General Terminal Corporation
    Terminal:                          SW 80
-------------------------------------------------------------------------
```

41. Information provided by:
    MANUFACTURER

42. PROGRAM FUNCTION KEYS   NOTES
    1.   3. 25th status line.
                                    30. Additional attribute combinations
                                        available.
    2.   36. 96 ASCII characters, 32 systems
                                        characters, 96 graphic and special
                                        characters.
    3.   42. 12 programmable function keys plus
                                        12 in shift mode, each capable of
                                        storing up to 254 characters.
    4.

    5.

    6.

    7.

    8.

    9.

   10.

   11.

   12.

   13.

   14.

   15.

   16.

```
------------------------------------------------------------------------
1. Manufacturer:              GraphOn Corporation
2. Terminal:                  GO-100
------------------------------------------------------------------------
```

SCREEN LAYOUT
3. Number of rows: 24
4. Number of columns: 80
5. Top Row: 1
6. Left Column: 1
7. Printing in bottom right
   cause scroll?   PROG

CURSOR ADDRESSING
8. Lead-in sequence:
          ESC [
          1B 5B
9. Row or column first: ROW
10. Numeric form of row and column:
    VARIABLE-LENGTH ASCII
11. Add offset to: Row: 0
                            Col: 0
12. Separator sequence:
          ;
          3B
13. End sequence:
          H
          48
14. Cursor to top row, left column:
ESC [1   ;   1   H
1B 5B 31 3B 31 48
15. 10th Row, 50th Column:
ESC [1   0   ;   5   0   H
1B 5B 31 30 3B 35 30 48
16. Delay after positioning: 0
17. Cursor home:
          ESC [H
          1B 5B 48

ERASURE   DELAY
18. Entire screen:
          ESC [2   J   0
          1B 5B 32 4A
19. Cursor to end of screen:
          ESC [J   0
          1B 5B 4A
20. Beginning of screen to cursor:
          ESC [1   J   0
          1B 5B 31 4A
21. Cursor to end of line:
          ESC [K   0
          1B 5B 4B
22. Beginning of line to cursor:
          ESC [1   K   0
          1B 5B 31 4B
23. Entire cursor line:
          ESC [2   K   0
          1B 5B 32 4B

VIDEO ATTRIBUTES
          ON   OFF
24. Blinking:
ESC [5   m   ESC [m
1B 5B 35 6D   1B 5B   6D
25. Reverse video:
ESC [7   m   ESC [m
1B 5B 37 6D   1B 5B   6D
26. Underline:
ESC [4   m   ESC [m
1B 5B 34 6D   1B 5B   6D
27. High intensity:
ESC [1   m   ESC [m
1B 5B 31 6D   1B 5B   6D
28. Half intensity:

29. Attributes occupy position: NO
30. Attributes cumulative: YES
31. All attributes off:
          ESC [m
          1B 5B   6D

CURSOR CONTROL KEYS
32. Cursor up:
          ESC [A
          1B 5B   41
33. Cursor down:
          ESC [B
          1B 5B   42
34. Cursor right:
          ESC [C
          1B 5B   43
35. Cursor left:
          ESC [D
          1B 5B   44

CHARACTER SET
36. Full upper and lower ASCII: YES
37. Generate all control codes: YES
38. Bell or tone sequence:
          ^G
          07

EMULATION
39. Conform to ANSI X3.64?   YES
40. Terminals Emulated:
    DEC VT100
    DEC VT52

153   CONTINUED ====>

41. Information provided by:
    MANUFACTURER

42. PROGRAM FUNCTION KEYS   NOTES
    1. ESC O   P   42. In addition to four program
       1B 4F 50   function keys shown (PF1-PF4),
                                   terminal supports 8 programmable
    2. ESC O   Q   function keys (F1-F8), in shift
       1B 4F 51   and unshift mode, for a total of
                                   16 programmable function keys
    3. ESC O   R   which may be set by the user or
       1B 4F 52   host.

    4. ESC O   S   Additional editing functions:
       1B 4F 53   Insert line   ESC [L
                                   Delete line   ESC [M
    5.   Delete character   ESC [P
                                   Enter char insert mode ESC [4 h
                                   Exit char insert mode ESC [4 1
    6.

    7.

    8.

    9.

    10.

    11.

    12.

    13.

    14.

    15.

    16.

---
1. Manufacturer: GraphOn Corporation
2. Terminal: GO-140

SCREEN LAYOUT   VIDEO ATTRIBUTES
3. Number of rows: 24   ON   OFF
4. Number of columns: 80   24. Blinking:
5. Top Row: 1   ESC [5   m   ESC [m
6. Left Column: 1   1B   5B   35   6D   1B   5B   6D
7. Printing in bottom right   25. Reverse video:
   cause scroll?   PROG   ESC [7   m   ESC [m
                                         1B   5B   37   6D   1B   5B   6D
CURSOR ADDRESSING   26. Underline:
8. Lead-in sequence: ESC [4   m   ESC [m
          ESC [1B   5B   34   6D   1B   5B   6D
          1B   5B   27. High intensity:
9. Row or column first: ROW   ESC [1   m   ESC [m
10. Numeric form of row and column: 1B   5B   31   6D   1B   5B   6D
    VARIABLE-LENGTH ASCII   28. Half intensity:
11. Add offset to: Row: 0
                         Col: 0
12. Separator sequence: 29. Attributes occupy position: NO
          ;   30. Attributes cumulative: YES
          3B   31. All attributes off:
13. End sequence: ESC [m
          H   1B   5B   6D
          48
14. Cursor to top row, left column: CURSOR CONTROL KEYS
ESC [1   ;   1   H   32. Cursor up:
1B   5B   31   3B   31   48   ESC [A
15. 10th Row, 50th Column: 1B   5B   41
ESC [1   0   ;   5   0   H   33. Cursor down:
1B   5B   31   30   3B   35   30   48   ESC [B
16. Delay after positioning: 0   1B   5B   42
17. Cursor home: 34. Cursor right:
          ESC [H   ESC [C
          1B   5B   48   1B   5B   43
                                          35. Cursor left:
ERASURE   DELAY   ESC [D
18. Entire screen: 1B   5B   44
          ESC [2   J   0
          1B   5B   32   4A   CHARACTER SET
19. Cursor to end of screen: 36. Full upper and lower ASCII: YES
          ESC [J   0   37. Generate all control codes: YES
          1B   5B   4A   38. Bell or tone sequence:
20. Beginning of screen to cursor: ^G
          ESC [1   J   0   07
          1B   5B   31   4A
21. Cursor to end of line: EMULATION
          ESC [K   0   39. Conform to ANSI X3.64?   YES
          1B   5B   4B   40. Terminals Emulated:
22. Beginning of line to cursor: DEC VT100
          ESC [1   K   0   DEC VT52
          1B   5B   31   4B
23. Entire cursor line:
          ESC [2   K   0
          1B   5B   32   4B

```
--------------------------------------------------------------------------------
      Manufacturer:              GraphOn Corporation
      Terminal:                  GO-140
--------------------------------------------------------------------------------
```

41. Information provided by:
    MANUFACTURER

42. PROGRAM FUNCTION KEYS   NOTES
    1. ESC O   P   36. Also graphics mode.
       1B   4F   50   42. In addition to four program
                                       function keys shown (PF1-PF4),
    2. ESC O   Q   terminal supports 8 programmable
       1B   4F   51   function keys (F1-F8), in shift
                                       and unshift mode, for a total of
    3. ESC O   R   16 programmable function keys
       1B   4F   52   which may be set by the user or
                                       host.
    4. ESC O   S
       1B   4F   53   Additional editing functions:
                                       Insert line   ESC [L
    5.   Delete line   ESC [M
                                       Delete character   ESC [P
                                       Enter char insert mode   ESC [4 h
    6.   Exit char insert mode   ESC [4 1

    7.

    8.

    9.

   10.

   11.

   12.

   13.

   14.

   15.

   16.

```
1. Manufacturer:                        Hewlett-Packard
2. Terminal:                            HP 262X, 264X and HP 2382A
```

```
SCREEN LAYOUT                           VIDEO ATTRIBUTES
 3. Number of rows:          24               ON                    OFF
 4. Number of columns:       80         24. Blinking:
 5. Top Row:                  0         ESC &    d    A        ESC &    d    @
 6. Left Column:              0         1B  26   64   41       1B  26   64   40
 7. Printing in bottom right            25. Reverse video:
    cause scroll?            YES        ESC &    d    B        ESC &    d    @
                                        1B  26   64   42       1B  26   64   40
CURSOR ADDRESSING                       26. Underline:
 8. Lead-in sequence:                   ESC &    d    D        ESC &    d    @
        ESC &    a                      1B  26   64   44       1B  26   64   40
        1B   26   61                    27. High intensity:
 9. Row or column first:      COL
10. Numeric form of row and column:
    VARIABLE-LENGTH ASCII               28. Half intensity:
11. Add offset to:        Row:    0     ESC &    d    H        ESC &    d    @
                          Col:    0     1B  26   64   48       1B  26   64   40
12. Separator sequence:                 29. Attributes occupy position: NO
                                        30. Attributes cumulative:      NO
                                        31. All attributes off:
13. End sequence:                               ESC &    d    @
                                                1B   26   64   40

14. Cursor to top row, left column:     CURSOR CONTROL KEYS
ESC &    a    0    c    0    R          32. Cursor up:
1B  26   61   30   63   30   52                 ESC A
15. 10th Row, 50th Column:                      1B   41
ESC &    a    4    9    c    9    R     33. Cursor down:
1B  26   61   34   39   63   39   52            ESC B
16. Delay after positioning:      0             1B   42
17. Cursor home:                        34. Cursor right:
        ESC h                                   ESC C
        1B   68                                 1B   43
                                        35. Cursor left:
ERASURE                     DELAY               ESC D
18. Entire screen:                              1B   44
        ESC h    ESC J         0
        1B   68  1B   4A               CHARACTER SET
19. Cursor to end of screen:            36. Full upper and lower ASCII: YES
        ESC J                  0        37. Generate all control codes: YES
        1B   4A                         38. Bell or tone sequence:
20. Beginning of screen to cursor:              ^G
                                                07

21. Cursor to end of line:              EMULATION
        ESC K                  0        39. Conform to ANSI X3.64?      NO
        1B   4B                         40. Terminals Emulated:
22. Beginning of line to cursor:


23. Entire cursor line:
```

41. Information provided by:
    MANUFACTURER

42. PROGRAM FUNCTION KEYS
    1. ESC p
       1B 70

    2. ESC q
       1B 71

    3. ESC r
       1B 72

    4. ESC s
       1B 73

    5. ESC t
       1B 74

    6. ESC u
       1B 75

    7. ESC v
       1B 76

    8. ESC w
       1B 77

    9.

    10.

    11.

    12.

    13.

    14.

    15.

    16.

NOTES
2. This data applies to the alphanumeric capabilities of the following HP terminals:
   2621B   2622A   2623A   2624B
   2626A   2645A   2648A   2647F
   2382A
9. Either row or column first is
   acceptable, depending on sequence
   sent. See notes 12, 13, 14, and 15.
12. To send row first, use r (72H).
13. To send row first, use C (43H).
14. To send row first:
    ESC &   a   0   r   0   C
    1B   26   61   30   72   30   43
15. To send row first:
    ESC &   a   9   r   4   9   C
    1B   26   61   39   72   34   39   43
23. To delete entire cursor line:
    ESC &   a   0   C   ESC K
    1B   26   61   30   43   1B   4B
30. Combinations preceeded by ESC & d:
                    @ABCDEFGHIJKLMNOS
    Half-intensity   XXXXXXXX
    Underline   XXXX   XXXX
    Reverse   XX XX XX XX
    Blinking   X X X X X X X X
    Security   X
    End enhancement   X
    Example: Reverse, blinking and
             underline:
             ESC &   d   G
             1B   26   64   47
36. Three complete 128-character sets
    (base, line drawing and mathematics)
    are available standard. The 8-bit
    extended ASCII code is used to
    generate an additional 128-charac-
    ter foreign set.
    ESC) @ selects base set
    ESC) A selects math set
    ESC) B selects line drawing set
42. Sequences shown are default. All 8
    function keys are programmable.

```
--------------------------------------------------------------------
1. Manufacturer:              Hewlett-Packard
2. Terminal:                  HP-150
--------------------------------------------------------------------

SCREEN LAYOUT                      VIDEO ATTRIBUTES
3. Number of rows:        24            ON                    OFF
4. Number of columns:     80       24. Blinking:
5. Top Row:                0       ESC &    d    A       ESC &    d    @
6. Left Column:            0       1B  26   64   41      1B  26   64   40
7. Printing in bottom right        25. Reverse video:
   cause scroll?         YES       ESC &    d    B       ESC &    d    @
                                   1B  26   64   42      1B  26   64   40
CURSOR ADDRESSING                  26. Underline:
8. Lead-in sequence:               ESC &    d    D       ESC &    d    @
        ESC &    a                 1B  26   64   44      1B  26   64   40
        1B  26   61                27. High intensity:
9. Row or column first:     COL
10. Numeric form of row and column:
    VARIABLE-LENGTH ASCII          28. Half intensity:
11. Add offset to:      Row:   0   ESC &    d    H       ESC &    d    @
                        Col:   0   1B  26   64   48      1B  26   64   40
12. Separator sequence:            29. Attributes occupy position: NO
                                   30. Attributes cumulative:      NO
                                   31. All attributes off:
13. End sequence:                          ESC &    d    @
                                           1B   26   64   40


14. Cursor to top row, left column:  CURSOR CONTROL KEYS
ESC &    a    0    c    0    R      32. Cursor up:
1B  26   61   30   63   30   52             ESC A
15. 10th Row, 50th Column:                  1B  41
ESC &    a    4    9    c    9    R   33. Cursor down:
1B  26   61   34   39   63   39   52         ESC B
16. Delay after positioning:    0           1B  42
17. Cursor home:                   34. Cursor right:
        ESC h                              ESC C
        1B  68                             1B  43
                                   35. Cursor left:
ERASURE                   DELAY            ESC D
18. Entire screen:                         1B  44
        ESC h   ESC J           0
        1B  68  1B  4A             CHARACTER SET
19. Cursor to end of screen:       36. Full upper and lower ASCII: YES
        ESC J               0      37. Generate all control codes: YES
        1B  4A                     38. Bell or tone sequence:
20. Beginning of screen to cursor:         ^G
                                           07
21. Cursor to end of line:         EMULATION
        ESC K               0      39. Conform to ANSI X3.64?      NO
        1B  4B                     40. Terminals Emulated:
22. Beginning of line to cursor:


23. Entire cursor line:
```

41. Information provided by:
    MANUFACTURER

42. PROGRAM FUNCTION KEYS
1. ESC p
   1B 70

2. ESC q
   1B 71

3. ESC r
   1B 72

4. ESC s
   1B 73

5. ESC t
   1B 74

6. ESC u
   1B 75

7. ESC v
   1B 76

8. ESC w
   1B 77

9.

10.

11.

12.

13.

14.

15.

16.

NOTES

9. Either row or column first is
   acceptable, depending on sequence
   sent. See notes 12, 13, 14, and 15.

12. To send row first, use r (72H).

13. To send row first, use C (43H).

14. To send row first:

    ESC &   a   0   r   0   C
    1B   26 61 30 72 30 43

15. To send row first:

    ESC &   a   9   r   4   9   C
    1B   26 61 39 72 34 39 43

23. To delete entire cursor line:

    ESC &   a   0   C   ESC K
    1B   26 61 30 43 1B   4B

30. Combinations preceeded by ESC & d:

```
                         @ABCDEFGHIJKLMNOS
Half-intensity             XXXXXXXX
Underline                XXXX     XXXX
Reverse                    XX  XX  XX  XX
Blinking                 X X X X X X X X
Security                                X
End enhancement          X
```

    Example: Reverse, blinking and
             underline:
             ESC &   d   G
             1B   26 64 47

36. Three complete 128-character sets
    (base, line drawing and mathematics)
    are available standard. The 8-bit
    extended ASCII code is used to
    generate an additional 128-charac-
    ter foreign set.
    ESC) @ selects base set
    ESC) A selects math set
    ESC) B selects line drawing set

    The HP-150 also emulates certain
    features of the Tektronics 4010
    and 4014 graphics terminals.

37. Foreign language keyboards are
    available.

42. Sequences shown are default. All 8
    function keys are programmable.

```
-----------------------------------------------------------------------
1. Manufacturer:                    Honeywell Information Systems
2. Terminal:                        VIP 7201
-----------------------------------------------------------------------
```

SCREEN LAYOUT
3. Number of rows: 24
4. Number of columns: 80
5. Top Row: 1
6. Left Column: 1
7. Printing in bottom right
   cause scroll?   YES

CURSOR ADDRESSING
8. Lead-in sequence:
              ESC f
              1B 66
9. Row or column first: ROW
10. Numeric form of row and column:
    BINARY
11. Add offset to: Row: 1F
                        Col: 1F
12. Separator sequence:

13. End sequence:

14. Cursor to top row, left column:
ESC f   SP   SP
1B 66   20   20
15. 10th Row, 50th Column:
ESC f   )   Q
1B 66   29   51
16. Delay after positioning: 0
17. Cursor home:
              ESC H
              1B 48

ERASURE   DELAY
18. Entire screen:
        ESC `   0
        1B 60
19. Cursor to end of screen:
        ESC J   0
        1B 4A
20. Beginning of screen to cursor:

21. Cursor to end of line:
        ESC K   0
        1B 4B
22. Beginning of line to cursor:

23. Entire cursor line:

VIDEO ATTRIBUTES
        ON   OFF
24. Blinking:
    ESC 4   ESC 3
    1B 34   1B 33
25. Reverse video:
    ESC 4   ESC 3
    1B 34   1B 33
26. Underline:
    ESC 4   ESC 3
    1B 34   1B 33
27. High intensity:
    ESC 4   ESC 3
    1B 34   1B 33
28. Half intensity:
    ESC 4   ESC 3
    1B 34   1B 33
29. Attributes occupy position: NO
30. Attributes cumulative: YES
31. All attributes off:
              ESC 3
              1B 33

CURSOR CONTROL KEYS
32. Cursor up:
              ESC A
              1B 41
33. Cursor down:
              ESC B
              1B 42
34. Cursor right:
              ESC C
              1B 43
35. Cursor left:
              ESC D
              1B 44

CHARACTER SET
36. Full upper and lower ASCII: YES
37. Generate all control codes: YES
38. Bell or tone sequence:
              ^G
              07

EMULATION
39. Conform to ANSI X3.64?   NO
40. Terminals Emulated:
    Honeywell VIP 7200, VIP 7205

CONTINUED ====>

41. Information provided by:
    MANUFACTURER

42. PROGRAM FUNCTION KEYS   NOTES
    1. ESC 0   24.-28. Operator selects video
       1B   30   attributes by terminal set-up
                                   instruction.
    2. ESC 2   42. Function keys shown are unshift.
       1B   32   Shifted function keys are:
                                   F1   ESC 1
    3. ESC 6   F2   ESC 5
       1B   36   F3   ESC 7
                                   F4   ESC 9
    4. ESC 8   F5   ESC ;
       1B   38   F6   ESC =
                                   F7   ESC ?

    5. ESC :
       1B   3A

    6. ESC <
       1B   3C

    7. ESC >
       1B   3E

    8.

    9.

   10.

   11.

   12.

   13.

   14.

   15.

   16.

```
--------------------------------------------------------------------------------
 1. Manufacturer:                        Honeywell Information Systems
 2. Terminal:                            VIP 7301
--------------------------------------------------------------------------------
```

SCREEN LAYOUT   VIDEO ATTRIBUTES
 3. Number of rows: 24   ON   OFF
 4. Number of columns: 80   24. Blinking:
 5. Top Row: 1   ESC s   B   ESC s   R
 6. Left Column: 1   1B 73   42   1B 73   52
 7. Printing in bottom right   25. Reverse video:
    cause scroll?   YES   ESC s   I   ESC s   R
                                         1B 73   49   1B 73   52
CURSOR ADDRESSING   26. Underline:
 8. Lead-in sequence: ESC s   _   ESC s   R
            ESC f   1B 73   5F   1B 73   52
            1B 66   27. High intensity:
 9. Row or column first: ROW   ESC s   ESC s   R
10. Numeric form of row and column: 1B 73   1B 73   52
    BINARY   28. Half intensity:
11. Add offset to: Row: 1F   ESC s   L   ESC s   R
                         Col: 1F   1B 73   4C   1B 73   52
12. Separator sequence: 29. Attributes occupy position: NO
                                         30. Attributes cumulative: YES
                                         31. All attributes off:
13. End sequence: ESC s   R
                                                    1B 73   52

14. Cursor to top row, left column: CURSOR CONTROL KEYS
ESC f   SP SP   32. Cursor up:
1B 66   20 20   ESC A
15. 10th Row, 50th Column: 1B 41
ESC f   )   Q   33. Cursor down:
1B 66   29 51   ESC B
16. Delay after positioning: 0   1B 42
17. Cursor home: 34. Cursor right:
            ESC H   ESC C
            1B 48   1B 43
                                         35. Cursor left:
ERASURE   DELAY   ESC D
18. Entire screen: 1B 44
            ESC `   0
            1B 60   CHARACTER SET
19. Cursor to end of screen: 36. Full upper and lower ASCII: YES
            ESC J   0   37. Generate all control codes: YES
            1B 4A   38. Bell or tone sequence:
20. Beginning of screen to cursor: ^G
                                                    07
21. Cursor to end of line: EMULATION
            ESC K   0   39. Conform to ANSI X3.64?   NO
            1B 4B   40. Terminals Emulated:
22. Beginning of line to cursor:

23. Entire cursor line:

                              163   CONTINUED ====>

41. Information provided by:
    MANUFACTURER

42. PROGRAM FUNCTION KEYS
    1. ESC 0
       1B   30

    2. ESC 2
       1B   32

    3. ESC 6
       1B   36

    4. ESC 8
       1B   38

    5. ESC :
       1B   3A

    6. ESC <
       1B   3C

    7. ESC >
       1B   3E

    8. ESC P
       1B   50

    9. ESC R
       1B   52

   10. ESC T
       1B   54

   11. ESC \
       1B   5C

   12. ESC ^
       1B   5E

   13.

   14.

   15.

   16.

NOTES
42. Function keys are shown unshift.
    Shifted function keys are:
    PF1   ESC 1
    PF2   ESC 5
    PF3   ESC 7
    PF4   ESC 9
    PF5   ESC ;
    PF6   ESC =
    PF7   ESC ?
    PF8   ESC Q
    PF9   ESC S
    PF10   ESC V
    PF11   ESC]
    PF12   ESC _

| 1. Manufacturer: | Human Designed Systems, Inc. |
| 2. Terminal: | Concept AVT Series |

SCREEN LAYOUT
3. Number of rows: 24
4. Number of columns: 80
5. Top Row: 1
6. Left Column: 1
7. Printing in bottom right
   cause scroll?   YES

CURSOR ADDRESSING
8. Lead-in sequence:
            ESC [
            1B 5B
9. Row or column first: ROW
10. Numeric form of row and column:
    VARIABLE-LENGTH ASCII
11. Add offset to: Row: 0
                         Col: 0
12. Separator sequence:
            ;
            3B
13. End sequence:
            H
            48
14. Cursor to top row, left column:
ESC [1   ;   1   H
1B 5B 31 3B 31 48
15. 10th Row, 50th Column:
ESC [1   0   ;   5   0   H
1B 5B 31 30 3B 35 30 48
16. Delay after positioning: 0
17. Cursor home:
            ESC [H
            1B 5B 48

ERASURE   DELAY
18. Entire screen:
        ESC [2   J   38
        1B 5B 32 4A
19. Cursor to end of screen:
        ESC [J   96
        1B 5B 4A
20. Beginning of screen to cursor:
        ESC [1   J   96
        1B 5B 31 4A
21. Cursor to end of line:
        ESC [K   6
        1B 5B 4B
22. Beginning of line to cursor:
        ESC [1   K   6
        1B 5B 31 4B
23. Entire cursor line:
        ESC [2   K   6
        1B 5B 32 4B

VIDEO ATTRIBUTES
            ON   OFF
24. Blinking:
    ESC [5   m   ESC [m
    1B 5B 35 6D   1B 5B 6D
25. Reverse video:
    ESC [7   m   ESC [m
    1B 5B 37 6D   1B 5B 6D
26. Underline:
    ESC [4   m   ESC [m
    1B 5B 34 6D   1B 5B 6D
27. High intensity:
    ESC [1   m   ESC [m
    1B 5B 31 6D   1B 5B 6D
28. Half intensity:

29. Attributes occupy position: NO
30. Attributes cumulative: YES
31. All attributes off:
            ESC [m
            1B 5B 6D

CURSOR CONTROL KEYS
32. Cursor up:
            ESC [A
            1B 5B 41
33. Cursor down:
            ESC [B
            1B 5B 42
34. Cursor right:
            ESC [C
            1B 5B 43
35. Cursor left:
            ESC [D
            1B 5B 44

CHARACTER SET
36. Full upper and lower ASCII: YES
37. Generate all control codes: YES
38. Bell or tone sequence:
            ^G
            07

EMULATION
39. Conform to ANSI X3.64?   YES
40. Terminals Emulated:
    DEC VT100, DEC VT52
    Tektronix 4010/4013 (GVT+ and
       GVT-APL+)

                      CONTINUED ====>

41. Information provided by:
    MANUFACTURER

42. PROGRAM FUNCTION KEYS
    1. ^\ 0   0   1   ^M
       1C 30 30 31 0D

    2. ^\ 0   0   2   ^M
       1C 30 30 32 0D

    3. ^\ 0   0   3   ^M
       1C 30 30 33 0D

    4. ^\ 0   0   4   ^M
       1C 30 30 34 0D

    5. ^\ 0   0   5   ^M
       1C 30 30 35 0D

    6. ^\ 0   0   6   ^M
       1C 30 30 36 0D

    7. ^\ 0   0   7   ^M
       1C 30 30 37 0D

    8. ^\ 0   0   8   ^M
       1C 30 30 38 0D

    9. ^\ 0   0   9   ^M
       1C 30 30 39 0D

   10. ^\ 0   1   0   ^M
       1C 30 31 30 0D

   11. ^\ 0   1   1   ^M
       1C 30 31 31 0D

   12. ^\ 0   1   2   ^M
       1C 30 31 32 0D

   13. ^\ 0   1   3   ^M
       1C 30 31 33 0D

   14. ^\ 0   1   4   ^M
       1C 30 31 34 0D

   15. ^\ 0   1   5   ^M
       1C 30 31 35 0D

   16. ^\ 0   1   6   ^M
       1C 30 31 36 0D

NOTES

2. Series includes:
   AVT+   ASCII alphanumeric
   AVT-APL+ APL/ASCII alphanumeric
   GVT+   Graphics and alphanumeric
   GVT-APL+ Graphics and alphanumeric
3. All of display memory is accessible
   (96 or 192 lines) but only 24 lines
   appear on the screen at a time.
4. Software selectable 132.
18. Also FF (0CH). Delay is 38 ms per
    page. One page equals 24 lines.
    Delay required depends on how large
    a window is being cleared.
19. Delay is 96 ms per page. See note
    18.
20. Delay is 96 ms per page. See note
    18.
36. Also VT100/Concept Special Graphics
    characters and other optional (up
    to 4) software selectable character
    sets.
42. Each of the 46 programmable key
    functions can either execute a
    terminal function or transmit a
    sequence of characters to the host
    system.

ADDITIONAL FEATURES
4-8 pages of display memory
1-4 user-definable windows
4 software selectable character
   sets (total of 512 characters)
full editing functions (insert/
   delete line, character; erase,
   etc.)
multiple attribute lists
46 programmable key functions
   (execute, transmit, or disabled)

---

1. Manufacturer: IBM
2. Terminal: 3101

SCREEN LAYOUT   VIDEO ATTRIBUTES
3. Number of rows: 24   ON   OFF
4. Number of columns: 80   24. Blinking:
5. Top Row: 1
6. Left Column: 1
7. Printing in bottom right   25. Reverse video:
   cause scroll?   PROG

CURSOR ADDRESSING   26. Underline:
8. Lead-in sequence:
        ESC Y
        1B 59   27. High intensity:
9. Row or column first: ROW
10. Numeric form of row and column:
    BINARY   28. Half intensity:
11. Add offset to: Row: 1F
                         Col: 1F
12. Separator sequence: 29. Attributes occupy position: NO
                                    30. Attributes cumulative: NO
                                    31. All attributes off:
13. End sequence:

14. Cursor to top row, left column: CURSOR CONTROL KEYS
ESC Y   SP   SP   32. Cursor up:
1B   59   20   20   ESC A
15. 10th Row, 50th Column: 1B   41
ESC Y   )   Q   33. Cursor down:
1B   59   29   51   ESC B
16. Delay after positioning: 0   1B   42
17. Cursor home: 34. Cursor right:
        ESC H   ESC C
        1B 48   1B   43
                                     35. Cursor left:
ERASURE   DELAY   ESC D
18. Entire screen: 1B   44
        ESC K   0
        1B 4B   CHARACTER SET
19. Cursor to end of screen: 36. Full upper and lower ASCII: YES
        ESC J   0   37. Generate all control codes: YES
        1B 4A   38. Bell or tone sequence:
20. Beginning of screen to cursor: ^G
                                             07

21. Cursor to end of line: EMULATION
        ESC K   0   39. Conform to ANSI X3.64?   NO
        1B 4B   40. Terminals Emulated:
22. Beginning of line to cursor:

23. Entire cursor line:

     Manufacturer: IBM
     Terminal: 3101
----

41. Information provided by:
    PUBLISHER

42. PROGRAM FUNCTION KEYS   NOTES
 1. ESC a   ^C   18. ESC H ESC J will also clear the
    1B   61 03   screen by homing the cursor then
                                         clearing to end of screen and
 2. ESC b   ^C   will maintain complete
    1B   62 03   compability with the DEC VT52
                                         except for PF keys.
 3. ESC c   ^C   24.-28. 3101/20 has attributes but
    1B   63 03   only in the block mode.

 4. ESC d   ^C
    1B   64 03

 5. ESC e   ^C
    1B   65 03

 6. ESC f   ^C
    1B   66 03

 7. ESC g   ^C
    1B   67 03

 8. ESC h   ^C
    1B   68 03

 9.

10.

11.

12.

13.

14.

15.

16.

```
------------------------------------------------------------------------
    1. Manufacturer:              Intecolor Corporation
    2. Terminal:                  2405
------------------------------------------------------------------------
```

SCREEN LAYOUT
3. Number of rows: 24
4. Number of columns: 80
5. Top Row: 1
6. Left Column: 1
7. Printing in bottom right
   cause scroll?   NO

CURSOR ADDRESSING
8. Lead-in sequence:
        ESC [
        1B 5B
9. Row or column first: ROW
10. Numeric form of row and column:
    VARIABLE-LENGTH ASCII
11. Add offset to: Row: 0
                          Col: 0
12. Separator sequence:
        ;
        3B
13. End sequence:
        H
        48
14. Cursor to top row, left column:
    ESC [1   ;   1   H
    1B 5B 31 3B 31 48
15. 10th Row, 50th Column:
    ESC [1   0   ;   5   0   H
    1B 5B 31 30 3B 35 30 48
16. Delay after positioning: 0
17. Cursor home:
        ESC [H
        1B 5B 48

ERASURE   DELAY
18. Entire screen:
        ESC [2   J   0
        1B 5B 32 4A
19. Cursor to end of screen:
        ESC [J   0
        1B 5B 4A
20. Beginning of screen to cursor:
        ESC [1   J   0
        1B 5B 31 4A
21. Cursor to end of line:
        ESC [K   0
        1B 5B 4B
22. Beginning of line to cursor:
        ESC [1   K   0
        1B 5B 31 4B
23. Entire cursor line:
        ESC [2   K   0
        1B 5B 32 4B

VIDEO ATTRIBUTES
         ON   OFF
24. Blinking:
    ESC [5   m   ESC [m
    1B 5B 35 6D   1B 5B 6D
25. Reverse video:
    ESC [7   m   ESC [m
    1B 5B 37 6D   1B 5B 6D
26. Underline:
    ESC [4   m   ESC [m
    1B 5B 34 6D   1B 5B 6D
27. High intensity:

28. Half intensity:

29. Attributes occupy position: NO
30. Attributes cumulative: YES
31. All attributes off:
        ESC [m
        1B 5B 6D

CURSOR CONTROL KEYS
32. Cursor up:
        ESC [A
        1B 5B 41
33. Cursor down:
        ESC [B
        1B 5B 42
34. Cursor right:
        ESC [C
        1B 5B 43
35. Cursor left:
        ESC [D
        1B 5B 44

CHARACTER SET
36. Full upper and lower ASCII: YES
37. Generate all control codes: YES
38. Bell or tone sequence:
        ^G
        07

EMULATION
39. Conform to ANSI X3.64?   YES
40. Terminals Emulated:
    VT100, VT52

169   CONTINUED ====>

Manufacturer: Intecolor Corporation
Terminal: 2405

41. Information provided by:
    MANUFACTURER

42. PROGRAM FUNCTION KEYS   NOTES
    1. ESC O   P
       1B 4F 50

    2. ESC O   Q
       1B 4F 51

    3. ESC O   R
       1B 4F 52

    4. ESC O   S
       1B 4F 53

    5.

    6.

    7.

    8.

    9.

   10.

   11.

   12.

   13.

   14.

   15.

   16.

```
--------------------------------------------------------------------------
  1. Manufacturer:              Intecolor Corporation
  2. Terminal:                  2427
--------------------------------------------------------------------------
```

SCREEN LAYOUT   VIDEO ATTRIBUTES
  3. Number of rows: 24   ON   OFF
  4. Number of columns: 80   24. Blinking:
  5. Top Row: 1   ESC [5   m   ESC [m
  6. Left Column: 1   1B 5B 35 6D   1B 5B 6D
  7. Printing in bottom right   25. Reverse video:
     cause scroll?   NO   ESC [7   m   ESC [m
                                 1B 5B 37 6D   1B 5B 6D
CURSOR ADDRESSING   26. Underline:
  8. Lead-in sequence: ESC [4   m   ESC [m
         ESC [1B 5B 34 6D   1B 5B 6D
         1B 5B   27. High intensity:
  9. Row or column first: ROW
 10. Numeric form of row and column:
     VARIABLE-LENGTH ASCII   28. Half intensity:
 11. Add offset to: Row: 0
                         Col: 0
 12. Separator sequence: 29. Attributes occupy position: NO
         ;   30. Attributes cumulative: YES
         3B   31. All attributes off:
 13. End sequence: ESC [m
         H   1B 5B 6D
         48
 14. Cursor to top row, left column: CURSOR CONTROL KEYS
 ESC [1   ;   1   H   32. Cursor up:
 1B 5B 31 3B 31 48   ESC [A
 15. 10th Row, 50th Column: 1B 5B 41
 ESC [1   0   ;   5   0   H   33. Cursor down:
 1B 5B 31 30 3B 35 30 48   ESC [B
 16. Delay after positioning: 0   1B 5B 42
 17. Cursor home: 34. Cursor right:
         ESC [H   ESC [C
         1B 5B 48   1B 5B 43
                                 35. Cursor left:
ERASURE   DELAY   ESC [D
 18. Entire screen: 1B 5B 44
         ESC [2   J   0
         1B 5B 32 4A   CHARACTER SET
 19. Cursor to end of screen: 36. Full upper and lower ASCII: YES
         ESC [J   0   37. Generate all control codes: YES
         1B 5B 4A   38. Bell or tone sequence:
 20. Beginning of screen to cursor: ^G
         ESC [1   J   0   07
         1B 5B 31 4A
 21. Cursor to end of line: EMULATION
         ESC [K   0   39. Conform to ANSI X3.64?   YES
         1B 5B 4B   40. Terminals Emulated:
 22. Beginning of line to cursor: VT100, VT52, 4010, 4027
         ESC [1   K   0
         1B 5B 31 4B
 23. Entire cursor line:
         ESC [2   K   0
         1B 5B 32 4B

                         171   CONTINUED ====>

Manufacturer: Intecolor Corporation
Terminal: 2427

41. Information provided by:
    MANUFACTURER

42. PROGRAM FUNCTION KEYS   NOTES
 1. ESC O   P
    1B   4F 50

 2. ESC O   Q
    1B   4F 51

 3. ESC O   R
    1B   4F 52

 4. ESC O   S
    1B   4F 53

 5.

 6.

 7.

 8.

 9.

10.

11.

12.

13.

14.

15.

16.

---

1. Manufacturer: Intecolor Corporation
2. Terminal: E8001G

SCREEN LAYOUT   VIDEO ATTRIBUTES
3. Number of rows: 48   ON   OFF
4. Number of columns: 80   24. Blinking:
5. Top Row: 0   ^   ^0
6. Left Column: 0   1F   OF
7. Printing in bottom right   25. Reverse video:
   cause scroll?   YES   ^F ^P   ^F ^B
                                    06 10   06 02
CURSOR ADDRESSING   26. Underline:
8. Lead-in sequence:
            ^C
            03   27. High intensity:
9. Row or column first: COL
10. Numeric form of row and column:
    BINARY   28. Half intensity:
11. Add offset to: Row: 0
                        Col: 0
12. Separator sequence: 29. Attributes occupy position: NO
                                    30. Attributes cumulative: YES
                                    31. All attributes off:
13. End sequence: ^F ^B ^0
                                            06 02 OF

14. Cursor to top row, left column: CURSOR CONTROL KEYS
 ^C NUL NUL   32. Cursor up:
 03 00 00   ^\
15. 10th Row, 50th Column: 1C
 ^C 1   ^I   33. Cursor down:
 03 31 09   ^J
16. Delay after positioning: 51   0A
17. Cursor home: 34. Cursor right:
            ^H   ^Y
            08   19
                                    35. Cursor left:
ERASURE   DELAY   ^Z
18. Entire screen: 1A
            ^L   46
            0C   CHARACTER SET
19. Cursor to end of screen: 36. Full upper and lower ASCII: YES
                                    37. Generate all control codes: YES
                                    38. Bell or tone sequence:
20. Beginning of screen to cursor: ^G
                                            07

21. Cursor to end of line: EMULATION
                                    39. Conform to ANSI X3.64?   NO
                                    40. Terminals Emulated:
22. Beginning of line to cursor:

23. Entire cursor line:
            ^K   46
            0B

173   CONTINUED ====>

41. Information provided by:
    MANUFACTURER

42. PROGRAM FUNCTION KEYS   NOTES
  1.   36. ISA Available.
       F0

  2.
       F1

  3.
       F2

  4.
       F3

  5.
       F4

  6.
       F5

  7.
       F6

  8.
       F7

  9.
       F8

 10.
       F9

 11.
       FA

 12.
       FB

 13.
       FC

 14.
       FD

 15.
       FE

 16.
       FF

```
--------------------------------------------------------------------------------
 1. Manufacturer:                    Intecolor Corporation
 2. Terminal:                        E8001R
--------------------------------------------------------------------------------

SCREEN LAYOUT                        VIDEO ATTRIBUTES
 3. Number of rows:          48           ON                    OFF
 4. Number of columns:       80      24. Blinking:
 5. Top Row:                  0      ^                   ^O
 6. Left Column:              0      1F                  OF
 7. Printing in bottom right         25. Reverse video:
    cause scroll?           YES      ^F  ^P              ^F  ^B
                                     06  10              06  02
CURSOR ADDRESSING                    26. Underline:
 8. Lead-in sequence:
        ^C
        03                           27. High intensity:
 9. Row or column first:     COL
10. Numeric form of row and column:
    BINARY                           28. Half intensity:
11. Add offset to:      Row:  0
                        Col:  0
12. Separator sequence:              29. Attributes occupy position: NO
                                     30. Attributes cumulative:      YES
                                     31. All attributes off:
13. End sequence:                              ^F  ^B  ^O
                                               06  02  OF


14. Cursor to top row, left column:  CURSOR CONTROL KEYS
^C  NUL NUL                          32. Cursor up:
03  00  00                                      ^\
15. 10th Row, 50th Column:                      1C
^C  1   ^I                           33. Cursor down:
03  31  09                                      ^J
16. Delay after positioning:   51               0A
17. Cursor home:                     34. Cursor right:
            ^H                                  ^Y
            08                                  19
                                     35. Cursor left:
ERASURE                    DELAY                ^Z
18. Entire screen:                              1A
        ^L                  146
        0C                           CHARACTER SET
19. Cursor to end of screen:         36. Full upper and lower ASCII: YES
                                     37. Generate all control codes: YES
                                     38. Bell or tone sequence:
20. Beginning of screen to cursor:              ^G
                                                07

21. Cursor to end of line:           EMULATION
                                     39. Conform to ANSI X3.64?     NO
                                     40. Terminals Emulated:
22. Beginning of line to cursor:         E8001R


23. Entire cursor line:
        ^K                  146
        0B
```

CONTINUED ====>

41. Information provided by:
    MANUFACTURER

42. PROGRAM FUNCTION KEYS   NOTES
  1.   36. ISA Available.
      F0

  2.
      F1

  3.
      F2

  4.
      F3

  5.
      F4

  6.
      F5

  7.
      F6

  8.
      F7

  9.
      F8

 10.
      F9

 11.
      FA

 12.
      FB

 13.
      FC

 14.
      FD

 15.
      FE

 16.
      FF

```
--------------------------------------------------------------------------------
  1. Manufacturer:                    Intecolor Corporation
  2. Terminal:                        VHR19
--------------------------------------------------------------------------------
```

SCREEN LAYOUT   VIDEO ATTRIBUTES
  3. Number of rows: 32   ON   OFF
  4. Number of columns: 80   24. Blinking:
  5. Top Row: 1   ESC [5   m   ESC [m
  6. Left Column: 1   1B 5B 35   6D   1B 5B   6D
  7. Printing in bottom right   25. Reverse video:
     cause scroll?   NO   ESC [7   m   ESC [m
                                        1B 5B 37   6D   1B 5B   6D
CURSOR ADDRESSING   26. Underline:
  8. Lead-in sequence: ESC [4   m   ESC [m
               ESC [1B 5B 34   6D   1B 5B   6D
               1B 5B   27. High intensity:
  9. Row or column first: ROW
 10. Numeric form of row and column:
     VARIABLE-LENGTH ASCII   28. Half intensity:
 11. Add offset to: Row: 0
                         Col: 0
 12. Separator sequence: 29. Attributes occupy position: NO
             ;   30. Attributes cumulative: YES
             3B   31. All attributes off:
 13. End sequence: ESC [m
             H   1B 5B   6D
             48
 14. Cursor to top row, left column: CURSOR CONTROL KEYS
 ESC [1   ;   1   H   32. Cursor up:
 1B 5B 31 3B 31 48   ESC [A
 15. 10th Row, 50th Column: 1B 5B 41
 ESC [1   0   ;   5   0   H   33. Cursor down:
 1B 5B 31 30 3B 35 30 48   ESC [B
 16. Delay after positioning: 0   1B 5B 42
 17. Cursor home: 34. Cursor right:
             ESC [H   ESC [C
             1B 5B 48   1B 5B 43
                                        35. Cursor left:
                                                    ESC [D
ERASURE   DELAY   1B 5B 44
 18. Entire screen:
         ESC [2   J   0
         1B 5B 32 4A   CHARACTER SET
 19. Cursor to end of screen: 36. Full upper and lower ASCII: YES
         ESC [J   0   37. Generate all control codes: YES
         1B 5B 4A   38. Bell or tone sequence:
 20. Beginning of screen to cursor: ^G
         ESC [1   J   0   07
         1B 5B 31 4A
 21. Cursor to end of line: EMULATION
         ESC [K   0   39. Conform to ANSI X3.64?   YES
         1B 5B 4B   40. Terminals Emulated:
 22. Beginning of line to cursor: VT100, VT52, 4014
         ESC [1   K   0
         1B 5B 31 4B
 23. Entire cursor line:
         ESC [2   K   0
         1B 5B 32 4B
```

CONTINUED  ====>
```

41. Information provided by:
    MANUFACTURER

42. PROGRAM FUNCTION KEYS   NOTES
    1. ESC O   P
       1B   4F   50

    2. ESC O   Q
       1B   4F   51

    3. ESC O   R
       1B   4F   52

    4. ESC O   S
       1B   4F   53

    5.

    6.

    7.

    8.

    9.

    10.

    11.

    12.

    13.

    14.

    15.

    16.

```
--------------------------------------------------------------------------------
 1. Manufacturer:                    Interaction Systems Inc.
 2. Terminal:                        TT150
--------------------------------------------------------------------------------
```

SCREEN LAYOUT   VIDEO ATTRIBUTES
 3. Number of rows: 24   ON   OFF
 4. Number of columns: 80   24. Blinking:
 5. Top Row: 1   ESC G   ^B   ESC G   NUL
 6. Left Column: 1   1B 47 02   1B 47 00
 7. Printing in bottom right   25. Reverse video:
    cause scroll?   YES   ESC X   ^X
                                          1B 58   18
CURSOR ADDRESSING   26. Underline:
 8. Lead-in sequence: ESC G   ^H   ESC G   NUL
              ESC =   1B 47 08   1B 47 00
              1B 3D   27. High intensity:
 9. Row or column first: ROW
10. Numeric form of row and column:
    BINARY   28. Half intensity:
11. Add offset to: Row: 1F   ESC)   ESC (
                       Col: 1F   1B 29   1B 28
12. Separator sequence: 29. Attributes occupy position: NO
                                        30. Attributes cumulative: NO
                                        31. All attributes off:
13. End sequence: ESC G   NUL
                                                   1B 47 00

14. Cursor to top row, left column: CURSOR CONTROL KEYS
    ESC =   SP   SP   32. Cursor up:
    1B 3D   20   20   ^K
15. 10th Row, 50th Column: OB
    ESC =   )   Q   33. Cursor down:
    1B 3D   29   51   ^V
16. Delay after positioning: 0   16
17. Cursor home: 34. Cursor right:
              ESC H   ^L
              1B 48   0C
                                        35. Cursor left:
ERASURE   DELAY   ^H
18. Entire screen: 08
         ^Z   0
         1A   CHARACTER SET
19. Cursor to end of screen: 36. Full upper and lower ASCII: YES
         ESC Y   0   37. Generate all control codes: YES
         1B 59   38. Bell or tone sequence:
20. Beginning of screen to cursor: ^G
                                  0   07
21. Cursor to end of line: EMULATION
         ESC T   0   39. Conform to ANSI X3.64?   NO
         1B 54   40. Terminals Emulated:
22. Beginning of line to cursor: TT100, Televideo 950

23. Entire cursor line:

CONTINUED ====>

41. Information provided by:
    MANUFACTURER

42. PROGRAM FUNCTION KEYS   NOTES
   1. ^A   @   ^M   42. 20 function keys.
      01   40   0D

   2. ^A   A   ^M
      01   41   0D

   3. ^A   B   ^M
      01   42   0D

   4. ^A   C   ^M
      01   43   0D

   5. ^A   D   ^M
      01   44   0D

   6. ^A   E   ^M
      01   45   0D

   7. ^A   F   ^M
      01   46   0D

   8. ^A   G   ^M
      01   47   0D

   9. ^A   H   ^M
      01   48   0D

  10. ^A   I   ^M
      01   49   0D

  11. ^A   P   ^M
      01   50   0D

  12. ^A   Q   ^M
      01   51   0D

  13. ^A   R   ^M
      01   52   0D

  14. ^A   S   ^M
      01   53   0D

  15. ^A   T   ^M
      01   54   0D

  16. ^A   U   ^M
      01   55   0D

---

1. Manufacturer: Ithaca Intersystems, Inc.
2. Terminal: Graphos I

SCREEN LAYOUT
3. Number of rows: 30
4. Number of columns: 80
5. Top Row: 1
6. Left Column: 1
7. Printing in bottom right
   cause scroll?   PROG

CURSOR ADDRESSING
8. Lead-in sequence:
                ESC [
                1B   5B
9. Row or column first: ROW
10. Numeric form of row and column:
    VARIABLE-LENGTH ASCII
11. Add offset to: Row: 0
                           Col: 0
12. Separator sequence:
                ;
                3B
13. End sequence:
                H
                48
14. Cursor to top row, left column:
ESC [1   ;   1   H
1B   5B   31   3B   31   48
15. 10th Row, 50th Column:
ESC [1   0   ;   5   0   H
1B   5B   31   30   3B   35   30   48
16. Delay after positioning: 0
17. Cursor home:
                ESC [H
                1B   5B   48

ERASURE   DELAY
18. Entire screen:
        ESC [2   J   0
        1B   5B   32   4A
19. Cursor to end of screen:
        ESC [J   0
        1B   5B   4A
20. Beginning of screen to cursor:
        ESC [1   J   0
        1B   5B   31   4A
21. Cursor to end of line:
        ESC [K   0
        1B   5B   4B
22. Beginning of line to cursor:
        ESC [1   K   0
        1B   5B   31   4B
23. Entire cursor line:
        ESC [2   K   0
        1B   5B   32   4B

VIDEO ATTRIBUTES
        ON   OFF
24. Blinking:
ESC [5   m   ESC [m
1B   5B   35   6D   1B   5B   6D
25. Reverse video:
ESC [7   m   ESC [m
1B   5B   37   6D   1B   5B   6D
26. Underline:
ESC [4   m   ESC [m
1B   5B   34   6D   1B   5B   6D
27. High intensity:
ESC [1   m   ESC [m
1B   5B   31   6D   1B   5B   6D
28. Half intensity:

29. Attributes occupy position: NO
30. Attributes cumulative: YES
31. All attributes off:
                ESC [m
                1B   5B   6D

CURSOR CONTROL KEYS
32. Cursor up:
                ESC [A
                1B   5B   41
33. Cursor down:
                ESC [B
                1B   5B   42
34. Cursor right:
                ESC [C
                1B   5B   43
35. Cursor left:
                ESC [D
                1B   5B   44

CHARACTER SET
36. Full upper and lower ASCII: YES
37. Generate all control codes: YES
38. Bell or tone sequence:
                ^G
                07

EMULATION
39. Conform to ANSI X3.64?   YES
40. Terminals Emulated:
    DEC VT100
    Tektronix 4010

181   CONTINUED ====>

41. Information provided by:
    MANUFACTURER

42. PROGRAM FUNCTION KEYS   NOTES
 1. ESC O   P
    1B   4F   50

 2. ESC O   Q
    1B   4F   51

 3. ESC O   R
    1B   4F   52

 4. ESC O   S
    1B   4F   53

 5.

 6.

 7.

 8.

 9.

10.

11.

12.

13.

14.

15.

16.

```
------------------------------------------------------------------------
1. Manufacturer:                    Ithaca Intersystems, Inc.
2. Terminal:                        Graphos II
------------------------------------------------------------------------
```

SCREEN LAYOUT
3. Number of rows: 30
4. Number of columns: 80
5. Top Row: 1
6. Left Column: 1
7. Printing in bottom right
   cause scroll?   PROG

CURSOR ADDRESSING
8. Lead-in sequence:
        ESC [
        1B   5B
9. Row or column first: ROW
10. Numeric form of row and column:
    VARIABLE-LENGTH ASCII
11. Add offset to: Row: 0
                           Col: 0
12. Separator sequence:
        ;
        3B
13. End sequence:
        H
        48
14. Cursor to top row, left column:
ESC [1   ;   1   H
1B   5B   31   3B   31   48
15. 10th Row, 50th Column:
ESC [1   0   ;   5   0   H
1B   5B   31   30   3B   35   30   48
16. Delay after positioning: 0
17. Cursor home:
        ESC [H
        1B   5B   48

ERASURE   DELAY
18. Entire screen:
        ESC [2   J   0
        1B   5B   32   4A
19. Cursor to end of screen:
        ESC [J   0
        1B   5B   4A
20. Beginning of screen to cursor:
        ESC [1   J   0
        1B   5B   31   4A
21. Cursor to end of line:
        ESC [K   0
        1B   5B   4B
22. Beginning of line to cursor:
        ESC [1   K   0
        1B   5B   31   4B
23. Entire cursor line:
        ESC [2   K   0
        1B   5B   32   4B

VIDEO ATTRIBUTES
            ON   OFF
24. Blinking:
ESC [5   m   ESC [m
1B   5B   35   6D   1B   5B   6D
25. Reverse video:
ESC [7   m   ESC [m
1B   5B   37   6D   1B   5B   6D
26. Underline:
ESC [4   m   ESC [m
1B   5B   34   6D   1B   5B   6D
27. High intensity:
ESC [1   m   ESC [m
1B   5B   31   6D   1B   5B   6D
28. Half intensity:

29. Attributes occupy position: NO
30. Attributes cumulative: YES
31. All attributes off:
        ESC [m
        1B   5B   6D

CURSOR CONTROL KEYS
32. Cursor up:
        ESC [A
        1B   5B   41
33. Cursor down:
        ESC [B
        1B   5B   42
34. Cursor right:
        ESC [C
        1B   5B   43
35. Cursor left:
        ESC [D
        1B   5B   44

CHARACTER SET
36. Full upper and lower ASCII: YES
37. Generate all control codes: YES
38. Bell or tone sequence:
        ^G
        07

EMULATION
39. Conform to ANSI X3.64?   YES
40. Terminals Emulated:
    DEC VT100
    Tektronix 4010

                    CONTINUED ====>

```
--------------------------------------------------------------------------
     Manufacturer:                    Ithaca Intersystems, Inc.
     Terminal:                        Graphos II
--------------------------------------------------------------------------
```

41. Information provided by:
    MANUFACTURER

42. PROGRAM FUNCTION KEYS   NOTES
 1. ESC O   P
    1B 4F 50

 2. ESC O   Q
    1B 4F 51

 3. ESC O   R
    1B 4F 52

 4. ESC O   S
    1B 4F 53

 5.

 6.

 7.

 8.

 9.

10.

11.

12.

13.

14.

15.

16.

---

1. Manufacturer: Ithaca Intersystems, Inc.
2. Terminal: Graphos III

SCREEN LAYOUT
3. Number of rows: 30
4. Number of columns: 80
5. Top Row: 1
6. Left Column: 1
7. Printing in bottom right
   cause scroll?   PROG

CURSOR ADDRESSING
8. Lead-in sequence:
        ESC [
        1B 5B
9. Row or column first: ROW
10. Numeric form of row and column:
    VARIABLE-LENGTH ASCII
11. Add offset to: Row: 0
                          Col: 0
12. Separator sequence:
        ;
        3B
13. End sequence:
        H
        48
14. Cursor to top row, left column:
    ESC [1   ;   1   H
    1B 5B 31 3B 31 48
15. 10th Row, 50th Column:
    ESC [1   0   ;   5   0   H
    1B 5B 31 30 3B 35 30 48
16. Delay after positioning: 0
17. Cursor home:
        ESC [H
        1B 5B 48

ERASURE   DELAY
18. Entire screen:
        ESC [2   J   0
        1B 5B 32 4A
19. Cursor to end of screen:
        ESC [J   0
        1B 5B 4A
20. Beginning of screen to cursor:
        ESC [1   J   0
        1B 5B 31 4A
21. Cursor to end of line:
        ESC [K   0
        1B 5B 4B
22. Beginning of line to cursor:
        ESC [1   K   0
        1B 5B 31 4B
23. Entire cursor line:
        ESC [2   K   0
        1B 5B 32 4B

VIDEO ATTRIBUTES
            ON   OFF
24. Blinking:
    ESC [5   m   ESC [m
    1B 5B 35 6D   1B 5B   6D
25. Reverse video:
    ESC [7   m   ESC [m
    1B 5B 37 6D   1B 5B   6D
26. Underline:
    ESC [4   m   ESC [m
    1B 5B 34 6D   1B 5B   6D
27. High intensity:
    ESC [1   m   ESC [m
    1B 5B 31 6D   1B 5B   6D
28. Half intensity:

29. Attributes occupy position: NO
30. Attributes cumulative: YES
31. All attributes off:
        ESC [m
        1B 5B   6D

CURSOR CONTROL KEYS
32. Cursor up:
        ESC [A
        1B 5B 41
33. Cursor down:
        ESC [B
        1B 5B 42
34. Cursor right:
        ESC [C
        1B 5B 43
35. Cursor left:
        ESC [D
        1B 5B 44

CHARACTER SET
36. Full upper and lower ASCII: YES
37. Generate all control codes: YES
38. Bell or tone sequence:
        ^G
        07

EMULATION
39. Conform to ANSI X3.64?   YES
40. Terminals Emulated:
    DEC VT100
    Tektronix 4010

                        CONTINUED ====>

41. Information provided by:
    MANUFACTURER

42. PROGRAM FUNCTION KEYS   NOTES
  1. ESC O   P
     1B   4F 50

  2. ESC O   Q
     1B   4F 51

  3. ESC O   R
     1B   4F 52

  4. ESC O   S
     1B   4F 53

  5.

  6.

  7.

  8.

  9.

 10.

 11.

 12.

 13.

 14.

 15.

 16.

```
-------------------------------------------------------------------
1. Manufacturer:                    Kaypro Corporation
2. Terminal:                        Kaypro 2´84, 4´84, 10 and Robie
-------------------------------------------------------------------
```

SCREEN LAYOUT   VIDEO ATTRIBUTES
3. Number of rows: 24   ON   OFF
4. Number of columns: 80   24. Blinking:
5. Top Row: 1   ESC B   2   ESC C   2
6. Left Column: 1   1B   42   32   1B   43   32
7. Printing in bottom right   25. Reverse video:
   cause scroll?   YES   ESC B   0   ESC C   0
                                       1B   42   30   1B   43   30
CURSOR ADDRESSING   26. Underline:
8. Lead-in sequence: ESC B   3   ESC C   3
              ESC =   1B   42   33   1B   43   33
              1B 3D   27. High intensity:
9. Row or column first: ROW
10. Numeric form of row and column:
    BINARY   28. Half intensity:
11. Add offset to: Row: 1F   ESC B   1   ESC B   1
                        Col: 1F   1B   42   31   1B   42   31
12. Separator sequence: 29. Attributes occupy position: NO
                                    30. Attributes cumulative: YES
                                    31. All attributes off:
13. End sequence:

14. Cursor to top row, left column: CURSOR CONTROL KEYS
ESC =   SP SP   32. Cursor up:
1B   3D 20 20   ^E
15. 10th Row, 50th Column: 05
ESC =   )   Q   33. Cursor down:
1B   3D 29 51   ^X
16. Delay after positioning: 0   18
17. Cursor home: 34. Cursor right:
          ^^   ^D
          1E   04
                                    35. Cursor left:
ERASURE   DELAY   ^S
18. Entire screen: 13
        ^Z   0
        1A   CHARACTER SET
19. Cursor to end of screen: 36. Full upper and lower ASCII: YES
        ^W   0   37. Generate all control codes: YES
        17   38. Bell or tone sequence:
20. Beginning of screen to cursor: ^G
                                                 07
21. Cursor to end of line: EMULATION
        ^X   0   39. Conform to ANSI X3.64?   NO
        18   40. Terminals Emulated:
22. Beginning of line to cursor: ADM 3A (Partial)

23. Entire cursor line:
        ESC R   0
        1B   52

                              187   CONTINUED ====>
```
```

41. Information provided by:
    MANUFACTURER

42. PROGRAM FUNCTION KEYS   NOTES
   1.   Models 2´84 and 4´84 identified by
                                half-high drives and two serial ports.

   2.

   3.

   4.

   5.

   6.

   7.

   8.

   9.

  10.

  11.

  12.

  13.

  14.

  15.

  16.

```
-----------------------------------------------------------------------
1. Manufacturer:                    Kaypro Corporation
2. Terminal:                        KP 2´83, KP 4´83
-----------------------------------------------------------------------
```

SCREEN LAYOUT   VIDEO ATTRIBUTES
3. Number of rows: 24   ON   OFF
4. Number of columns: 80   24. Blinking:
5. Top Row: 1
6. Left Column: 1
7. Printing in bottom right   25. Reverse video:
   cause scroll?   YES

CURSOR ADDRESSING   26. Underline:
8. Lead-in sequence:
        ESC =
        1B 3D   27. High intensity:
9. Row or column first: ROW
10. Numeric form of row and column:
    BINARY   28. Half intensity:
11. Add offset to: Row: 1F
                         Col: 1F
12. Separator sequence: 29. Attributes occupy position: NO
                                    30. Attributes cumulative: NO
                                    31. All attributes off:

13. End sequence:

14. Cursor to top row, left column: CURSOR CONTROL KEYS
ESC =   SP SP   32. Cursor up:
1B 3D   20 20   ^K
15. 10th Row, 50th Column: 0B
ESC =   )   Q   33. Cursor down:
1B 3D   29 51   ^J
16. Delay after positioning: 0   0A
17. Cursor home: 34. Cursor right:
        ^^   ^L
        1E   0C
                                    35. Cursor left:
ERASURE   DELAY   ^H
18. Entire screen: 08
        ^Z   0
        1A   CHARACTER SET
19. Cursor to end of screen: 36. Full upper and lower ASCII: YES
        ^W   0   37. Generate all control codes: YES
        17   38. Bell or tone sequence:
20. Beginning of screen to cursor: ^G
                                            07

21. Cursor to end of line: EMULATION
        ^X   0   39. Conform to ANSI X3.64?   NO
        18   40. Terminals Emulated:
22. Beginning of line to cursor: ADM 3A (Partial)

23. Entire cursor line:
        ESC R   0
        1B   52

                            189   CONTINUED ====>

```
--------------------------------------------------------------------------
      Manufacturer:                    Kaypro Corporation
      Terminal:                        KP 2´83, KP 4´83
--------------------------------------------------------------------------
```

41. Information provided by:
    MANUFACTURER

42. PROGRAM FUNCTION KEYS   NOTES
    1.   The ´83 series were the original 2 and
                                   4 with full height drives and one
                                   serial port.
    2.

    3.

    4.

    5.

    6.

    7.

    8.

    9.

    10.

    11.

    12.

    13.

    14.

    15.

    16.

```
-------------------------------------------------------------------------
1. Manufacturer:               Kimtron Corporation
2. Terminal:                   KT-10
-------------------------------------------------------------------------
```

SCREEN LAYOUT
3. Number of rows: 24
4. Number of columns: 80
5. Top Row: 1
6. Left Column: 1
7. Printing in bottom right
   cause scroll?   PROG

CURSOR ADDRESSING
8. Lead-in sequence:
            ESC [
            1B 5B
9. Row or column first: ROW
10. Numeric form of row and column:
    VARIABLE-LENGTH ASCII
11. Add offset to: Row: 0
                          Col: 0
12. Separator sequence:
            ;
            3B
13. End sequence:
            H
            48
14. Cursor to top row, left column:
ESC [1   ;   1   H
1B 5B 31 3B 31 48
15. 10th Row, 50th Column:
ESC [1   0   ;   5   0   H
1B 5B 31 30 3B 35 30 48
16. Delay after positioning: 0
17. Cursor home:
            ESC [H
            1B 5B 48

ERASURE   DELAY
18. Entire screen:
        ESC [2   J   0
        1B 5B 32 4A
19. Cursor to end of screen:
        ESC [J   0
        1B 5B 4A
20. Beginning of screen to cursor:
        ESC [1   J   0
        1B 5B 31 4A
21. Cursor to end of line:
        ESC [K   0
        1B 5B 4B
22. Beginning of line to cursor:
        ESC [1   K   0
        1B 5B 31 4B
23. Entire cursor line:
        ESC [2   K   0
        1B 5B 32 4B

VIDEO ATTRIBUTES
       ON   OFF
24. Blinking:
ESC [5   m   ESC [m
1B 5B 35 6D   1B 5B 6D
25. Reverse video:
ESC [7   m   ESC [m
1B 5B 37 6D   1B 5B 6D
26. Underline:
ESC [4   m   ESC [m
1B 5B 34 6D   1B 5B 6D
27. High intensity:
ESC [1   m   ESC [m
1B 5B 31 6D   1B 5B 6D
28. Half intensity:

29. Attributes occupy position: NO
30. Attributes cumulative: YES
31. All attributes off:
            ESC [m
            1B 5B 6D

CURSOR CONTROL KEYS
32. Cursor up:
            ESC [A
            1B 5B 41
33. Cursor down:
            ESC [B
            1B 5B 42
34. Cursor right:
            ESC [C
            1B 5B 43
35. Cursor left:
            ESC [D
            1B 5B 44

CHARACTER SET
36. Full upper and lower ASCII: YES
37. Generate all control codes: YES
38. Bell or tone sequence:
            ^G
            07

EMULATION
39. Conform to ANSI X3.64?   YES
40. Terminals Emulated:

CONTINUED ====>

41. Information provided by:
    MANUFACTURER

42. PROGRAM FUNCTION KEYS   NOTES
  1.

  2.

  3.

  4.

  5.

  6.

  7.

  8.

  9.

 10.

 11.

 12.

 13.

 14.

 15.

 16.

---
1. Manufacturer: Lear Siegler, Inc.
2. Terminal: ADM 11

SCREEN LAYOUT   VIDEO ATTRIBUTES
3. Number of rows: 24   ON   OFF
4. Number of columns: 80   24. Blinking:
5. Top Row: 1   ESC G   2   ESC G   0
6. Left Column: 1   1B 47 32   1B 47 30
7. Printing in bottom right   25. Reverse video:
   cause scroll?   YES   ESC G   4   ESC G   0
                                            1B 47 34   1B 47 30
CURSOR ADDRESSING   26. Underline:
8. Lead-in sequence:
        ESC =
        1B 3D   27. High intensity:
9. Row or column first: ROW
10. Numeric form of row and column:
    BINARY   28. Half intensity:
11. Add offset to: Row: 1F   ESC)   ESC (
                        Col: 1F   1B 29   1B 28
12. Separator sequence: 29. Attributes occupy position: YES
                                          30. Attributes cumulative: NO
                                          31. All attributes off:
13. End sequence: ESC G   0
                                                   1B 47 30

14. Cursor to top row, left column: CURSOR CONTROL KEYS
ESC =   SP SP   32. Cursor up:
1B 3D 20 20   ^K
15. 10th Row, 50th Column: 0B
ESC =   )   Q   33. Cursor down:
1B 3D 29 51   ^J
16. Delay after positioning: 0   0A
17. Cursor home: 34. Cursor right:
        ^^   ^L
        1E   0C
                                          35. Cursor left:
ERASURE   DELAY   ^H
18. Entire screen: 08
        ^Z   0
        1A   CHARACTER SET
19. Cursor to end of screen: 36. Full upper and lower ASCII: YES
        ESC y   0   37. Generate all control codes: YES
        1B 79   38. Bell or tone sequence:
20. Beginning of screen to cursor: ^G
                                                    07
21. Cursor to end of line: EMULATION
        ESC t   0   39. Conform to ANSI X3.64?   NO
        1B 74   40. Terminals Emulated:
22. Beginning of line to cursor:

23. Entire cursor line:

                    193   CONTINUED ====>

Manufacturer:	Lear Siegler, Inc.
Terminal:	ADM 11

41. Information provided by:
    MANUFACTURER

42. PROGRAM FUNCTION KEYS   NOTES

1. ^A @   ^M   29. Half intensity does not occupy
   01 40 0D   a character position, all others
                                       do.
2. ^A A   ^M   30. Combinations as follows:
   01 41 0D   ESC G 0   Normal video
                                       ESC G 1   Blank
3. ^A B   ^M   ESC G 2   Blink
   01 42 0D   ESC G 3   Blank and blink
                                       ESC G 4   Reverse
4. ^A C   ^M   ESC G 5   Reverse and blank
   01 43 0D   ESC G 6   Reverse and blink
                                       ESC G 7   Blank, blink and reverse
5. ^A D   ^M   ESC G 8   Business graphics
   01 44 0D   ESC G 9   Bus. graphics and blank
                                       ESC G A   Bus. graphics and blink
6. ^A E   ^M   ESC G B   Bus. graph., blank & blink
   01 45 0D   ESC G C   Bus. graphics and reverse
                                       ESC G D   Bus. graph., rev. & blank
7. ^A F   ^M   ESC G E   Bus. graph., rev. & blink
   01 46 0D   ESC G F   Bus. graph., rev., blank &
                                                 blink
8. ^A G   ^M   ESC G)   Set reduced intensity
   01 47 0D   ESC G (Reset reduced intensity
                                   36. 128 displayable characters, includ-
9.   ing control codes. Optional inter-
                                       national sets available. Block
                                       graphics, wide point graphics and
10.   line drawing characters.
                                   42. F5-F8 are F1-F4 shifted. Defaults
                                       shown, all function keys are pro-
11.   grammable up to 8 characters each.

12.

13.

14.

15.

16.

```
--------------------------------------------------------------------
1. Manufacturer:                      Lear Siegler, Inc.
2. Terminal:                          ADM 12
--------------------------------------------------------------------
```

SCREEN LAYOUT		VIDEO ATTRIBUTES			

SCREEN LAYOUT
3. Number of rows: 24
4. Number of columns: 80
5. Top Row: 1
6. Left Column: 1
7. Printing in bottom right
   cause scroll?   YES

CURSOR ADDRESSING
8. Lead-in sequence:
            ESC =
            1B   3D
9. Row or column first: ROW
10. Numeric form of row and column:
    BINARY
11. Add offset to: Row: 1F
                         Col: 1F
12. Separator sequence:

13. End sequence:

14. Cursor to top row, left column:
ESC =   SP   SP
1B   3D   20   20
15. 10th Row, 50th Column:
ESC =   )   Q
1B   3D   29   51
16. Delay after positioning: 0
17. Cursor home:
            ^^
            1E

ERASURE   DELAY
18. Entire screen:
       ^Z   0
       1A
19. Cursor to end of screen:
       ESC y   0
       1B   79
20. Beginning of screen to cursor:

21. Cursor to end of line:
       ESC t   0
       1B   74
22. Beginning of line to cursor:

23. Entire cursor line:

VIDEO ATTRIBUTES
                 ON   OFF
24. Blinking:
    ESC G   2   ESC G   0
    1B   47   32   1B   47   30
25. Reverse video:
    ESC G   4   ESC G   0
    1B   47   34   1B   47   30
26. Underline:
    ESC G   8   ESC G   0
    1B   47   38   1B   47   30
27. High intensity:

28. Half intensity:
    ESC G   @   ESC G   0
    1B   47   40   1B   47   30
29. Attributes occupy position: NO
30. Attributes cumulative: NO
31. All attributes off:
                 ESC G   0
                 1B   47   30

CURSOR CONTROL KEYS
32. Cursor up:
                 ^K
                 0B
33. Cursor down:
                 ^J
                 0A
34. Cursor right:
                 ^L
                 0C
35. Cursor left:
                 ^H
                 08

CHARACTER SET
36. Full upper and lower ASCII: YES
37. Generate all control codes: YES
38. Bell or tone sequence:
                 ^G
                 07

EMULATION
39. Conform to ANSI X3.64?   NO
40. Terminals Emulated:

CONTINUED ====>

```
-------------------------------------------------------------------------
        Manufacturer:                        Lear Siegler, Inc.
        Terminal:                            ADM 12
-------------------------------------------------------------------------
```

41. Information provided by:
    MANUFACTURER

42. PROGRAM FUNCTION KEYS   NOTES
    1. ^A   @   ^M   3. Optionally 48.
       01   40   0D   4. Optionally 158 (x24 rows).
                                         29. Embedded attributes also available.
    2. ^A   A   ^M   36. 128 displayable characters, includ-
       01   41   0D   ing control codes. Optional inter-
                                             national sets available. Block
    3. ^A   B   ^M   graphics, wide point graphics and
       01   42   0D   line drawing characters.
                                         42. F17-F32 are F1-F16 shifted. Defaults
    4. ^A   C   ^M   shown, all function keys are pro-
       01   43   0D   grammable up to 8 characters each.
                                             F17   SOH P CR   F25   SOH X CR
    5. ^A   D   ^M   F18   SOH Q CR   F26   SOH Y CR
       01   44   0D   F19   SOH R CR   F27   SOH Z CR
                                             F20   SOH S CR   F28   SOH [CR
    6. ^A   E   ^M   F21   SOH T CR   F29   SOH \ CR
       01   45   0D   F22   SOH U CR   F30   SOH] CR
                                             F23   SOH V CR   F31   SOH ^ CR
    7. ^A   F   ^M   F24   SOH W CR   F32   SOH _ CR
       01   46   0D

    8. ^A   G   ^M
       01   47   0D

    9. ^A   H   ^M
       01   48   0D

   10. ^A   I   ^M
       01   49   0D

   11. ^A   J   ^M
       01   4A   0D

   12. ^A   K   ^M
       01   4B   0D

   13. ^A   L   ^M
       01   4C   0D

   14. ^A   M   ^M
       01   4D   0D

   15. ^A   N   ^M
       01   4E   0D

   16. ^A   O   ^M
       01   4F   0D

---

1. Manufacturer: Lear Siegler, Inc.
2. Terminal: ADM 22

SCREEN LAYOUT   VIDEO ATTRIBUTES
3. Number of rows: 24   ON   OFF
4. Number of columns: 80   24. Blinking:
5. Top Row: 1
6. Left Column: 1
7. Printing in bottom right   25. Reverse video:
   cause scroll?   YES

CURSOR ADDRESSING   26. Underline:
8. Lead-in sequence:
           ESC =
           1B 3D   27. High intensity:
9. Row or column first: ROW
10. Numeric form of row and column:
    BINARY   28. Half intensity:
11. Add offset to: Row: 1F
                          Col: 1F
12. Separator sequence: 29. Attributes occupy position: NO
                                          30. Attributes cumulative: NO
                                          31. All attributes off:
13. End sequence:

14. Cursor to top row, left column: CURSOR CONTROL KEYS
ESC =   SP SP   32. Cursor up:
1B   3D 20 20   ^K
15. 10th Row, 50th Column: 0B
ESC =   )   Q   33. Cursor down:
1B   3D 29 51   ^J
16. Delay after positioning: 0   0A
17. Cursor home: 34. Cursor right:
           ^^   ^L
           1E   0C
                                          35. Cursor left:
ERASURE   DELAY   ^H
18. Entire screen: 08
           ^Z   0
           1A   CHARACTER SET
19. Cursor to end of screen: 36. Full upper and lower ASCII: YES
           ESC y   0   37. Generate all control codes: YES
           1B 79   38. Bell or tone sequence:
20. Beginning of screen to cursor: ^G
                                                         07

21. Cursor to end of line: EMULATION
           ESC t   0   39. Conform to ANSI X3.64?   NO
           1B 74   40. Terminals Emulated:
22. Beginning of line to cursor: Hazeltine 1500, ADDS Regent 25

23. Entire cursor line:
           ESC >   0
           1B 3E

CONTINUED ====>

41. Information provided by:
    MANUFACTURER

42. PROGRAM FUNCTION KEYS   NOTES
    1. ^A   @   ^M   24.-28. Blinking, reverse video,
       01   40   0D   underline, half-intensity and
                                           combinations thereof may be
    2. ^A   A   ^M   selected by switch settings
       01   41   0D   and used with write protected
                                           fields.
    3. ^A   B   ^M   36. Plus 32 graphics characters.
       01   42   0D

    4. ^A   C   ^M
       01   43   0D

    5. ^A   D   ^M
       01   44   0D

    6. ^A   E   ^M
       01   45   0D

    7. ^A   F   ^M
       01   46   0D

    8.

    9.

   10.

   11.

   12.

   13.

   14.

   15.

   16.

```
--------------------------------------------------------------------------------
1. Manufacturer:                    Lear Siegler, Inc.
2. Terminal:                        ADM 24E
--------------------------------------------------------------------------------
```

SCREEN LAYOUT   VIDEO ATTRIBUTES
3. Number of rows: 24   ON   OFF
4. Number of columns: 80   24. Blinking:
5. Top Row: 1   ESC G   2   ESC c
6. Left Column: 1   1B 47 32   1B 63
7. Printing in bottom right   25. Reverse video:
   cause scroll?   YES   ESC G   4   ESC c
                                    1B 47 34   1B 63
CURSOR ADDRESSING   26. Underline:
8. Lead-in sequence: ESC G   8   ESC c
              ESC =   1B 47 38   1B 63
              1B 3D   27. High intensity:
9. Row or column first: ROW
10. Numeric form of row and column:
    BINARY   28. Half intensity:
11. Add offset to: Row: 1F   ESC G   @   ESC c
                       Col: 1F   1B 47 40   1B 63
12. Separator sequence: 29. Attributes occupy position: NO
                                    30. Attributes cumulative: NO
                                    31. All attributes off:
13. End sequence: ESC c
                                              1B 63

14. Cursor to top row, left column: CURSOR CONTROL KEYS
ESC =   SP SP   32. Cursor up:
1B 3D   20 20   ^K
15. 10th Row, 50th Column: 0B
ESC =   )   Q   33. Cursor down:
1B 3D   29 51   ^J
16. Delay after positioning: 0   0A
17. Cursor home: 34. Cursor right:
        ^^   ^L
        1E   0C
                                    35. Cursor left:
ERASURE   DELAY   ^H
18. Entire screen: 08
        ^Z   0
        1A   CHARACTER SET
19. Cursor to end of screen: 36. Full upper and lower ASCII: YES
                                    37. Generate all control codes: YES
                                    38. Bell or tone sequence:
20. Beginning of screen to cursor: ^G
                                              07

21. Cursor to end of line: EMULATION
                                    39. Conform to ANSI X3.64?   NO
                                    40. Terminals Emulated:

22. Beginning of line to cursor:

23. Entire cursor line:

                         199   CONTINUED ====>
```
```

```
--------------------------------------------------------------------------------
     Manufacturer:                          Lear Siegler, Inc.
     Terminal:                              ADM 24E
--------------------------------------------------------------------------------
```

41. Information provided by:
    MANUFACTURER

42. PROGRAM FUNCTION KEYS   NOTES
    1. ^A @   ^M   3. 48-line display configurable
       01 40 0D   in 1 or 2 user definable pages.
                                   30. Cumulative attributes use
    2. ^A A   ^M   separate codes. See manual.
       01 41 0D   36. Foreign language sets available.
                                   42. F1 through F8 are shiftable to
    3. ^A B   ^M   F9 through F16.
       01 42 0D   All function keys are programmable
                                       through set-up mode. Values shown
    4. ^A C   ^M   are default.
       01 43 0D

    5. ^A D   ^M
       01 44 0D

    6. ^A E   ^M
       01 45 0D

    7. ^A F   ^M
       01 46 0D

    8. ^A G   ^M
       01 47 0D

    9. ^A H   ^M
       01 48 0D

   10. ^A I   ^M
       01 49 0D

   11. ^A J   ^M
       01 4A 0D

   12. ^A K   ^M
       01 4B 0D

   13. ^A L   ^M
       01 4C 0D

   14. ^A M   ^M
       01 4D 0D

   15. ^A N   ^M
       01 4E 0D

   16. ^A O   ^M
       01 4F 0D

----
1. Manufacturer: Lear Siegler, Inc.
2. Terminal: ADM 3A

SCREEN LAYOUT   VIDEO ATTRIBUTES
3. Number of rows: 24   ON   OFF
4. Number of columns: 80   24. Blinking:
5. Top Row: 1
6. Left Column: 1
7. Printing in bottom right   25. Reverse video:
   cause scroll?   YES

CURSOR ADDRESSING   26. Underline:
8. Lead-in sequence:
        ESC =
        1B   3D   27. High intensity:
9. Row or column first: ROW
10. Numeric form of row and column:
    BINARY   28. Half intensity:
11. Add offset to: Row: 1F
                         Col: 1F
12. Separator sequence: 29. Attributes occupy position: NO
                                    30. Attributes cumulative: NO
                                    31. All attributes off:
13. End sequence:

14. Cursor to top row, left column: CURSOR CONTROL KEYS
ESC =   SP   SP   32. Cursor up:
1B   3D 20   20   ^K
15. 10th Row, 50th Column: OB
ESC =   )   Q   33. Cursor down:
1B   3D 29   51   ^J
16. Delay after positioning: 0   0A
17. Cursor home: 34. Cursor right:
        ^^   ^L
        1E   0C
                                    35. Cursor left:
ERASURE   DELAY   ^H
18. Entire screen: 08
     ^Z   0
     1A   CHARACTER SET
19. Cursor to end of screen: 36. Full upper and lower ASCII: NO
                                    37. Generate all control codes: YES
                                    38. Bell or tone sequence:
20. Beginning of screen to cursor: ^G
                                             07

21. Cursor to end of line: EMULATION
                                    39. Conform to ANSI X3.64?   NO
                                    40. Terminals Emulated:
22. Beginning of line to cursor:

23. Entire cursor line:

```
-----------------------------------------------------------------------
     Manufacturer:                    Lear Siegler, Inc.
     Terminal:                        ADM 3A
-----------------------------------------------------------------------
```

41. Information provided by:
    MANUFACTURER

42. PROGRAM FUNCTION KEYS   NOTES
    1.   36. 64-character ASCII standard,
                                       95-character ASCII optional
                                   37. Generates 128 ASCII characters
    2.

    3.

    4.

    5.

    6.

    7.

    8.

    9.

    10.

    11.

    12.

    13.

    14.

    15.

    16.

```
--------------------------------------------------------------------------
  1. Manufacturer:                    Lear Siegler, Inc.
  2. Terminal:                        ADM 5
--------------------------------------------------------------------------
```

SCREEN LAYOUT   VIDEO ATTRIBUTES
  3. Number of rows: 24   ON   OFF
  4. Number of columns: 80   24. Blinking:
  5. Top Row: 1
  6. Left Column: 1
  7. Printing in bottom right   25. Reverse video:
     cause scroll?   YES   ESC G   ESC G
                                       1B 47   1B 47
CURSOR ADDRESSING   26. Underline:
  8. Lead-in sequence:
           ESC =
           1B   3D   27. High intensity:
  9. Row or column first: ROW
 10. Numeric form of row and column:
     BINARY   28. Half intensity:
 11. Add offset to: Row: 1F   ESC)   ESC (
                        Col: 1F   1B 29   1B 28
 12. Separator sequence: 29. Attributes occupy position: NO
                                       30. Attributes cumulative: NO
                                       31. All attributes off:
 13. End sequence: ESC (
                                                1B 28

 14. Cursor to top row, left column: CURSOR CONTROL KEYS
  ESC =   SP SP   32. Cursor up:
  1B 3D   20 20   ^K
 15. 10th Row, 50th Column: 0B
  ESC =   )   Q   33. Cursor down:
  1B 3D   29 51   ^J
 16. Delay after positioning: 0   0A
 17. Cursor home: 34. Cursor right:
           ^^   ^L
                                               0C
           1E   35. Cursor left:
                                               ^H
ERASURE   DELAY   08
 18. Entire screen:
       ^Z   0   CHARACTER SET
       1A   36. Full upper and lower ASCII: YES
 19. Cursor to end of screen: 37. Generate all control codes: YES
                                       38. Bell or tone sequence:
                                               ^G
 20. Beginning of screen to cursor: 07

 21. Cursor to end of line: EMULATION
                                       39. Conform to ANSI X3.64?   NO
                                       40. Terminals Emulated:
 22. Beginning of line to cursor:

 23. Entire cursor line:

                     CONTINUED ====>

41. Information provided by:
    MANUFACTURER

42. PROGRAM FUNCTION KEYS   NOTES
  1.

  2.

  3.

  4.

  5.

  6.

  7.

  8.

  9.

 10.

 11.

 12.

 13.

 14.

 15.

 16.

----
1. Manufacturer: Liberty Electronics
2. Terminal: Freedom 100

SCREEN LAYOUT   VIDEO ATTRIBUTES
3. Number of rows: 24   ON   OFF
4. Number of columns: 80   24. Blinking:
5. Top Row: 1   ESC G   2   ESC G   0
6. Left Column: 1   1B   47   32   1B   47   30
7. Printing in bottom right   25. Reverse video:
   cause scroll?   YES   ESC G   4   ESC G   0
                                     1B   47   34   1B   47   30
CURSOR ADDRESSING   26. Underline:
8. Lead-in sequence: ESC G   8   ESC G   0
        ESC =   1B   47   38   1B   47   30
        1B   3D   27. High intensity:
9. Row or column first: ROW
10. Numeric form of row and column:
    BINARY   28. Half intensity:
11. Add offset to: Row: 1F   ESC G   @   ESC G   0
                         Col: 1F   1B   47   40   1B   47   30
12. Separator sequence: 29. Attributes occupy position: NO
                                     30. Attributes cumulative: NO
                                     31. All attributes off:
13. End sequence: ESC G   0
                                              1B   47   30

14. Cursor to top row, left column: CURSOR CONTROL KEYS
ESC =   SP SP   32. Cursor up:
1B   3D   20   20   ^K
15. 10th Row, 50th Column: 0B
ESC =   )   Q   33. Cursor down:
1B   3D   29   51   ^V
16. Delay after positioning: 0   16
17. Cursor home: 34. Cursor right:
        ^^   ^L
        1E   0C
                                     35. Cursor left:
ERASURE   DELAY   ^H
18. Entire screen: 08
        ESC *   0
        1B   2A   CHARACTER SET
19. Cursor to end of screen: 36. Full upper and lower ASCII: YES
        ESC Y   0   37. Generate all control codes: YES
        1B   59   38. Bell or tone sequence:
20. Beginning of screen to cursor: ^G
                                                07
21. Cursor to end of line: EMULATION
        ESC T   0   39. Conform to ANSI X3.64?   NO
        1B   54   40. Terminals Emulated:
22. Beginning of line to cursor: Televideo 950
                                         ADM 31

23. Entire cursor line:
        ESC R   0
        1B   52

CONTINUED ====>

41. Information provided by:
    MANUFACTURER

42. PROGRAM FUNCTION KEYS   NOTES
  1. ^A @   ^M
     01 40 0D

  2. ^A A   ^M
     01 41 0D

  3. ^A B   ^M
     01 42 0D

  4. ^A C   ^M
     01 43 0D

  5. ^A D   ^M
     01 44 0D

  6. ^A E   ^M
     01 45 0D

  7. ^A F   ^M
     01 46 0D

  8. ^A G   ^M
     01 47 0D

  9. ^A H   ^M
     01 48 0D

 10. ^A I   ^M
     01 49 0D

 11.

 12.

 13.

 14.

 15.

 16.

```
--------------------------------------------------------------------------------
1. Manufacturer:                         Liberty Electronics
2. Terminal:                             Freedom 110
--------------------------------------------------------------------------------
```

SCREEN LAYOUT
3. Number of rows: 24
4. Number of columns: 80
5. Top Row: 1
6. Left Column: 1
7. Printing in bottom right
   cause scroll?   YES

CURSOR ADDRESSING
8. Lead-in sequence:
              ESC =
              1B   3D
9. Row or column first: ROW
10. Numeric form of row and column:
    BINARY
11. Add offset to: Row: 1F
                          Col: 1F
12. Separator sequence:

13. End sequence:

14. Cursor to top row, left column:
ESC =   SP SP
1B   3D   20 20
15. 10th Row, 50th Column:
ESC =   )   Q
1B   3D   29 51
16. Delay after positioning: 0
17. Cursor home:
              ^^
              1E

ERASURE   DELAY
18. Entire screen:
         ESC *   0
         1B   2A
19. Cursor to end of screen:
         ESC Y   0
         1B   59
20. Beginning of screen to cursor:

21. Cursor to end of line:
         ESC T   0
         1B   54
22. Beginning of line to cursor:

23. Entire cursor line:
         ESC R   0
         1B   52

VIDEO ATTRIBUTES
         ON   OFF
24. Blinking:
ESC G   2   ESC G   0
1B   47   32   1B   47   30
25. Reverse video:
ESC G   4   ESC G   0
1B   47   34   1B   47   30
26. Underline:
ESC G   8   ESC G   0
1B   47   38   1B   47   30
27. High intensity:

28. Half intensity:
ESC G   @   ESC G   0
1B   47   40   1B   47   30
29. Attributes occupy position: NO
30. Attributes cumulative: NO
31. All attributes off:
              ESC G   0
              1B   47   30

CURSOR CONTROL KEYS
32. Cursor up:
              ^K
              0B
33. Cursor down:
              ^V
              16
34. Cursor right:
              ^L
              0C
35. Cursor left:
              ^H
              08

CHARACTER SET
36. Full upper and lower ASCII: YES
37. Generate all control codes: YES
38. Bell or tone sequence:
              ^G
              07

EMULATION
39. Conform to ANSI X3.64?   NO
40. Terminals Emulated:
    Televideo 950
    ADM 31

CONTINUED ====>

41. Information provided by:
    MANUFACTURER

42. PROGRAM FUNCTION KEYS   NOTES
    1. ^A @   ^M   42. All function keys are user-
       01 40 0D   programmable up to 256 bytes.

    2. ^A A   ^M
       01 41 0D

    3. ^A B   ^M
       01 42 0D

    4. ^A C   ^M
       01 43 0D

    5. ^A D   ^M
       01 44 0D

    6. ^A E   ^M
       01 45 0D

    7. ^A F   ^M
       01 46 0D

    8. ^A G   ^M
       01 47 0D

    9. ^A H   ^M
       01 48 0D

   10. ^A I   ^M
       01 49 0D

   11.

   12.

   13.

   14.

   15.

   16.

```
-----------------------------------------------------------------------
   1. Manufacturer:                  Liberty Electronics
   2. Terminal:                      Freedom 200
-----------------------------------------------------------------------
```

SCREEN LAYOUT
  3. Number of rows: 24
  4. Number of columns: 80
  5. Top Row: 1
  6. Left Column: 1
  7. Printing in bottom right
     cause scroll?   YES

CURSOR ADDRESSING
  8. Lead-in sequence:
                  ESC =
                  1B 3D
  9. Row or column first: ROW
 10. Numeric form of row and column:
     BINARY
 11. Add offset to: Row: 1F
                         Col: 1F
 12. Separator sequence:

 13. End sequence:

 14. Cursor to top row, left column:
     ESC =   SP SP
     1B 3D   20 20
 15. 10th Row, 50th Column:
     ESC =   )   Q
     1B 3D   29 51
 16. Delay after positioning: 0
 17. Cursor home:
                  ^^
                  1E

ERASURE   DELAY
 18. Entire screen:
          ESC *   0
          1B 2A
 19. Cursor to end of screen:
          ESC Y   0
          1B 59
 20. Beginning of screen to cursor:

 21. Cursor to end of line:
          ESC T   0
          1B 54
 22. Beginning of line to cursor:

 23. Entire cursor line:
          ESC R   0
          1B 52

VIDEO ATTRIBUTES
             ON   OFF
 24. Blinking:
     ESC G   2   ESC G   0
     1B 47 32   1B 47 30
 25. Reverse video:
     ESC G   4   ESC G   0
     1B 47 34   1B 47 30
 26. Underline:
     ESC G   8   ESC G   0
     1B 47 38   1B 47 30
 27. High intensity:

 28. Half intensity:
     ESC G   @   ESC G   0
     1B 47 40   1B 47 30
 29. Attributes occupy position: NO
 30. Attributes cumulative: NO
 31. All attributes off:
              ESC G   0
              1B 47 30

CURSOR CONTROL KEYS
 32. Cursor up:
              ^K
              0B
 33. Cursor down:
              ^V
              16
 34. Cursor right:
              ^L
              0C
 35. Cursor left:
              ^H
              08

CHARACTER SET
 36. Full upper and lower ASCII: YES
 37. Generate all control codes: YES
 38. Bell or tone sequence:
              ^G
              07

EMULATION
 39. Conform to ANSI X3.64?   NO
 40. Terminals Emulated:
         Televideo 910
         ADM 3A/5
         Hazeltine 1420
         ADDS Regent 25

                    CONTINUED ====>

Manufacturer: Liberty Electronics
Terminal: Freedom 200

41. Information provided by:
    MANUFACTURER

42. PROGRAM FUNCTION KEYS   NOTES
 1. ^A @   ^M   42. All function keys are user-
    01 40 0D   programmable up to 256 bytes.

 2. ^A A   ^M
    01 41 0D

 3. ^A B   ^M
    01 42 0D

 4. ^A C   ^M
    01 43 0D

 5. ^A D   ^M
    01 44 0D

 6. ^A E   ^M
    01 45 0D

 7. ^A F   ^M
    01 46 0D

 8. ^A G   ^M
    01 47 0D

 9. ^A H   ^M
    01 48 0D

10. ^A I   ^M
    01 49 0D

11.

12.

13.

14.

15.

16.

----

1. Manufacturer: Morrow Inc.
2. Terminal: MDT 60

SCREEN LAYOUT   VIDEO ATTRIBUTES
3. Number of rows: 24   ON   OFF
4. Number of columns: 80   24. Blinking:
5. Top Row: 1
6. Left Column: 1
7. Printing in bottom right   25. Reverse video:
   cause scroll?   YES   ESC G   4   ESC G   0
                                    1B   47   34   1B   47   30
CURSOR ADDRESSING   26. Underline:
8. Lead-in sequence: ESC G   1   ESC G   0
              ESC =   1B   47   31   1B   47   30
              1B   3D   27. High intensity:
9. Row or column first: ROW   ESC G   0   ESC G   0
10. Numeric form of row and column: 1B   47   30   1B   47   30
    BINARY   28. Half intensity:
11. Add offset to: Row: 1F   ESC G   2   ESC G   0
                      Col: 1F   1B   47   32   1B   47   30
12. Separator sequence: 29. Attributes occupy position: NO
                                    30. Attributes cumulative: NO
                                    31. All attributes off:
13. End sequence: ESC G   0
                                              1B   47   30

14. Cursor to top row, left column: CURSOR CONTROL KEYS
ESC =   SP   SP   32. Cursor up:
1B   3D   20   20   ^\   J
15. 10th Row, 50th Column: 1C   4A
ESC =   )   Q   33. Cursor down:
1B   3D   29   51   ^\   K
16. Delay after positioning: 0   1C   4B
17. Cursor home: 34. Cursor right:
          ^^   ^\   M
          1E   1C   4D
                                    35. Cursor left:
ERASURE   DELAY   ^\   L
18. Entire screen: 1C   4C
        ^Z   0
        1A   CHARACTER SET
19. Cursor to end of screen: 36. Full upper and lower ASCII: YES
        ESC Y   0   37. Generate all control codes: YES
        1B   59   38. Bell or tone sequence:
20. Beginning of screen to cursor: ^G
                                              07

21. Cursor to end of line: EMULATION
        ESC T   0   39. Conform to ANSI X3.64?   NO
        1B   54   40. Terminals Emulated:
22. Beginning of line to cursor: Televideo 925, Freedom 100

23. Entire cursor line:
        ESC R   0
        1B   52

                                 CONTINUED ====>

Manufacturer: Morrow Inc.
Terminal: MDT 60

41. Information provided by:
    MANUFACTURER

42. PROGRAM FUNCTION KEYS   NOTES
  1. ^\ @
     1C 40

  2. ^\ A
     1C 41

  3. ^\ B
     1C 42

  4. ^\ C
     1C 43

  5. ^\ D
     1C 44

  6. ^\ E
     1C 45

  7. ^\ F
     1C 46

  8. ^\ G
     1C 47

  9. ^\ H
     1C 48

10.

11.

12.

13.

14.

15.

16.

```
-------------------------------------------------------------------------------
  1. Manufacturer:                     NCR Corp.
  2. Terminal:                         NCR 7910 (ANSI mode)
-------------------------------------------------------------------------------
```

SCREEN LAYOUT
  3. Number of rows: 24
  4. Number of columns: 80
  5. Top Row: 1
  6. Left Column: 1
  7. Printing in bottom right
     cause scroll?   PROG

CURSOR ADDRESSING
  8. Lead-in sequence:
              ESC [
              1B   5B
  9. Row or column first: ROW
 10. Numeric form of row and column:
     VARIABLE-LENGTH ASCII
 11. Add offset to: Row: 0
                           Col: 0
 12. Separator sequence:
              ;
              3B
 13. End sequence:
              H
              48
 14. Cursor to top row, left column:
     ESC [1   ;   1   H
     1B   5B   31   3B   31   48
 15. 10th Row, 50th Column:
     ESC [1   0   ;   5   0   H
     1B   5B   31   30   3B   35   30   48
 16. Delay after positioning: 0
 17. Cursor home:
              ESC [H
              1B   5B   48

ERASURE   DELAY
 18. Entire screen:
              ^L   0
              0C
 19. Cursor to end of screen:
              ESC [0   0
              1B   5B   4F
 20. Beginning of screen to cursor:

 21. Cursor to end of line:
              ESC [K   0
              1B   5B   4B
 22. Beginning of line to cursor:

 23. Entire cursor line:
              ESC [2   K   0
              1B   5B   32   4B

VIDEO ATTRIBUTES
                 ON   OFF
 24. Blinking:

 25. Reverse video:

 26. Underline:

 27. High intensity:

 28. Half intensity:

 29. Attributes occupy position: YES
 30. Attributes cumulative: NO
 31. All attributes off:
              ESC P   @   @   ESC \
              1B   50 40   40   1B   5C
CURSOR CONTROL KEYS
 32. Cursor up:
              ESC [A
              1B   5B   41
 33. Cursor down:
              ESC [B
              1B   5B   42
 34. Cursor right:
              ESC [C
              1B   5B   43
 35. Cursor left:
              ESC [D
              1B   5B   44

CHARACTER SET
 36. Full upper and lower ASCII: YES
 37. Generate all control codes: YES
 38. Bell or tone sequence:
              ^G
              07

EMULATION
 39. Conform to ANSI X3.64?   YES
 40. Terminals Emulated:
     NCR 7900 Model 1
     NCR 7900 Model 4
     ANSI Standard X3.64

Manufacturer: NCR Corp.
Terminal: NCR 7910 (ANSI mode)

----

41. Information provided by:
    MANUFACTURER

42. PROGRAM FUNCTION KEYS   NOTES
    1. ^B 1   ^M   3. Terminal may be configured to have
       02 31 0D   a total of 24, 48, 72 or 96 lines,
                                      of which 24 are displayed on the
    2. ^B 2   ^M   screen at one time (plus status
       02 32 0D   line).
                                   4. Terminal may be configured to
    3. ^B 3   ^M   either 80 or 132 columns.
       02 33 0D   7. Terminal may be configured so that
                                      entering a character in the last
    4. ^B 4   ^M   column of any row (including the
       02 34 0D   last one on the screen) will not
                                      cause a scroll to the next line
    5. ^B 5   ^M   until a CR LF (or another control
       02 35 0D   sequence) is entered.
                                  14. Row 1 and column 1 are default
    6. ^B 6   ^M   paramaters that do not need to be
       02 36 0D   specifically transmitted.
                                  24.-28. Field attributes:
    7. ^B 7   ^M   Blinking   ESC P @ C ESC \
       02 37 0D   Reverse   ESC P @ B ESC \
                                      Underline   ESC P @ A ESC \
    8. ^B 8   ^M   High intensity   ESC P P @ ESC \
       02 38 0D   Normal   ESC P @ @ ESC \
                                  29. Attributes in 24-28 are field
    9. ^B 9   ^M   attributes, which do take up char-
       02 39 0D   acter positions. Character attri-
                                      butes, which do not take up a
   10. ^B 0   ^M   character position, can also be
       02 30 0D   accessed by using different
                                      parameters [see ANSI X3.64].
   11.   30. Combinations of attributes (plus
                                      double wide, protected, and
                                      numeric entry) are possible in one
   12.   sequence by changing the middle
                                      two parameters of the sequence.
                                      Concatenated attribute sequences
   13.   are not cumulative. See manual.
                                  31. The sequence to clear character
                                      attributes is ESC P b @ ESC \.
   14.   36. An extended character set, con-
                                      taining international language and
                                      block graphics characters is also
   15.   available.
                                  42. Terminal has PF0-PF9. PF10 shown
                                      here is PF0 on the terminal.
   16.   Besides the 10 PF keys, there are
                                      20 user keys that can be programmed
                                      with any sequence desired.

```
--------------------------------------------------------------------------
1. Manufacturer:                    NCR Corp.
2. Terminal:                        NCR 7910 (Model 1 mode)
--------------------------------------------------------------------------

SCREEN LAYOUT                       VIDEO ATTRIBUTES
3. Number of rows:        24             ON                    OFF
4. Number of columns:     80        24. Blinking:
5. Top Row:                0        ESC 0    B          ESC 0   @
6. Left Column:            0        1B  30   42         1B  30  40
7. Printing in bottom right         25. Reverse video:
   cause scroll?         YES        ESC 0    P          ESC 0   @
                                    1B  30   50         1B  30  40
CURSOR ADDRESSING                   26. Underline:
8. Lead-in sequence:                ESC 0    `          ESC 0   @
           ESC 1                    1B  30   60         1B  30  40
           1B  31                   27. High intensity:
9. Row or column first:   COL       ESC 0    A          ESC 0   @
10. Numeric form of row and column: 1B  30   41         1B  30  40
    BINARY                          28. Half intensity:
11. Add offset to:      Row:   0
                        Col:   0
12. Separator sequence:             29. Attributes occupy position: YES
                                    30. Attributes cumulative:      NO
                                    31. All attributes off:
13. End sequence:                            ESC 0    @
                                             1B   30   40

14. Cursor to top row, left column: CURSOR CONTROL KEYS
ESC 1    P    0                     32. Cursor up:
1B   31   50   30                            ^Z
15. 10th Row, 50th Column:                   1A
ESC 1    1    9                     33. Cursor down:
1B   31   31   39                            ^J
16. Delay after positioning:    0            0A
17. Cursor home:                    34. Cursor right:
           ^A                                ^F
           01                                06
                                    35. Cursor left:
ERASURE                     DELAY            ^U
18. Entire screen:                           15
           ^L                  0
           0C                       CHARACTER SET
19. Cursor to end of screen:        36. Full upper and lower ASCII: YES
           ESC k               0    37. Generate all control codes: YES
           1B  6B                   38. Bell or tone sequence:
20. Beginning of screen to cursor:           ^G
                                             07

21. Cursor to end of line:          EMULATION
           ESC K               0    39. Conform to ANSI X3.64?      NO
           1B  4B                   40. Terminals Emulated:
22. Beginning of line to cursor:       NCR 7900 Model 1
                                       NCR 7900 Model 4
                                       ANSI Standard X3.64
23. Entire cursor line:
```

CONTINUED ====>

41. Information provided by:
    MANUFACTURER

42. PROGRAM FUNCTION KEYS   NOTES

1.	^B	1	^M
	02	31	0D
2.	^B	2	^M
	02	32	0D
3.	^B	3	^M
	02	33	0D
4.	^B	4	^M
	02	34	0D
5.	^B	5	^M
	02	35	0D
6.	^B	6	^M
	02	36	0D
7.	^B	7	^M
	02	37	0D
8.	^B	8	^M
	02	38	0D
9.	^B	9	^M
	02	39	0D
10.	^B	0	^M
	02	30	0D

11.

12.

13.

14.

15.

16.

NOTES

3. Terminal may be configured to have a total of 24, 48, 72 or 96 lines, of which 24 are displayed on the screen at one time (plus a status line).

4. Terminal may be configured to have either 80 or 132 columns.

7. Terminal may be configured so that entering a character in the last column of any row (including the last one on the screen) will not cause a scroll to the next line until a CR LF (or another control sequence) is entered.

5. & 11. In 7900 Model 1 mode, row and column parameters are binary, but the column parameter is taken modulo 80, and the row parameter is taken modulo 24.

17. If the terminal is configured to scroll data rather than wrap the cursor to the top of screen, the home position is the lower left-hand corner.

30. Some combinations of these attributes are possible in one sequence by changing the last parameter of the sequence. Concatenated attribute sequences are not cumulative.

36. An extended character set, containing international language and block graphics characters is also available.

42. Terminal uses PF0-PF9. PF10 shown here is PF0 on the terminal.
The CR character shown can be configured to send CR, ETX, EOT or none.

```
--------------------------------------------------------------------
1. Manufacturer:                        NCR Corp.
2. Terminal:                            NCR 7910 (Model 4 mode)
--------------------------------------------------------------------
```

SCREEN LAYOUT   VIDEO ATTRIBUTES
  3. Number of rows: 24   ON   OFF
  4. Number of columns: 80   24. Blinking:
  5. Top Row: 0   ^N   ^O
  6. Left Column: 0   0E   0F
  7. Printing in bottom right   25. Reverse video:
     cause scroll?   YES   ^N   ^O
                                          0E   0F
CURSOR ADDRESSING   26. Underline:
  8. Lead-in sequence: ^N   ^O
        ^K   0E   0F
        0B   27. High intensity:
  9. Row or column first: ROW
10. Numeric form of row and column:
     SEE NOTE 10   28. Half intensity:
11. Add offset to: Row: 40
                          Col: 0
12. Separator sequence: 29. Attributes occupy position: NO
     ESC ^E   30. Attributes cumulative: NO
     1B 05   31. All attributes off:
13. End sequence: ^O
                                                    0F

14. Cursor to top row, left column: CURSOR CONTROL KEYS
^K @   32. Cursor up:
0B 40
15. 10th Row, 50th Column:
^K I   ESC ^E   4   9   33. Cursor down:
0B 49   1B 05   34   39
16. Delay after positioning: 0
17. Cursor home: 34. Cursor right:
        ^K @
        0B 40
                                       35. Cursor left:
ERASURE   DELAY
18. Entire screen:
     ^L   0   CHARACTER SET
     0C   36. Full upper and lower ASCII: YES
19. Cursor to end of screen: 37. Generate all control codes: YES
                                       38. Bell or tone sequence:
                                                    ^G
20. Beginning of screen to cursor: 07

                                       EMULATION
21. Cursor to end of line: 39. Conform to ANSI X3.64?   NO
                                       40. Terminals Emulated:
                                          NCR 7900 Model 1
22. Beginning of line to cursor: NCR 7900 Model 4
                                          ANSI Standard X3.64

23. Entire cursor line:

```
-------------------------------------------------------------------------
        Manufacturer:                    NCR Corp.
        Terminal:                        NCR 7910 (Model 4 mode)
-------------------------------------------------------------------------
```

41. Information provided by:
    MANUFACTURER

42. PROGRAM FUNCTION KEYS

1. ^B 1 ^M	
02 31 0D	
2. ^B 2 ^M	
02 32 0D	
3. ^B 3 ^M	
02 33 0D	
4. ^B 4 ^M	
02 34 0D	
5. ^B 5 ^M	
02 35 0D	
6. ^B 6 ^M	
02 36 0D	
7. ^B 7 ^M	
02 37 0D	
8. ^B 8 ^M	
02 38 0D	
9. ^B 9 ^M	
02 39 0D	
10. ^B 0 ^M	
02 30 0D	

11.

12.

13.

14.

15.

16.

NOTES

3. Terminal may be configured to have 24, 48, 72 or 96 lines, of which 24 are displayed on the screen at one time (plus a status line).

4. Terminal may be configured to either 80 or 132 columns.

7. Terminal may be configured so that entering a character in the last column of any row (including the last one on the screen) will not cause a scroll to the next line until a CR LF (or another control sequence) is entered.

10. 7900 Model 4 uses two separate sequences for cursor positioning: line address, and horizontal address. The listed row/column sequence separator is really the lead-in sequence for the horizontal address command. Row is binary plus 40H offset. Column is 2-byte or 3-byte ASCII.

12. See note 10.

19. & 21. Although there are no sequences for these functions that can be transmitted by the host, the following erasure functions can be be done from the keyboard:
    From cursor to end of screen.
    From cursor to end of line.

30. The 7900 Model 4 can only use one video attribute at a time. There can not be cumulative or multiple attributes.

32.-35. All are local in block mode only. No sequence generated.

36. A limited set of block graphics characters is also available.

42. Terminal has PF0-PF9. PF10 shown is PF0 on the terminal. The CR character may be CR, ETX, EOT or none.

```
-----------------------------------------------------------------------
1. Manufacturer:                    Paradyne
2. Terminal:                        7811-01 Async
-----------------------------------------------------------------------
```

SCREEN LAYOUT   VIDEO ATTRIBUTES
3. Number of rows: 24   ON   OFF
4. Number of columns: 80   24. Blinking:
5. Top Row: 1
6. Left Column: 1
7. Printing in bottom right   25. Reverse video:
   cause scroll?   YES   ESC G   4   ESC G   0
                                    1B   47   34   1B   47   30
CURSOR ADDRESSING   26. Underline:
8. Lead-in sequence: ESC G   1   ESC G   0
          ESC =   1B   47   31   1B   47   30
          1B   3D   27. High intensity:
9. Row or column first: ROW
10. Numeric form of row and column:
   BINARY   28. Half intensity:
11. Add offset to: Row: 1F   ESC G   2   ESC G   0
                       Col: 1F   1B   47   32   1B   47   30
12. Separator sequence: 29. Attributes occupy position: YES
                                    30. Attributes cumulative: YES
                                    31. All attributes off:
13. End sequence: ESC G   0
                                              1B   47   30

14. Cursor to top row, left column: CURSOR CONTROL KEYS
ESC =   SP SP   32. Cursor up:
1B   3D   20 20   ^A   J   ^M
15. 10th Row, 50th Column: 01   4A 0D
ESC =   )   Q   33. Cursor down:
1B   3D   29 51   ^A   K   ^M
16. Delay after positioning: 0   01   4B 0D
17. Cursor home: 34. Cursor right:
          ^N   ^A   M   ^M
          0E   01   4D 0D
                                    35. Cursor left:
ERASURE   DELAY   ^A   L   ^M
18. Entire screen: 01   4C 0D
          ESC +   0
          1B   2B   CHARACTER SET
19. Cursor to end of screen: 36. Full upper and lower ASCII: YES
          ESC Y   0   37. Generate all control codes: YES
          1B   59   38. Bell or tone sequence:
20. Beginning of screen to cursor: ^G
                                              07

21. Cursor to end of line: EMULATION
          ESC T   0   39. Conform to ANSI X3.64?   NO
          1B   54   40. Terminals Emulated:
22. Beginning of line to cursor: Televideo 910
                                              ADM 31

23. Entire cursor line:
          ESC R   0
          1B   52

                            219   CONTINUED ====>
```
```

41. Information provided by:
    MANUFACTURER

42. PROGRAM FUNCTION KEYS   NOTES
 1. ˆA @   ˆM   30. ESC G 5 gives reverse video and
    01 40 0D   underline.

 2. ˆA A   ˆM
    01 41 0D

 3. ˆA B   ˆM
    01 42 0D

 4. ˆA C   ˆM
    01 43 0D

 5. ˆA D   ˆM
    01 44 0D

 6. ˆA E   ˆM
    01 45 0D

 7. ˆA F   ˆM
    01 46 0D

 8. ˆA G   ˆM
    01 47 0D

 9. ˆA H   ˆM
    01 48 0D

10. ˆA P   ˆM
    01 50 0D

11. ˆA ˆ\ ˆM
    01 1C 0D

12. ˆA ˆ] ˆM
    01 1D 0D

13. ˆA ˆˆ ˆM
    01 1E 0D

14. ˆA ˆ_ ˆM
    01 1F 0D

15.

16.

```
-----------------------------------------------------------------------
1. Manufacturer:                     Pickles & Trout
2. Terminal:                         CP/M - TRS-80 Models II, 12, 16
-----------------------------------------------------------------------
```

SCREEN LAYOUT   VIDEO ATTRIBUTES
3. Number of rows: 24   ON   OFF
4. Number of columns: 80   24. Blinking:
5. Top Row: 0
6. Left Column: 0
7. Printing in bottom right   25. Reverse video:
   cause scroll?   PROG   ^N   ^O
                                      OE   OF
CURSOR ADDRESSING   26. Underline:
8. Lead-in sequence:
         ESC Y
         1B 59   27. High intensity:
9. Row or column first: ROW
10. Numeric form of row and column:
    BINARY   28. Half intensity:
11. Add offset to: Row: 20
                        Col: 20
12. Separator sequence: 29. Attributes occupy position: NO
                                      30. Attributes cumulative: NO
                                      31. All attributes off:
13. End sequence: ^O   ^T
                                             OF   14

14. Cursor to top row, left column: CURSOR CONTROL KEYS
ESC Y   SP SP   32. Cursor up:
1B 59   20 20   ^^
15. 10th Row, 50th Column: 1E
ESC Y   )   Q   33. Cursor down:
1B 59   29 51   ^
16. Delay after positioning: 0   1F
17. Cursor home: 34. Cursor right:
         ^F   ^]
         06   1D
                                     35. Cursor left:
ERASURE   DELAY   ^\
18. Entire screen: 1C
         ^L   0
         0C   CHARACTER SET
19. Cursor to end of screen: 36. Full upper and lower ASCII: YES
         ^B   0   37. Generate all control codes: YES
         02   38. Bell or tone sequence:
20. Beginning of screen to cursor: ^G
                                                 07

21. Cursor to end of line: EMULATION
         ^A   0   39. Conform to ANSI X3.64?   NO
         01   40. Terminals Emulated:
22. Beginning of line to cursor: ADM 3A

23. Entire cursor line:
         ^K   0
         0B

                                221   CONTINUED ====>
```
```

41. Information provided by:
    MANUFACTURER

42. PROGRAM FUNCTION KEYS   NOTES
    1. ^A   1.-2. This is a version of the CP/M
       01   operating system which runs on the
                                         stated micro-computers. Pickles &
    2. ^B   Trout is not the manufacturer of
       02   the micro-computers.
                                   7. If line wrap is enabled, yes;
    3. ^D   if line wrap is disabled, no.
       04

    4. ^L
       0C

    5. ^U
       15

    6. ^P
       10

    7. ^C
       03

    8. ^S
       13

    9.

   10.

   11.

   12.

   13.

   14.

   15.

   16.

```
---------------------------------------------------------------------
  1. Manufacturer:                      Prime Computer, Inc.
  2. Terminal:                          PST100
---------------------------------------------------------------------
```

SCREEN LAYOUT
3. Number of rows: 24
4. Number of columns: 80
5. Top Row: 1
6. Left Column: 1
7. Printing in bottom right
   cause scroll?   PROG

CURSOR ADDRESSING
8. Lead-in sequence:
            ESC [
            1B 5B
9. Row or column first: ROW
10. Numeric form of row and column:
    VARIABLE-LENGTH ASCII
11. Add offset to: Row: 0
                         Col: 0
12. Separator sequence:
            ;
            3B
13. End sequence:
            H
            48
14. Cursor to top row, left column:
ESC [1   ;   1   H
1B   5B   31   3B   31   48
15. 10th Row, 50th Column:
ESC [1   0   ;   5   0   H
1B   5B   31   30   3B   35   30   48
16. Delay after positioning: 0
17. Cursor home:
            ESC [H
            1B 5B   48

ERASURE   DELAY
18. Entire screen:
        ESC [2   J   0
        1B 5B   32   4A
19. Cursor to end of screen:
        ESC [J   0
        1B 5B   4A
20. Beginning of screen to cursor:
        ESC [1   J   0
        1B 5B   31   4A
21. Cursor to end of line:
        ESC [K   0
        1B 5B   4B
22. Beginning of line to cursor:
        ESC [1   K   0
        1B 5B   31   4B
23. Entire cursor line:
        ESC [2   K   0
        1B 5B   32   4B

VIDEO ATTRIBUTES
          ON   OFF
24. Blinking:
ESC [5   m   ESC [m
1B   5B   35   6D   1B   5B   6D
25. Reverse video:
ESC [7   m   ESC [m
1B   5B   37   6D   1B   5B   6D
26. Underline:
ESC [4   m   ESC [m
1B   5B   34   6D   1B   5B   6D
27. High intensity:

28. Half intensity:
ESC [2   m   ESC [m
1B   5B   32   6D   1B   5B   6D
29. Attributes occupy position: NO
30. Attributes cumulative: YES
31. All attributes off:
            ESC [m
            1B 5B   6D

CURSOR CONTROL KEYS
32. Cursor up:
            ESC [A
            1B 5B   41
33. Cursor down:
            ESC [B
            1B 5B   42
34. Cursor right:
            ESC [C
            1B 5B   43
35. Cursor left:
            ESC [D
            1B 5B   44

CHARACTER SET
36. Full upper and lower ASCII: YES
37. Generate all control codes: YES
38. Bell or tone sequence:
            ^G
            07

EMULATION
39. Conform to ANSI X3.64?   YES
40. Terminals Emulated:

CONTINUED ====>

41. Information provided by:
    MANUFACTURER

42. PROGRAM FUNCTION KEYS   NOTES
   1. ESC O   !   3. Plus 25th status line.
      1B   4F   21   36. 128 ASCII characters, 8 graphic
                                        symbols, 64 block graphic symbols.
   2. ESC O   "   42. F1-F8 shown unaugmented.
      1B   4F   22   F1-F8 and PF1-PF14 may be used
                                        unaugmented, shifted, control or
   3. ESC O   #   control-shift. All 22 keys are
      1B   4F   23   user programmable.

   4. ESC O $
      1B   4F   24

   5. ESC O   %
      1B   4F   25

   6. ESC O   &
      1B   4F   26

   7. ESC O   ´
      1B   4F   27

   8. ESC O   (
      1B   4F   28

   9.

  10.

  11.

  12.

  13.

  14.

  15.

  16.

```
------------------------------------------------------------------------
1. Manufacturer:                        Qume
2. Terminal:                            QVT-102
------------------------------------------------------------------------

SCREEN LAYOUT                           VIDEO ATTRIBUTES
 3. Number of rows:          24              ON                      OFF
 4. Number of columns:       80         24. Blinking:
 5. Top Row:                  1         ESC G   2               ESC G   0
 6. Left Column:              1         1B  47  32              1B  47  30
 7. Printing in bottom right            25. Reverse video:
    cause scroll?           YES         ESC G   4               ESC G   0
                                        1B  47  34              1B  47  30
CURSOR ADDRESSING                       26. Underline:
 8. Lead-in sequence:                   ESC G   8               ESC G   0
            ESC =                       1B  47  38              1B  47  30
            1B  3D                      27. High intensity:
 9. Row or column first:     ROW        ESC (                   ESC )
10. Numeric form of row and column:     1B  28                  1B  29
    BINARY                              28. Half intensity:
11. Add offset to:      Row:  1F        ESC )                   ESC (
                        Col:  1F        1B  29                  1B  28
12. Separator sequence:                 29. Attributes occupy position: YES
                                        30. Attributes cumulative:      NO
                                        31. All attributes off:
13. End sequence:                               ESC *
                                                1B  2A

14. Cursor to top row, left column:     CURSOR CONTROL KEYS
ESC =   SP  SP                          32. Cursor up:
1B  3D  20  20                                  ^K
15. 10th Row, 50th Column:                      0B
ESC =   )   Q                           33. Cursor down:
1B  3D  29  51                                  ^V
16. Delay after positioning:     0              16
17. Cursor home:                        34. Cursor right:
            ESC =   SP  SP                      ^L
            1B  3D  20  20                       0C
                                        35. Cursor left:
ERASURE                     DELAY               ^H
18. Entire screen:                              08
        ESC *                16
        1B  2A                          CHARACTER SET
19. Cursor to end of screen:            36. Full upper and lower ASCII: YES
        ESC Y                 2         37. Generate all control codes: YES
        1B  59                          38. Bell or tone sequence:
20. Beginning of screen to cursor:              ^G
                                                07

21. Cursor to end of line:              EMULATION
        ESC T                 2         39. Conform to ANSI X3.64?       NO
        1B  54                          40. Terminals Emulated:
22. Beginning of line to cursor:            Lear Siegler ADM 3A/5
                                            Televideo 910
                                            Hazeltine 1500
23. Entire cursor line:
        ESC R                 0
        1B  52
```

CONTINUED ====>

41. Information provided by:
    MANUFACTURER

42. PROGRAM FUNCTION KEYS   NOTES
    1. ^A @   ^M   16. For current page the execution time
       01 40 0D   is negligible. For different page
                                       it will take 20ms waiting time
    2. ^A A   ^M   (worst case).
       01 41 0D   29. High/Half intensity do not occupy
                                       screen position.
    3. ^A B   ^M   42. PF1-PF4 shown unshifted.
       01 42 0D   Shifted:
                                       PF1   SOH D CR
    4. ^A C   ^M   PF2   SOH E CR
       01 43 0D   PF3   SOH F CR
                                       PF4   SOH G CR
    5.   Control:
                                       PF1   SOH H CR
                                       PF2   SOH I CR
    6.   PF3   SOH J CR
                                       PF4   SOH K CR

    7.

    8.

    9.

    10.

    11.

    12.

    13.

    14.

    15.

    16.

---

1. Manufacturer: Qume
2. Terminal: QVT-108

SCREEN LAYOUT
3. Number of rows: 24
4. Number of columns: 80
5. Top Row: 1
6. Left Column: 1
7. Printing in bottom right
   cause scroll? YES

CURSOR ADDRESSING
8. Lead-in sequence:
   ESC =
   1B   3D
9. Row or column first: ROW
10. Numeric form of row and column:
    BINARY
11. Add offset to: Row: 1F
                   Col: 1F
12. Separator sequence:

13. End sequence:

14. Cursor to top row, left column:
    ESC =   SP SP
    1B   3D 20 20
15. 10th Row, 50th Column:
    ESC =   )   Q
    1B   3D 29 51
16. Delay after positioning: 0
17. Cursor home:
            ESC =   SP SP
            1B   3D 20 20

ERASURE   DELAY
18. Entire screen:
        ESC *   16
        1B   2A
19. Cursor to end of screen:
        ESC Y   2
        1B   59
20. Beginning of screen to cursor:

21. Cursor to end of line:
        ESC T   2
        1B   54
22. Beginning of line to cursor:

23. Entire cursor line:
        ESC R   0
        1B   52

VIDEO ATTRIBUTES
                 ON   OFF
24. Blinking:
    ESC G   2   ESC G   0
    1B   47 32   1B   47 30
25. Reverse video:
    ESC G   4   ESC G   0
    1B   47 34   1B   47 30
26. Underline:
    ESC G   8   ESC G   0
    1B   47 38   1B   47 30
27. High intensity:
    ESC (ESC)
    1B   28   1B   29
28. Half intensity:
    ESC)   ESC (
    1B   29   1B   28
29. Attributes occupy position: YES
30. Attributes cumulative: NO
31. All attributes off:
            ESC *
            1B   2A

CURSOR CONTROL KEYS
32. Cursor up:
            ^K
            0B
33. Cursor down:
            ^V
            16
34. Cursor right:
            ^L
            0C
35. Cursor left:
            ^H
            08

CHARACTER SET
36. Full upper and lower ASCII: YES
37. Generate all control codes: YES
38. Bell or tone sequence:
            ^G
            07

EMULATION
39. Conform to ANSI X3.64?   NO
40. Terminals Emulated:
       Televideo 925, 920, 912

41. Information provided by:
    MANUFACTURER

42. PROGRAM FUNCTION KEYS   NOTES
    1. ^A @   ^M   16. For current page the execution time
       01 40 0D   is negligible. For different page
                                     it will take 20ms waiting time
    2. ^A A   ^M   (worst case).
       01 41 0D   29. High/Half intensity do not occupy
                                     screen position.
    3. ^A B   ^M   42. All 11 function keys are program-
       01 42 0D   mable. Refer to operator's manual.

    4. ^A C   ^M
       01 43 0D

    5. ^A D   ^M
       01 44 0D

    6. ^A E   ^M
       01 45 0D

    7. ^A F   ^M
       01 46 0D

    8. ^A G   ^M
       01 47 0D

    9. ^A H   ^M
       01 48 0D

   10. ^A I   ^M
       01 49 0D

   11. ^A J   ^M
       01 4A 0D

   12.

   13.

   14.

   15.

   16.

```
1. Manufacturer:              Radio Shack
2. Terminal:                  TRS-80 DT-1
```

SCREEN LAYOUT
```
3. Number of rows:        24
4. Number of columns:     80
5. Top Row:                1
6. Left Column:            1
7. Printing in bottom right
   cause scroll?         PROG
```

CURSOR ADDRESSING
```
8. Lead-in sequence:
          ESC >
          1B  3E
9. Row or column first:     ROW
10. Numeric form of row and column:
    BINARY
11. Add offset to:      Row:  1F
                        Col:  1F
12. Separator sequence:


13. End sequence:


14. Cursor to top row, left column:
ESC >   SP  SP
1B  3E  20  20
15. 10th Row, 50th Column:
ESC >   )   Q
1B  3E  29  51
16. Delay after positioning:    0
17. Cursor home:
        ^ ^
        1E
```

ERASURE   DELAY
```
18. Entire screen:
       ESC *                  0
       1B  2A
19. Cursor to end of screen:
       ESC Y                  0
       1B  59
20. Beginning of screen to cursor:


21. Cursor to end of line:
       ESC T                  0
       1B  54
22. Beginning of line to cursor:


23. Entire cursor line:
```

VIDEO ATTRIBUTES
```
        ON                      OFF
24. Blinking:
ESC G    2            ESC G   0
1B  47  32           1B  47  30
25. Reverse video:
ESC G    4            ESC G   0
1B  47  34           1B  47  30
26. Underline:
ESC G    8            ESC G   0
1B  47  38           1B  47  30
27. High intensity:


28. Half intensity:
ESC (                ESC )
1B  28               1B  29
29. Attributes occupy position: YES
30. Attributes cumulative:       NO
31. All attributes off:
             ESC G   0
             1B  47  30
```

CURSOR CONTROL KEYS
```
32. Cursor up:
             ^K
             0B
33. Cursor down:
             ^J
             0A
34. Cursor right:
             ^L
             0C
35. Cursor left:
             ^H
             08
```

CHARACTER SET
```
36. Full upper and lower ASCII: YES
37. Generate all control codes: YES
38. Bell or tone sequence:
             ^G
             07
```

EMULATION
```
39. Conform to ANSI X3.64?      NO
40. Terminals Emulated:
    Televideo 910
    ADDS 25
    Lear Siegler ADM-5
    Hazeltine 1410
```

CONTINUED ====>

```
----------------------------------------------------------------------
        Manufacturer:                 Radio Shack
        Terminal:                     TRS-80 DT-1
----------------------------------------------------------------------
```

41. Information provided by:
    MANUFACTURER

42. PROGRAM FUNCTION KEYS   NOTES
    1.   This terminal emulates any of the
                                      four terminals shown in item 40.
                                      It has no "native" mode. Codes
    2.   shown are for Televideo 910.

    3.

    4.

    5.

    6.

    7.

    8.

    9.

    10.

    11.

    12.

    13.

    14.

    15.

    16.

```
--------------------------------------------------------------------
1. Manufacturer:                     RCA
2. Terminal:                         APT VP3801/VP4801
--------------------------------------------------------------------


SCREEN LAYOUT                        VIDEO ATTRIBUTES
3. Number of rows:          24            ON                    OFF
4. Number of columns:       80       24. Blinking:
5. Top Row:                  1          ESC ESC S   4    ^N   ^O
6. Left Column:              1          1B  1B  53  34   0E   0F
7. Printing in bottom right          25. Reverse video:
   cause scroll?           YES          ESC ESC S   3    ^N   ^O
                                        1B  1B  53  33   0E   0F
CURSOR ADDRESSING                    26. Underline:
8. Lead-in sequence:
         ESC Y
         1B  59                       27. High intensity:
9. Row or column first:     ROW
10. Numeric form of row and column:
    BINARY                           28. Half intensity:
11. Add offset to:      Row:  1F
                        Col:  1F
12. Separator sequence:              29. Attributes occupy position: NO
                                     30. Attributes cumulative:      NO
                                     31. All attributes off:
13. End sequence:                            ESC ESC S   0
                                             1B  1B  53  30


14. Cursor to top row, left column:  CURSOR CONTROL KEYS
ESC Y   SP  SP                       32. Cursor up:
1B  59  20  20                                   ESC A
15. 10th Row, 50th Column:                       1B  41
ESC Y   )   Q                        33. Cursor down:
1B  59  29  51                                   ESC B
16. Delay after positioning:    0                1B  42
17. Cursor home:                     34. Cursor right:
         ESC H                                   ESC C
         1B  48                                  1B  43
                                     35. Cursor left:
ERASURE                     DELAY                ESC D
18. Entire screen:                               1B  44
         ESC j              0
         1B  6A                      CHARACTER SET
19. Cursor to end of screen:         36. Full upper and lower ASCII: YES
         ESC J              0        37. Generate all control codes: YES
         1B  4A                      38. Bell or tone sequence:
20. Beginning of screen to cursor:               ^G
                                                 07
21. Cursor to end of line:           EMULATION
         ESC K              0        39. Conform to ANSI X3.64?       NO
         1B  4B                      40. Terminals Emulated:
22. Beginning of line to cursor:


23. Entire cursor line:
```

231   CONTINUED ====>

41. Information provided by:
    MANUFACTURER

42. PROGRAM FUNCTION KEYS   NOTES
    1. ESC 1   3. Or 23.
       1B   31   4. Or 40.
                              8. User-definable.
    2. ESC 2   17. User-definable.
       1B   32   18. Or ^L (OCH). User-definable.
                        19. User-definable.
    3. ESC 3   21. User-definable.
       1B   33   31. Or ^O (OFH). User-definable.
                        32.-35. No dedicated cursor keys.
    4. ESC 4   38. User-definable.
       1B   34   42. All function keys can be user or
                            host programmed to send any string
    5. ESC 5   of up to 31 ASCII characters. The
       1B   35   default strings are shown.

    6. ESC 6
       1B   36   RCA APT terminals allow the user to
                            redefine the lead-in sequence for
    7. ESC 7   all command functions.
       1B   37

    8. ESC 8
       1B   38

    9.

    10.

    11.

    12.

    13.

    14.

    15.

    16.

```
--------------------------------------------------------------------------------
1. Manufacturer:                    Sanyo
2. Terminal:                        CRX-1100
--------------------------------------------------------------------------------
```

SCREEN LAYOUT   VIDEO ATTRIBUTES
3. Number of rows: 24   ON   OFF
4. Number of columns: 80   24. Blinking:
5. Top Row: 1   ESC T   A   ESC T   @
6. Left Column: 1   1B   54 41   1B   54 40
7. Printing in bottom right   25. Reverse video:
   cause scroll?   NO   ESC T   D   ESC T   @
                                      1B   54 44   1B   54 40
CURSOR ADDRESSING   26. Underline:
8. Lead-in sequence: ESC T   B   ESC T   @
          ESC F   1B   54 42   1B   54 40
          1B 46   27. High intensity:
9. Row or column first: ROW
10. Numeric form of row and column:
    BINARY   28. Half intensity:
11. Add offset to: Row: 20   ESC)   ESC (
                        Col: 20   1B   29   1B   28
12. Separator sequence: 29. Attributes occupy position: NO
                                     30. Attributes cumulative: NO
                                     31. All attributes off:
13. End sequence: ESC -
                                              1B   2D

14. Cursor to top row, left column: CURSOR CONTROL KEYS
ESC F   SP SP   32. Cursor up:
1B   46 20 20   ESC A
15. 10th Row, 50th Column: 1B   41
ESC F   )   Q   33. Cursor down:
1B   46 29 51   ESC B
16. Delay after positioning: 0   1B   42
17. Cursor home: 34. Cursor right:
          ESC H   ESC C
          1B 48   1B   43
                                     35. Cursor left:
ERASURE   DELAY   ESC D
18. Entire screen: 1B   44
          ^L   0
          0C   CHARACTER SET
19. Cursor to end of screen: 36. Full upper and lower ASCII: YES
          ESC J   0   37. Generate all control codes: YES
          1B 4A   38. Bell or tone sequence:
20. Beginning of screen to cursor: ^G
                                              07

21. Cursor to end of line: EMULATION
          ESC K   0   39. Conform to ANSI X3.64?   NO
          1B 4B   40. Terminals Emulated:
22. Beginning of line to cursor: Televideo 910
                                          Hazeltine 1410
                                          ADDS R25
23. Entire cursor line:
          ESC M   0
          1B 4D

                                233   CONTINUED ====>

Manufacturer: Sanyo
Terminal: CRX-1100

41. Information provided by:
    MANUFACTURER

42. PROGRAM FUNCTION KEYS   NOTES
  1.   18. Or ESC E (1BH 45H).
                                  42. 8 ASCII programmable function
                                      keys.
  2.

  3.

  4.

  5.

  6.

  7.

  8.

  9.

 10.

 11.

 12.

 13.

 14.

 15.

 16.

```
--------------------------------------------------------------------------
  1. Manufacturer:                      Sanyo
  2. Terminal:                          MBC-1100
--------------------------------------------------------------------------

SCREEN LAYOUT                          VIDEO ATTRIBUTES
  3. Number of rows:          25            ON              OFF
  4. Number of columns:       80       24. Blinking:
  5. Top Row:                  0        ESC t    ^A        ESC t    NUL
  6. Left Column:              0        1B   74   01       1B   74   00
  7. Printing in bottom right           25. Reverse video:
     cause scroll?           YES        ESC t    ^D        ESC t    NUL
                                        1B   74   04       1B   74   00
CURSOR ADDRESSING                       26. Underline:
  8. Lead-in sequence:                  ESC t    ^B        ESC t    NUL
                ESC F                   1B   74   02       1B   74   00
                1B  46                  27. High intensity:
  9. Row or column first:     ROW
 10. Numeric form of row and column:
     BINARY                             28. Half intensity:
 11. Add offset to:      Row:  20       ESC t    @         ESC t    NUL
                         Col:  20       1B   74   40       1B   74   00
 12. Separator sequence:                29. Attributes occupy position: NO
                                        30. Attributes cumulative:     NO
                                        31. All attributes off:
 13. End sequence:                                   ESC t    NUL
                                                     1B   74   00

 14. Cursor to top row, left column:   CURSOR CONTROL KEYS
 ESC F    SP   SP                       32. Cursor up:
 1B   46   20   20                                   ESC A
 15. 10th Row, 50th Column:                          1B   41
 ESC F    )    Q                        33. Cursor down:
 1B   46   29   51                                   ESC B
 16. Delay after positioning:    0                   1B   42
 17. Cursor home:                       34. Cursor right:
                ESC H                                ESC C
                1B  48                               1B   43
                                        35. Cursor left:
ERASURE                    DELAY                     ESC D
 18. Entire screen:                                  1B   44
        ^Z                     0
        1A                              CHARACTER SET
 19. Cursor to end of screen:           36. Full upper and lower ASCII: YES
        ESC J                  0        37. Generate all control codes: YES
        1B   4A                         38. Bell or tone sequence:
 20. Beginning of screen to cursor:                  ^G
                                                     07
 21. Cursor to end of line:            EMULATION
        ESC K                  0        39. Conform to ANSI X3.64?      NO
        1B   4B                         40. Terminals Emulated:
 22. Beginning of line to cursor:           ADM-3A

 23. Entire cursor line:
        ESC M                  0
        1B   4D
```

CONTINUED ====>

```
----------------------------------------------------------------
     Manufacturer:              Sanyo
     Terminal:                  MBC-1100
----------------------------------------------------------------
```

41. Information provided by:
    MANUFACTURER

42. PROGRAM FUNCTION KEYS   NOTES
  1.   8. Or ESC = (1BH 3DH).
                                    18. Or ESC E (1BH 45H).
                                    42. 15 function keys.
  2.

  3.

  4.

  5.

  6.

  7.

  8.

  9.

 10.

 11.

 12.

 13.

 14.

 15.

 16.

```
-------------------------------------------------------------------------
 1. Manufacturer:                    Sanyo
 2. Terminal:                        MBC-1200
-------------------------------------------------------------------------

SCREEN LAYOUT                        VIDEO ATTRIBUTES
 3. Number of rows:            33        ON                    OFF
 4. Number of columns:         80    24. Blinking:
 5. Top Row:                    0
 6. Left Column:                0
 7. Printing in bottom right         25. Reverse video:
    cause scroll?              YES    ESC t    ^D          ESC t    NUL
                                      1B   74   04         1B   74   00
CURSOR ADDRESSING                    26. Underline:
 8. Lead-in sequence:                 ESC t    ^B          ESC t    NUL
       ESC =                          1B   74   02         1B   74   00
       1B   3D                       27. High intensity:
 9. Row or column first:      ROW
10. Numeric form of row and column:
    BINARY                           28. Half intensity:
11. Add offset to:       Row:  20
                         Col:  20
12. Separator sequence:              29. Attributes occupy position: NO
                                     30. Attributes cumulative:      NO
                                     31. All attributes off:
13. End sequence:                         ESC t    NUL
                                          1B   74   00

14. Cursor to top row, left column:  CURSOR CONTROL KEYS
ESC F    SP   SP                     32. Cursor up:
1B   46   20   20
15. 10th Row, 50th Column:
ESC F    )    Q                      33. Cursor down:
1B   46   29   51
16. Delay after positioning:    0
17. Cursor home:                     34. Cursor right:
         ESC F    SP   SP
         1B   46   20   20
                                     35. Cursor left:
ERASURE                    DELAY
18. Entire screen:
      ^Z                     0
      1A                             CHARACTER SET
19. Cursor to end of screen:         36. Full upper and lower ASCII: YES
                                     37. Generate all control codes: YES
                                     38. Bell or tone sequence:
20. Beginning of screen to cursor:        ^G
                                          07

21. Cursor to end of line:           EMULATION
      ESC T                  0       39. Conform to ANSI X3.64?      NO
      1B   54                        40. Terminals Emulated:
22. Beginning of line to cursor:


23. Entire cursor line:
      ESC B                  0
      1B   42
```

CONTINUED ====>

```
--------------------------------------------------------------------------------
      Manufacturer:                     Sanyo
      Terminal:                         MBC-1200
--------------------------------------------------------------------------------
```

41. Information provided by:
    MANUFACTURER

42. PROGRAM FUNCTION KEYS   NOTES
    1.   3. Or 40.
                                   36. Dot graphics computer.
                                   42. 15 function keys.
    2.

    3.

    4.

    5.

    6.

    7.

    8.

    9.

   10.

   11.

   12.

   13.

   14.

   15.

   16.

```
--------------------------------------------------------------------------
1. Manufacturer:                    Sanyo
2. Terminal:                        MBC-4000 (CP/M-86 O.S.)
--------------------------------------------------------------------------
```

SCREEN LAYOUT   VIDEO ATTRIBUTES
3. Number of rows: 25   ON   OFF
4. Number of columns: 80   24. Blinking:
5. Top Row: 0   ESC   ESC @
6. Left Column: 0   1B 60   1B   40
7. Printing in bottom right   25. Reverse video:
   cause scroll?   YES   ESC P   ESC @
                                    1B 50   1B   40
CURSOR ADDRESSING   26. Underline:
8. Lead-in sequence:
        ESC F
        1B 46   27. High intensity:
9. Row or column first: ROW   ESC G   ESC C
10. Numeric form of row and column: 1B 47   1B   43
   BINARY   28. Half intensity:
11. Add offset to: Row: 20   ESC A   ESC C
                        Col: 20   1B 41   1B   43
12. Separator sequence: 29. Attributes occupy position: NO
                                    30. Attributes cumulative: NO
                                    31. All attributes off:
13. End sequence: ESC C
                                            1B 43

14. Cursor to top row, left column: CURSOR CONTROL KEYS
ESC F   SP SP   32. Cursor up:
1B 46 20 20   ESC A
15. 10th Row, 50th Column: 1B 41
ESC F   )   Q   33. Cursor down:
1B 46 29 51   ESC B
16. Delay after positioning: 0   1B 42
17. Cursor home: 34. Cursor right:
        ESC H   ESC C
        1B 48   1B 43
                                    35. Cursor left:
ERASURE   DELAY   ESC D
18. Entire screen: 1B 44
        ^Z   0
        1A   CHARACTER SET
19. Cursor to end of screen: 36. Full upper and lower ASCII: YES
        ESC J   0   37. Generate all control codes: YES
        1B 4A   38. Bell or tone sequence:
20. Beginning of screen to cursor: ^G
                                            07

21. Cursor to end of line: EMULATION
        ESC K   0   39. Conform to ANSI X3.64?   NO
        1B 4B   40. Terminals Emulated:
22. Beginning of line to cursor:

23. Entire cursor line:
        ESC M   0
        1B 4D

                            239   CONTINUED ====>
```
```

```
-----------------------------------------------------------------------
        Manufacturer:                Sanyo
        Terminal:                    MBC-4000 (CP/M-86 O.S.)
-----------------------------------------------------------------------
```

41. Information provided by:
    MANUFACTURER

42. PROGRAM FUNCTION KEYS   NOTES
    1.   8. Or ESC = (1BH 3DH).
                                    18. Or ESC E (1BH 45H).
                                    42. 15 ASCII programmable function
    2.   keys.

    3.

    4.

    5.

    6.

    7.

    8.

    9.

    10.

    11.

    12.

    13.

    14.

    15.

    16.

```
-----------------------------------------------------------------------
  1. Manufacturer:                      Sony Corporation of America
  2. Terminal:                          SMC-70 (IBM 3101)
-----------------------------------------------------------------------
```

SCREEN LAYOUT   VIDEO ATTRIBUTES
  3. Number of rows: 25   ON   OFF
  4. Number of columns: 80   24. Blinking:
  5. Top Row: 1   ESC 3   I   ESC 3   H
  6. Left Column: 1   1B 33 49   1B 33 48
  7. Printing in bottom right   25. Reverse video:
     cause scroll?   YES   ESC 3   E   ESC 3   D
                                        1B 33 45   1B 33 44
CURSOR ADDRESSING   26. Underline:
  8. Lead-in sequence:
           ESC Y
           1B 59   27. High intensity:
  9. Row or column first: ROW
 10. Numeric form of row and column:
     BINARY   28. Half intensity:
 11. Add offset to: Row: 1F
                         Col: 1F
 12. Separator sequence: 29. Attributes occupy position: NO
                                        30. Attributes cumulative: YES
                                        31. All attributes off:

 13. End sequence:

 14. Cursor to top row, left column: CURSOR CONTROL KEYS
 ESC Y   SP SP   32. Cursor up:
 1B 59 20 20   ^W
 15. 10th Row, 50th Column: 17
 ESC Y   )   Q   33. Cursor down:
 1B 59 29 51   ^\
 16. Delay after positioning: 0   1C
 17. Cursor home: 34. Cursor right:
            ESC H   ^Y
            1B 48   19
                                       35. Cursor left:
ERASURE   DELAY   ^V
 18. Entire screen: 16
        ESC L   0
        1B 4C   CHARACTER SET
 19. Cursor to end of screen: 36. Full upper and lower ASCII: YES
        ESC J   0   37. Generate all control codes: YES
        1B 4A   38. Bell or tone sequence:
 20. Beginning of screen to cursor: ^G
                                                  07

 21. Cursor to end of line: EMULATION
        ESC I   0   39. Conform to ANSI X3.64?   NO
        1B 49   40. Terminals Emulated:
 22. Beginning of line to cursor: IBM 3101 emulation built into
                                           CP/M. Multiterminal emulator:
                                           DEC VT100, Lear Siegler ADM 3A,
 23. Entire cursor line: ADM 31, Televideo 910, ADDS
                                           Viewpoint, Hazeltine Esprit,
                                           IBM 3101, Dasher 0200.

                         241   CONTINUED ====>

41. Information provided by:
    MANUFACTURER

42. PROGRAM FUNCTION KEYS   NOTES
    1. ^A   18. Or FF (0CH).
       01   42. F1-F5 shown unshifted.
                                       F6-10 are F1-F5 shifted.
    2. ^B   F11-F15 are CTRL F1-F5.
       02

    3. ^C
       03

    4. ^D
       04

    5. ^E
       05

    6. ^I
       09

    7. ^J
       0A

    8. ^K
       0B

    9. ^L
       0C

   10. ^M
       0D

   11. ^Q
       11

   12. ^R
       12

   13. ^S
       13

   14. ^T
       14

   15. ^U
       15

   16.

```
---------------------------------------------------------------------
  1. Manufacturer:              Soroc
  2. Terminal:                  Challenger Series
---------------------------------------------------------------------
```

SCREEN LAYOUT
  3. Number of rows: 24
  4. Number of columns: 80
  5. Top Row: 1
  6. Left Column: 1
  7. Printing in bottom right
     cause scroll?   YES

CURSOR ADDRESSING
  8. Lead-in sequence:
              ESC =
              1B 3D
  9. Row or column first: ROW
 10. Numeric form of row and column:
     BINARY
 11. Add offset to: Row: 1F
                          Col: 1F
 12. Separator sequence:

 13. End sequence:

 14. Cursor to top row, left column:
     ESC =   SP SP
     1B 3D   20 20
 15. 10th Row, 50th Column:
     ESC =   )   Q
     1B 3D   29 51
 16. Delay after positioning: 0
 17. Cursor home:
              ^^
              1E

ERASURE   DELAY
 18. Entire screen:
              ESC *   0
              1B 2A
 19. Cursor to end of screen:
              ESC Y   0
              1B 59
 20. Beginning of screen to cursor:

 21. Cursor to end of line:
              ESC T   0
              1B 54
 22. Beginning of line to cursor:

 23. Entire cursor line:

VIDEO ATTRIBUTES
                ON   OFF
 24. Blinking:
     ESC ^G   ESC ^D
     1B 07   1B 04
 25. Reverse video:
     ESC ^F   ESC ^D
     1B 06   1B 04
 26. Underline:
     ESC ^U   ESC ^D
     1B 15   1B 04
 27. High intensity:

 28. Half intensity:
     ESC)   ESC (
     1B 29   1B 28
 29. Attributes occupy position: YES
 30. Attributes cumulative: NO
 31. All attributes off:
              ESC ^D
              1B 04

CURSOR CONTROL KEYS
 32. Cursor up:
              ^K
              0B
 33. Cursor down:
              ^J
              0A
 34. Cursor right:
              ^L
              0C
 35. Cursor left:
              ^H
              08

CHARACTER SET
 36. Full upper and lower ASCII: YES
 37. Generate all control codes: YES
 38. Bell or tone sequence:
              ^G
              07

EMULATION
 39. Conform to ANSI X3.64?   YES
 40. Terminals Emulated:
     Televideo 925 (Challenger 525)
     Lear Siegler ADM1, 2, 3
       (Challenger 550)
     Tandum 6510 (Challenger 550)

          CONTINUED ====>

41. Information provided by:
    MANUFACTURER

42. PROGRAM FUNCTION KEYS
    1. ^A @   ^M
       01 40 0D

    2. ^A A   ^M
       01 41 0D

    3. ^A B   ^M
       01 42 0D

    4. ^A C   ^M
       01 43 0D

    5. ^A D   ^M
       01 44 0D

    6. ^A E   ^M
       01 45 0D

    7. ^A F   ^M
       01 46 0D

    8. ^A G   ^M
       01 47 0D

    9. ^A H   ^M
       01 48 0D

    10. ^A I   ^M
        01 49 0D

    11. ^A J   ^M
        01 4A 0D

    12. ^A K   ^M
        01 4B 0D

    13. ^A L   ^M
        01 4C 0D

    14. ^A M   ^M
        01 4D 0D

    15. ^A N   ^M
        01 4E 0D

    16. ^A O   ^M
        01 4F 0D

NOTES
30. Terminal has combination
    attribute codes.

```
--------------------------------------------------------------------------
1. Manufacturer:                    Tab Products
2. Terminal:                        TAB 132/15
--------------------------------------------------------------------------
```

SCREEN LAYOUT   VIDEO ATTRIBUTES
3. Number of rows: 24   ON   OFF
4. Number of columns: 80   24. Blinking:
5. Top Row: 1   ESC [5   m   ESC [m
6. Left Column: 1   1B   5B 35   6D   1B   5B   6D
7. Printing in bottom right   25. Reverse video:
   cause scroll?   YES   ESC [7   m   ESC [m
                                      1B   5B 37   6D   1B   5B   6D
CURSOR ADDRESSING   26. Underline:
8. Lead-in sequence: ESC [4   m   ESC [m
         ESC [1B   5B 34   6D   1B   5B   6D
         1B   5B   27. High intensity:
9. Row or column first: ROW   ESC [1   m   ESC [m
10. Numeric form of row and column: 1B   5B 31   6D   1B   5B   6D
    VARIABLE-LENGTH ASCII   28. Half intensity:
11. Add offset to: Row: 0
                         Col: 0
12. Separator sequence: 29. Attributes occupy position: NO
         ;   30. Attributes cumulative: YES
         3B   31. All attributes off:
13. End sequence: ESC [m
         H   1B   5B   6D
         48
14. Cursor to top row, left column: CURSOR CONTROL KEYS
ESC [1   ;   1   H   32. Cursor up:
1B   5B 31   3B   31 48   ESC [A
15. 10th Row, 50th Column: 1B   5B   41
ESC [1   0   ;   5   0   H   33. Cursor down:
1B   5B 31   30   3B   35   30 48   ESC [B
16. Delay after positioning: 0   1B   5B   42
17. Cursor home: 34. Cursor right:
         ESC [H   ESC [C
         1B   5B 48   1B   5B   43
                                      35. Cursor left:
ERASURE   DELAY   ESC [D
18. Entire screen: 1B   5B   44
         ESC [2   J   0
         1B   5B 32   4A   CHARACTER SET
19. Cursor to end of screen: 36. Full upper and lower ASCII: YES
         ESC [J   0   37. Generate all control codes: YES
         1B   5B 4A   38. Bell or tone sequence:
20. Beginning of screen to cursor: ^G
         ESC [1   J   0   07
         1B   5B 31   4A
21. Cursor to end of line: EMULATION
         ESC [K   0   39. Conform to ANSI X3.64?   YES
         1B   5B 4B   40. Terminals Emulated:
22. Beginning of line to cursor: DEC VT100, VT132, VT52
         ESC [1   K   0
         1B   5B 31   4B
23. Entire cursor line:
         ESC [2   K   0
         1B   5B 32   4B

                              245   CONTINUED ====>
```

CONTINUED ====>
```

41. Information provided by:
    MANUFACTURER

42. PROGRAM FUNCTION KEYS   NOTES
    1. ESC O   P   4. Or 132.
       1B   4F   50   42. 14 user-programmable function
                                       keys.
    2. ESC O   Q   8 host-programmable function keys.
       1B   4F   51

    3. ESC O   R
       1B   4F   52

    4. ESC O   S
       1B   4F   53

    5.

    6.

    7.

    8.

    9.

   10.

   11.

   12.

   13.

   14.

   15.

   16.

```
------------------------------------------------------------------------
1. Manufacturer:                    Tandberg Data, Inc.
2. Terminal:                        TDV 2220
------------------------------------------------------------------------
```

SCREEN LAYOUT
3. Number of rows: 25
4. Number of columns: 80
5. Top Row: 1
6. Left Column: 1
7. Printing in bottom right
   cause scroll?   PROG

CURSOR ADDRESSING
8. Lead-in sequence:
                ESC [
                1B   5B
9. Row or column first: ROW
10. Numeric form of row and column:
    VARIABLE-LENGTH ASCII
11. Add offset to: Row: 0
                          Col: 0
12. Separator sequence:
                ;
                3B
13. End sequence:
                H
                48
14. Cursor to top row, left column:
ESC [1   ;   1   H
1B   5B   31   3B   31   48
15. 10th Row, 50th Column:
ESC [1   0   ;   5   0   H
1B   5B   31   30   3B   35   30   48
16. Delay after positioning: 0
17. Cursor home:
                ESC [H
                1B   5B   48

ERASURE   DELAY
18. Entire screen:
         ESC [2   J   0
         1B   5B   32   4A
19. Cursor to end of screen:
         ESC [J   0
         1B   5B   4A
20. Beginning of screen to cursor:
         ESC [1   J   0
         1B   5B   31   4A
21. Cursor to end of line:
         ESC [K   0
         1B   5B   4B
22. Beginning of line to cursor:
         ESC [1   K   0
         1B   5B   31   4B
23. Entire cursor line:
         ESC [2   K   0
         1B   5B   32   4B

VIDEO ATTRIBUTES
            ON   OFF
24. Blinking:
    ESC [5   m   ESC [m
    1B   5B   35   6D   1B   5B   6D
25. Reverse video:
    ESC [7   m   ESC [m
    1B   5B   37   6D   1B   5B   6D
26. Underline:
    ESC [4   m   ESC [m
    1B   5B   34   6D   1B   5B   6D
27. High intensity:

28. Half intensity:
    ESC [2   m   ESC [m
    1B   5B   32   6D   1B   5B   6D
29. Attributes occupy position: NO
30. Attributes cumulative: YES
31. All attributes off:
                ESC [m
                1B   5B   6D

CURSOR CONTROL KEYS
32. Cursor up:
                ESC [A
                1B   5B   41
33. Cursor down:
                ESC [B
                1B   5B   42
34. Cursor right:
                ESC [C
                1B   5B   43
35. Cursor left:
                ESC [D
                1B   5B   44

CHARACTER SET
36. Full upper and lower ASCII: YES
37. Generate all control codes: YES
38. Bell or tone sequence:
                ^G
                07

EMULATION
39. Conform to ANSI X3.64?   YES
40. Terminals Emulated:

CONTINUED ====>

41. Information provided by:
    MANUFACTURER

42. PROGRAM FUNCTION KEYS   NOTES
    1.   42. All function keys programmable.

    2.

    3.

    4.

    5.

    6.

    7.

    8.

    9.

   10.

   11.

   12.

   13.

   14.

   15.

   16.

```
--------------------------------------------------------------------------
1. Manufacturer:                    TEC Inc.
2. Terminal:                        ET 80B
--------------------------------------------------------------------------
```

SCREEN LAYOUT   VIDEO ATTRIBUTES
3. Number of rows: 24   ON   OFF
4. Number of columns: 80   24. Blinking:
5. Top Row: 1   ESC [5   m   ESC [m
6. Left Column: 1   1B 5B 35 6D   1B 5B 6D
7. Printing in bottom right   25. Reverse video:
   cause scroll?   PROG   ESC [7   m   ESC [m
                                       1B 5B 37 6D   1B 5B 6D
CURSOR ADDRESSING   26. Underline:
8. Lead-in sequence: ESC [4   m   ESC [m
        ESC [1B 5B 34 6D   1B 5B 6D
        1B 5B   27. High intensity:
9. Row or column first: ROW
10. Numeric form of row and column:
    VARIABLE-LENGTH ASCII   28. Half intensity:
11. Add offset to: Row: 0
                         Col: 0
12. Separator sequence: 29. Attributes occupy position: NO
        ;   30. Attributes cumulative: YES
        3B   31. All attributes off:
13. End sequence: ESC [m
        H   1B 5B 6D
        48
14. Cursor to top row, left column: CURSOR CONTROL KEYS
ESC [1   ;   1   H   32. Cursor up:
1B 5B 31 3B 31 48   ESC [A
15. 10th Row, 50th Column: 1B 5B 41
ESC [1   0   ;   5   0   H   33. Cursor down:
1B 5B 31 30 3B 35 30 48   ESC [B
16. Delay after positioning: 0   1B 5B 42
17. Cursor home: 34. Cursor right:
          ESC [H   ESC [C
          1B 5B 48   1B 5B 43
                                       35. Cursor left:
ERASURE   DELAY   ESC [D
18. Entire screen: 1B 5B 44
        ESC [2   J   0
        1B 5B 32 4A   CHARACTER SET
19. Cursor to end of screen: 36. Full upper and lower ASCII: YES
        ESC [J   0   37. Generate all control codes: YES
        1B 5B 4A   38. Bell or tone sequence:
20. Beginning of screen to cursor: ^G
        ESC [1   J   0   07
        1B 5B 31 4A
21. Cursor to end of line: EMULATION
        ESC [K   0   39. Conform to ANSI X3.64?   YES
        1B 5B 4B   40. Terminals Emulated:
22. Beginning of line to cursor:
        ESC [1   K   0
        1B 5B 31 4B
23. Entire cursor line:
        ESC [2   K   0
        1B 5B 32 4B

                              249   CONTINUED ====>

```
------------------------------------------------------------------------
      Manufacturer:                    TEC Inc.
      Terminal:                        ET 80B
------------------------------------------------------------------------
```

41. Information provided by:
    MANUFACTURER

42. PROGRAM FUNCTION KEYS   NOTES
    1.   4. Or 132.
                                    42. F1-F15 programmable to 17 chars.
                                        F16 programmable to 60 chars.
    2.

    3.

    4.

    5.

    6.

    7.

    8.

    9.

    10.

    11.

    12.

    13.

    14.

    15.

    16.

```
--------------------------------------------------------------------------
  1. Manufacturer:                    Tektronix
  2. Terminal:                        4105, 4107, 4109 (ANSI mode)
--------------------------------------------------------------------------
```

SCREEN LAYOUT
3. Number of rows: 30
4. Number of columns: 80
5. Top Row: 1
6. Left Column: 1
7. Printing in bottom right
   cause scroll?   NO

CURSOR ADDRESSING
8. Lead-in sequence:
          ESC [
          1B 5B
9. Row or column first: ROW
10. Numeric form of row and column:
    VARIABLE-LENGTH ASCII
11. Add offset to: Row: 0
                          Col: 0
12. Separator sequence:
          ;
          3B
13. End sequence:
          H
          48
14. Cursor to top row, left column:
ESC [1   ;   1   H
1B 5B 31 3B 31 48
15. 10th Row, 50th Column:
ESC [1   0   ;   5   0   H
1B 5B 31 30 3B 35 30 48
16. Delay after positioning: 0
17. Cursor home:
          ESC [H
          1B 5B 48

ERASURE   DELAY
18. Entire screen:
          ESC [2   J   0
          1B 5B 32 4A
19. Cursor to end of screen:
          ESC [J   0
          1B 5B 4A
20. Beginning of screen to cursor:
          ESC [1   J   0
          1B 5B 31 4A
21. Cursor to end of line:
          ESC [K   0
          1B 5B 4B
22. Beginning of line to cursor:
          ESC [1   K   0
          1B 5B 31 4B
23. Entire cursor line:
          ESC [2   K   0
          1B 5B 32 4B

VIDEO ATTRIBUTES
          ON   OFF
24. Blinking:
    ESC [5   m   ESC [m
    1B 5B 35 6D   1B 5B 6D
25. Reverse video:
    ESC [7   m   ESC [m
    1B 5B 37 6D   1B 5B 6D
26. Underline:
    ESC [4   m   ESC [m
    1B 5B 34 6D   1B 5B 6D
27. High intensity:
    ESC [1   m   ESC [m
    1B 5B 31 6D   1B 5B 6D
28. Half intensity:
    ESC [3   m   ESC [m
    1B 5B 33 6D   1B 5B 6D
29. Attributes occupy position: NO
30. Attributes cumulative: YES
31. All attributes off:
          ESC [m
          1B 5B 6D

CURSOR CONTROL KEYS
32. Cursor up:
          ESC [A
          1B 5B 41
33. Cursor down:
          ESC [B
          1B 5B 42
34. Cursor right:
          ESC [C
          1B 5B 43
35. Cursor left:
          ESC [D
          1B 5B 44

CHARACTER SET
36. Full upper and lower ASCII: YES
37. Generate all control codes: YES
38. Bell or tone sequence:
          ^G
          07

EMULATION
39. Conform to ANSI X3.64?   YES
40. Terminals Emulated:
    DEC VT100
    DEC VT52

41. Information provided by:
    MANUFACTURER

42. PROGRAM FUNCTION KEYS   NOTES
    1.   3. 30 for 4105,
                                     32 for 4107, 4109.
                                  4. Or 132 (all models).
    2.   42. All keys including function keys
                                     are definable by either the host
                                     or operator.
    3.

    4.

    5.

    6.

    7.

    8.

    9.

   10.

   11.

   12.

   13.

   14.

   15.

   16.

---

1. Manufacturer:	Teleray
2. Terminal:	Model 100

SCREEN LAYOUT
3. Number of rows: 24
4. Number of columns: 132
5. Top Row: 1
6. Left Column: 1
7. Printing in bottom right
   cause scroll? NO

CURSOR ADDRESSING
8. Lead-in sequence:
   ESC [
   1B 5B
9. Row or column first: ROW
10. Numeric form of row and column:
    VARIABLE-LENGTH ASCII
11. Add offset to: Row: 0
                        Col: 0
12. Separator sequence:
    ;
    3B
13. End sequence:
    H
    48
14. Cursor to top row, left column:
    ESC [1   ;   1   H
    1B 5B 31 3B 31 48
15. 10th Row, 50th Column:
    ESC [1   0   ;   5   0   H
    1B 5B 31 30 3B 35 30 48
16. Delay after positioning: 0
17. Cursor home:
    ESC [H
    1B 5B 48

ERASURE   DELAY
18. Entire screen:
    ESC [2   J   0
    1B 5B 32 4A
19. Cursor to end of screen:
    ESC [J   0
    1B 5B 4A
20. Beginning of screen to cursor:
    ESC [1   J   0
    1B 5B 31 4A
21. Cursor to end of line:
    ESC [K   0
    1B 5B 4B
22. Beginning of line to cursor:
    ESC [1   K   0
    1B 5B 31 4B
23. Entire cursor line:
    ESC [2   K   0
    1B 5B 32 4B

VIDEO ATTRIBUTES
                ON   OFF
24. Blinking:
    ESC [5   m   ESC [m
    1B 5B 35 6D   1B 5B   6D
25. Reverse video:
    ESC [7   m   ESC [m
    1B 5B 37 6D   1B 5B   6D
26. Underline:
    ESC [4   m   ESC [m
    1B 5B 34 6D   1B 5B   6D
27. High intensity:
    ESC [1   m   ESC [m
    1B 5B 31 6D   1B 5B   6D
28. Half intensity:

29. Attributes occupy position: NO
30. Attributes cumulative: YES
31. All attributes off:
    ESC [m
    1B 5B   6D

CURSOR CONTROL KEYS
32. Cursor up:
    ESC [A
    1B 5B 41
33. Cursor down:
    ESC [B
    1B 5B 42
34. Cursor right:
    ESC [C
    1B 5B 43
35. Cursor left:
    ESC [D
    1B 5B 44

CHARACTER SET
36. Full upper and lower ASCII: YES
37. Generate all control codes: YES
38. Bell or tone sequence:
    ^G
    07

EMULATION
39. Conform to ANSI X3.64?   YES
40. Terminals Emulated:
    DEC VT100, VT101, VT131, VT132,
    etc., VT52

253

CONTINUED ====>

41. Information provided by:
    MANUFACTURER

42. PROGRAM FUNCTION KEYS   NOTES
  1.   13. Or f (66H).
                                   42. All function keys user-defined.

  2.

  3.

  4.

  5.

  6.

  7.

  8.

  9.

 10.

 11.

 12.

 13.

 14.

 15.

 16.

| 1. Manufacturer: | Teleray |
| 2. Terminal: | Model 16 |

SCREEN LAYOUT
3. Number of rows: 24
4. Number of columns: 80
5. Top Row: 1
6. Left Column: 1
7. Printing in bottom right
   cause scroll? PROG

CURSOR ADDRESSING
8. Lead-in sequence:
   ESC [
   1B 5B
9. Row or column first: ROW
10. Numeric form of row and column:
    VARIABLE-LENGTH ASCII
11. Add offset to: Row: 0
                    Col: 0
12. Separator sequence:
    ;
    3B
13. End sequence:
    H
    48
14. Cursor to top row, left column:
    ESC [1 ; 1 H
    1B 5B 31 3B 31 48
15. 10th Row, 50th Column:
    ESC [1 0 ; 5 0 H
    1B 5B 31 30 3B 35 30 48
16. Delay after positioning: 0
17. Cursor home:
    ESC [H
    1B 5B 48

ERASURE   DELAY
18. Entire screen:
    ESC [2 J   0
    1B 5B 32 4A
19. Cursor to end of screen:
    ESC [J   0
    1B 5B 4A
20. Beginning of screen to cursor:
    ESC [1 J   0
    1B 5B 31 4A
21. Cursor to end of line:
    ESC [K   0
    1B 5B 4B
22. Beginning of line to cursor:
    ESC [1 K   0
    1B 5B 31 4B
23. Entire cursor line:
    ESC [2 K   0
    1B 5B 32 4B

VIDEO ATTRIBUTES
            ON   OFF
24. Blinking:
    ESC [5 m   ESC [m
    1B 5B 35 6D   1B 5B 6D
25. Reverse video:
    ESC [7 m   ESC [m
    1B 5B 37 6D   1B 5B 6D
26. Underline:
    ESC [4 m   ESC [m
    1B 5B 34 6D   1B 5B 6D
27. High intensity:

28. Half intensity:
    ESC [2 m   ESC [m
    1B 5B 32 6D   1B 5B 6D
29. Attributes occupy position: NO
30. Attributes cumulative: YES
31. All attributes off:
    ESC [m
    1B 5B 6D

CURSOR CONTROL KEYS
32. Cursor up:
    ESC [A
    1B 5B 41
33. Cursor down:
    ESC [B
    1B 5B 42
34. Cursor right:
    ESC [C
    1B 5B 43
35. Cursor left:
    ESC [D
    1B 5B 44

CHARACTER SET
36. Full upper and lower ASCII: YES
37. Generate all control codes: YES
38. Bell or tone sequence:
    ^G
    07

EMULATION
39. Conform to ANSI X3.64? YES
40. Terminals Emulated:
    DEC VT100 family.

CONTINUED ====>

```
-----------------------------------------------------------------------
     Manufacturer:                    Teleray
     Terminal:                        Model 16
-----------------------------------------------------------------------
```

41. Information provided by:
    MANUFACTURER

42. PROGRAM FUNCTION KEYS   NOTES
    1.   3. 24 to 555.
                                       4. 80 to 255.
                                      13. Or f (66H).
    2.   42. All function keys user-defined.

    3.

    4.

    5.

    6.

    7.

    8.

    9.

   10.

   11.

   12.

   13.

   14.

   15.

   16.

```
--------------------------------------------------------------------------
  1. Manufacturer:                    Teleray
  2. Terminal:                        Model 7
--------------------------------------------------------------------------
```

SCREEN LAYOUT
  3. Number of rows: 24
  4. Number of columns: 80
  5. Top Row: 1
  6. Left Column: 1
  7. Printing in bottom right
     cause scroll?   PROG

CURSOR ADDRESSING
  8. Lead-in sequence:
             ESC [
             1B   5B
  9. Row or column first: ROW
 10. Numeric form of row and column:
     VARIABLE-LENGTH ASCII
 11. Add offset to: Row: 0
                             Col: 0
 12. Separator sequence:
             ;
             3B
 13. End sequence:
             H
             48
 14. Cursor to top row, left column:
     ESC [1   ;   1   H
     1B   5B 31 3B 31 48
 15. 10th Row, 50th Column:
     ESC [1   0   ;   5   0   H
     1B   5B 31 30 3B 35 30 48
 16. Delay after positioning: 0
 17. Cursor home:
             ESC [H
             1B   5B 48

ERASURE   DELAY
 18. Entire screen:
         ESC [2   J   0
         1B   5B 32 4A
 19. Cursor to end of screen:
         ESC [J   0
         1B   5B 4A
 20. Beginning of screen to cursor:
         ESC [1   J   0
         1B   5B 31 4A
 21. Cursor to end of line:
         ESC [K   0
         1B   5B 4B
 22. Beginning of line to cursor:
         ESC [1   K   0
         1B   5B 31 4B
 23. Entire cursor line:
         ESC [2   K   0
         1B   5B 32 4B

VIDEO ATTRIBUTES
          ON   OFF
 24. Blinking:
     ESC [5   m   ESC [m
     1B   5B 35 6D   1B   5B   6D
 25. Reverse video:
     ESC [7   m   ESC [m
     1B   5B 37 6D   1B   5B   6D
 26. Underline:
     ESC [4   m   ESC [m
     1B   5B 34 6D   1B   5B   6D
 27. High intensity:

 28. Half intensity:
     ESC [2   m   ESC [m
     1B   5B 32 6D   1B   5B   6D
 29. Attributes occupy position: NO
 30. Attributes cumulative: YES
 31. All attributes off:
             ESC [m
             1B   5B   6D

CURSOR CONTROL KEYS
 32. Cursor up:
             ESC [A
             1B   5B 41
 33. Cursor down:
             ESC [B
             1B   5B 42
 34. Cursor right:
             ESC [C
             1B   5B 43
 35. Cursor left:
             ESC [D
             1B   5B 44

CHARACTER SET
 36. Full upper and lower ASCII: YES
 37. Generate all control codes: YES
 38. Bell or tone sequence:
             ^G
             07

EMULATION
 39. Conform to ANSI X3.64?   YES
 40. Terminals Emulated:
     All ASCII asychronous, non-
     polled. Protocol is user
     definable.

257   CONTINUED ====>

```
--------------------------------------------------------------------------
         Manufacturer:                   Teleray
         Terminal:                       Model 7
--------------------------------------------------------------------------
```

41. Information provided by:
    MANUFACTURER

42. PROGRAM FUNCTION KEYS   NOTES
    1.   3. 24 to 555.
                                     4. 80 to 255.
                                    13. Or f (66H).
    2.   42. All function keys user-defined.

                                    All sequences may be user
    3.   programmed to be the characters/
                                    sequences of his choice.

    4.

    5.

    6.

    7.

    8.

    9.

   10.

   11.

   12.

   13.

   14.

   15.

   16.

```
--------------------------------------------------------------------------
1. Manufacturer:                      Teletype Corporation
2. Terminal:                          5410
--------------------------------------------------------------------------
```

SCREEN LAYOUT
3. Number of rows: 24
4. Number of columns: 80
5. Top Row: 1
6. Left Column: 1
7. Printing in bottom right
   cause scroll?   YES

CURSOR ADDRESSING
8. Lead-in sequence:
       ESC [
       1B 5B
9. Row or column first: ROW
10. Numeric form of row and column:
    VARIABLE-LENGTH ASCII
11. Add offset to: Row: 0
                        Col: 0
12. Separator sequence:
       ;
       3B
13. End sequence:
       H
       48
14. Cursor to top row, left column:
ESC [1   ;   1   H
1B 5B 31 3B 31 48
15. 10th Row, 50th Column:
ESC [1   0   ;   5   0   H
1B 5B 31 30 3B 35 30 48
16. Delay after positioning: 0
17. Cursor home:
       ESC [H
       1B 5B 48

ERASURE   DELAY
18. Entire screen:
       ESC [2   J   0
       1B 5B 32 4A
19. Cursor to end of screen:
       ESC [J   0
       1B 5B 4A
20. Beginning of screen to cursor:
       ESC [1   J   0
       1B 5B 31 4A
21. Cursor to end of line:
       ESC [K   0
       1B 5B 4B
22. Beginning of line to cursor:
       ESC [1   K   0
       1B 5B 31 4B
23. Entire cursor line:
       ESC [2   K   0
       1B 5B 32 4B

VIDEO ATTRIBUTES
     ON   OFF
24. Blinking:
    ESC [5   m   ESC [m
    1B 5B 35 6D   1B 5B   6D
25. Reverse video:
    ESC [7   m   ESC [m
    1B 5B 37 6D   1B 5B   6D
26. Underline:
    ESC [4   m   ESC [m
    1B 5B 34 6D   1B 5B   6D
27. High intensity:

28. Half intensity:
    ESC [2   m
    1B 5B 32 6D
29. Attributes occupy position: NO
30. Attributes cumulative: YES
31. All attributes off:
            ESC [m
            1B 5B   6D

CURSOR CONTROL KEYS
32. Cursor up:
            ESC [A
            1B 5B 41
33. Cursor down:
            ESC [B
            1B 5B 42
34. Cursor right:
            ESC [C
            1B 5B 43
35. Cursor left:
            ESC [D
            1B 5B 44

CHARACTER SET
36. Full upper and lower ASCII: YES
37. Generate all control codes: YES
38. Bell or tone sequence:
            ^G
            07

EMULATION
39. Conform to ANSI X3.64?   YES
40. Terminals Emulated:

CONTINUED ====>

41. Information provided by:
    MANUFACTURER

42. PROGRAM FUNCTION KEYS   NOTES
    1.   3. 24 text lines plus host addressable
                                         25th line. Lines 26 and 27 contain
                                         downloadable and user-programmable
    2.   labels for PF keys.
                                      4. Or 132.
                                     36. 5 resident character sets:
    3.   United States ASCII
                                         United Kingdom
                                         Line Drawing Graphics
    4.   Securities Industry
                                         Mosaics
                                     42. 16 programmable function keys,
    5.   accessible 8 at a time.

    6.

    7.

    8.

    9.

    10.

    11.

    12.

    13.

    14.

    15.

    16.

---
1. Manufacturer: Teletype Corporation
2. Terminal: 5420

SCREEN LAYOUT   VIDEO ATTRIBUTES
3. Number of rows: 24   ON   OFF
4. Number of columns: 80   24. Blinking:
5. Top Row: 1   ESC [5   m   ESC [m
6. Left Column: 1   1B   5B   35   6D   1B   5B   6D
7. Printing in bottom right   25. Reverse video:
   cause scroll?   PROG   ESC [7   m   ESC [m
                                          1B   5B   37   6D   1B   5B   6D
CURSOR ADDRESSING   26. Underline:
8. Lead-in sequence: ESC [4   m   ESC [m
        ESC [1B   5B   34   6D   1B   5B   6D
        1B   5B   27. High intensity:
9. Row or column first: ROW
10. Numeric form of row and column:
    VARIABLE-LENGTH ASCII   28. Half intensity:
11. Add offset to: Row: 0   ESC [2   m
                         Col: 0   1B   5B   32   6D
12. Separator sequence: 29. Attributes occupy position: NO
        ;   30. Attributes cumulative: YES
        3B   31. All attributes off:
13. End sequence: ESC [m
        H   1B   5B   6D
        48
14. Cursor to top row, left column: CURSOR CONTROL KEYS
ESC [1   ;   1   H   32. Cursor up:
1B   5B   31   3B   31   48   ESC [A
15. 10th Row, 50th Column: 1B   5B   41
ESC [1   0   ;   5   0   H   33. Cursor down:
1B   5B   31   30   3B   35   30   48   ESC [B
16. Delay after positioning: 0   1B   5B   42
17. Cursor home: 34. Cursor right:
        ESC [H   ESC [C
        1B   5B   48   1B   5B   43
                                          35. Cursor left:
ERASURE   DELAY   ESC [D
18. Entire screen: 1B   5B   44
        ESC [2   J   0
        1B   5B   32   4A   CHARACTER SET
19. Cursor to end of screen: 36. Full upper and lower ASCII: YES
        ESC [J   0   37. Generate all control codes: YES
        1B   5B   4A   38. Bell or tone sequence:
20. Beginning of screen to cursor: ^G
        ESC [1   J   0   07
        1B   5B   31   4A
21. Cursor to end of line: EMULATION
        ESC [K   0   39. Conform to ANSI X3.64?   YES
        1B   5B   4B   40. Terminals Emulated:
22. Beginning of line to cursor:
        ESC [1   K   0
        1B   5B   31   4B
23. Entire cursor line:
        ESC [2   K   0
        1B   5B   32   4B

261   CONTINUED ====>

Manufacturer: Teletype Corporation
Terminal: 5420

41. Information provided by:
    MANUFACTURER

42. PROGRAM FUNCTION KEYS
    1.

    2.

    3.

    4.

    5.

    6.

    7.

    8.

    9.

    10.

    11.

    12.

    13.

    14.

    15.

    16.

NOTES
3. 24 text lines plus host addressable 25th line. Lines 26 and 27 contain downloadable and user-programmable labels for PF keys.
4. Or 132.
36. Plus 96 graphics characters.
42. 16 programmable function keys, accessible 8 at a time.

```
-----------------------------------------------------------------
1. Manufacturer:                     Televideo
2. Terminal:                         910
-----------------------------------------------------------------

SCREEN LAYOUT                        VIDEO ATTRIBUTES
3. Number of rows:          24          ON                 OFF
4. Number of columns:       80       24. Blinking:
5. Top Row:                  1       ESC G    2          ESC G    0
6. Left Column:              1       1B   47  32         1B   47  30
7. Printing in bottom right          25. Reverse video:
   cause scroll?           YES       ESC G    4          ESC G    0
                                     1B   47  34         1B   47  30
CURSOR ADDRESSING                    26. Underline:
8. Lead-in sequence:                 ESC G    8          ESC G    0
            ESC =                    1B   47  38         1B   47  30
            1B   3D                  27. High intensity:
9. Row or column first:     ROW      ESC G    0          ESC G    0
10. Numeric form of row and column:  1B   47  30         1B   47  30
    BINARY                           28. Half intensity:
11. Add offset to:      Row:  1F     ESC )               ESC (
                        Col:  1F     1B   29             1B   28
12. Separator sequence:              29. Attributes occupy position: YES
                                     30. Attributes cumulative:      NO
                                     31. All attributes off:
13. End sequence:                               ESC G    0
                                                1B   47  30

14. Cursor to top row, left column:  CURSOR CONTROL KEYS
ESC =    SP   SP                     32. Cursor up:
1B   3D  20   20                                ^K
15. 10th Row, 50th Column:                      0B
ESC =    )    Q                      33. Cursor down:
1B   3D  29   51                                ^J
16. Delay after positioning:    0               0A
17. Cursor home:                     34. Cursor right:
          ^^                                    ^L
          1E                                    0C
                                     35. Cursor left:
ERASURE                    DELAY                ^H
18. Entire screen:                              08
          ^Z                0
          1A                         CHARACTER SET
19. Cursor to end of screen:         36. Full upper and lower ASCII: YES
          ESC Y             0        37. Generate all control codes: YES
          1B   59                    38. Bell or tone sequence:
20. Beginning of screen to cursor:              ^G
                                                07

21. Cursor to end of line:           EMULATION
          ESC T             0        39. Conform to ANSI X3.64?      NO
          1B   54                    40. Terminals Emulated:
22. Beginning of line to cursor:         ADDS Regent 25
                                         Lear Siegler ADM 3A/5
                                         Hazeltine 1410
23. Entire cursor line:
          ^M   ESC T        0
          0D   1B   54
```

CONTINUED ====>

41. Information provided by:
    MANUFACTURER

42. PROGRAM FUNCTION KEYS   NOTES
    1.

    2.

    3.

    4.

    5.

    6.

    7.

    8.

    9.

   10.

   11.

   12.

   13.

   14.

   15.

   16.

```
--------------------------------------------------------------------------
1. Manufacturer:                      Televideo
2. Terminal:                          910+
--------------------------------------------------------------------------
```

SCREEN LAYOUT
3. Number of rows: 24
4. Number of columns: 80
5. Top Row: 1
6. Left Column: 1
7. Printing in bottom right
   cause scroll?   YES

CURSOR ADDRESSING
8. Lead-in sequence:
                    ESC =
                    1B   3D
9. Row or column first: ROW
10. Numeric form of row and column:
    BINARY
11. Add offset to: Row: 1F
                            Col: 1F
12. Separator sequence:

13. End sequence:

14. Cursor to top row, left column:
ESC =   SP   SP
1B   3D 20   20
15. 10th Row, 50th Column:
ESC =   )   Q
1B   3D 29   51
16. Delay after positioning: 0
17. Cursor home:
              ^^
              1E

ERASURE   DELAY
18. Entire screen:
         ^Z   0
         1A
19. Cursor to end of screen:
         ESC Y   0
         1B   59
20. Beginning of screen to cursor:

21. Cursor to end of line:
         ESC T   0
         1B   54
22. Beginning of line to cursor:

23. Entire cursor line:
         ^M ESC T   0
         0D 1B   54

VIDEO ATTRIBUTES
         ON   OFF
24. Blinking:
ESC G   2   ESC G   0
1B   47 32   1B   47 30
25. Reverse video:
ESC G   4   ESC G   0
1B   47 34   1B   47 30
26. Underline:
ESC G   8   ESC G   0
1B   47 38   1B   47 30
27. High intensity:
ESC G   0   ESC G   0
1B   47 30   1B   47 30
28. Half intensity:
ESC)   ESC (
1B   29   1B   28
29. Attributes occupy position: YES
30. Attributes cumulative: NO
31. All attributes off:
              ESC G   0
              1B   47 30

CURSOR CONTROL KEYS
32. Cursor up:
              ^K
              0B
33. Cursor down:
              ^J
              0A
34. Cursor right:
              ^L
              0C
35. Cursor left:
              ^H
              08

CHARACTER SET
36. Full upper and lower ASCII: YES
37. Generate all control codes: YES
38. Bell or tone sequence:
              ^G
              07

EMULATION
39. Conform to ANSI X3.64?   NO
40. Terminals Emulated:

CONTINUED ====>

41. Information provided by:
    MANUFACTURER

42. PROGRAM FUNCTION KEYS   NOTES
  1.

  2.

  3.

  4.

  5.

  6.

  7.

  8.

  9.

 10.

 11.

 12.

 13.

 14.

 15.

 16.

---
1. Manufacturer: Televideo
2. Terminal: 914

SCREEN LAYOUT   VIDEO ATTRIBUTES
3. Number of rows: 24   ON   OFF
4. Number of columns: 80   24. Blinking:
5. Top Row: 1   ESC G   2   ESC G   0
6. Left Column: 1   1B   47   32   1B   47   30
7. Printing in bottom right   25. Reverse video:
   cause scroll?   YES   ESC G   4   ESC G   0
                                     1B   47   34   1B   47   30
CURSOR ADDRESSING   26. Underline:
8. Lead-in sequence: ESC G   8   ESC G   0
            ESC =   1B   47   38   1B   47   30
            1B   3D   27. High intensity:
9. Row or column first: ROW   ESC G   0   ESC G   0
10. Numeric form of row and column: 1B   47   30   1B   47   30
    BINARY   28. Half intensity:
11. Add offset to: Row: 1F   ESC)   ESC (
                       Col: 1F   1B   29   1B   28
12. Separator sequence: 29. Attributes occupy position: YES
                                     30. Attributes cumulative: NO
                                     31. All attributes off:
13. End sequence: ESC G   0
                                                1B   47   30

14. Cursor to top row, left column: CURSOR CONTROL KEYS
ESC =   SP   SP   32. Cursor up:
1B   3D   20   20   ^K
15. 10th Row, 50th Column: 0B
ESC =   )   Q   33. Cursor down:
1B   3D   29   51   ^J
16. Delay after positioning: 0   0A
17. Cursor home: 34. Cursor right:
            ^^   ^L
            1E   0C
                                     35. Cursor left:
ERASURE   DELAY   ^H
18. Entire screen: 08
            ^Z   0
            1A   CHARACTER SET
19. Cursor to end of screen: 36. Full upper and lower ASCII: YES
            ESC Y   0   37. Generate all control codes: YES
            1B   59   38. Bell or tone sequence:
20. Beginning of screen to cursor: ^G
                                                07

21. Cursor to end of line: EMULATION
            ESC T   0   39. Conform to ANSI X3.64?   NO
            1B   54   40. Terminals Emulated:
22. Beginning of line to cursor: ADDS Viewpoint A-2

23. Entire cursor line:
            ^M   ESC T   0
            0D   1B   54

```
-------------------------------------------------------------------------
        Manufacturer:                Televideo
        Terminal:                    914
-------------------------------------------------------------------------
```

41. Information provided by:
    MANUFACTURER

42. PROGRAM FUNCTION KEYS   NOTES
    1. ^A @   ^M
       01 40 0D

    2. ^A A   ^M
       01 41 0D

    3. ^A B   ^M
       01 42 0D

    4.

    5.

    6.

    7.

    8.

    9.

    10.

    11.

    12.

    13.

    14.

    15.

    16.

```
------------------------------------------------------------------------
1. Manufacturer:                    Televideo
2. Terminal:                        924
------------------------------------------------------------------------
```

SCREEN LAYOUT   VIDEO ATTRIBUTES
3. Number of rows: 24   ON   OFF
4. Number of columns: 80   24. Blinking:
5. Top Row: 1   ESC G   2   ESC G   0
6. Left Column: 1   1B 47 32   1B 47 30
7. Printing in bottom right   25. Reverse video:
   cause scroll?   YES   ESC G   4   ESC G   0
                                        1B 47 34   1B 47 30
CURSOR ADDRESSING   26. Underline:
8. Lead-in sequence: ESC G   8   ESC G   0
           ESC =   1B 47 38   1B 47 30
           1B 3D   27. High intensity:
9. Row or column first: ROW   ESC G   0   ESC G   0
10. Numeric form of row and column: 1B 47 30   1B 47 30
    BINARY   28. Half intensity:
11. Add offset to: Row: 1F   ESC)   ESC (
                      Col: 1F   1B 29   1B 28
12. Separator sequence: 29. Attributes occupy position: YES
                                     30. Attributes cumulative: NO
                                     31. All attributes off:
13. End sequence: ESC G   0
                                              1B 47 30

14. Cursor to top row, left column: CURSOR CONTROL KEYS
ESC =   SP SP   32. Cursor up:
1B 3D   20 20   ^K
15. 10th Row, 50th Column: 0B
ESC =   )   Q   33. Cursor down:
1B 3D   29 51   ^J
16. Delay after positioning: 0   0A
17. Cursor home: 34. Cursor right:
           ^^   ^L
           1E   0C
                                     35. Cursor left:
ERASURE   DELAY   ^H
18. Entire screen: 08
           ^Z   0
           1A   CHARACTER SET
19. Cursor to end of screen: 36. Full upper and lower ASCII: YES
           ESC Y   0   37. Generate all control codes: YES
           1B 59   38. Bell or tone sequence:
20. Beginning of screen to cursor: ^G
                                                  07

21. Cursor to end of line: EMULATION
           ESC T   0   39. Conform to ANSI X3.64?   NO
           1B 54   40. Terminals Emulated:
22. Beginning of line to cursor:

23. Entire cursor line:
       ^M ESC T   0
       0D 1B 54

                            269   CONTINUED ====>
```
```

```
--------------------------------------------------------------------------
     Manufacturer:                    Televideo
     Terminal:                        924
--------------------------------------------------------------------------
```

41. Information provided by:
    MANUFACTURER

42. PROGRAM FUNCTION KEYS   NOTES
    1. ^A @   ^M
       01 40 0D

    2. ^A A   ^M
       01 41 0D

    3. ^A B   ^M
       01 42 0D

    4. ^A C   ^M
       01 43 0D

    5. ^A D   ^M
       01 44 0D

    6. ^A E   ^M
       01 45 0D

    7. ^A F   ^M
       01 46 0D

    8. ^A G   ^M
       01 47 0D

    9. ^A H   ^M
       01 48 0D

   10. ^A I   ^M
       01 49 0D

   11. ^A J   ^M
       01 4A 0D

   12. ^A K   ^M
       01 4B 0D

   13. ^A L   ^M
       01 4C 0D

   14. ^A M   ^M
       01 4D 0D

   15. ^A N   ^M
       01 4E 0D

   16. ^A O   ^M
       01 4F 0D

```
------------------------------------------------------------------------
1. Manufacturer:              Televideo
2. Terminal:                  925
------------------------------------------------------------------------
```

SCREEN LAYOUT   VIDEO ATTRIBUTES
3. Number of rows: 24   ON   OFF
4. Number of columns: 80   24. Blinking:
5. Top Row: 1   ESC G   2   ESC G   0
6. Left Column: 1   1B   47 32   1B   47 30
7. Printing in bottom right   25. Reverse video:
   cause scroll?   YES   ESC G   4   ESC G   0
                                   1B   47 34   1B   47 30
CURSOR ADDRESSING   26. Underline:
8. Lead-in sequence: ESC G   8   ESC G   0
            ESC =   1B   47 38   1B   47 30
            1B   3D   27. High intensity:
9. Row or column first: ROW   ESC G   0   ESC G   0
10. Numeric form of row and column: 1B 47 30   1B   47 30
    BINARY   28. Half intensity:
11. Add offset to: Row: 1F   ESC)   ESC (
                        Col: 1F   1B   29   1B   28
12. Separator sequence: 29. Attributes occupy position: YES
                                   30. Attributes cumulative: NO
                                   31. All attributes off:
13. End sequence: ESC G   0
                                              1B   47 30

14. Cursor to top row, left column: CURSOR CONTROL KEYS
ESC =   SP SP   32. Cursor up:
1B   3D 20 20   ^K
15. 10th Row, 50th Column: 0B
ESC =   )   Q   33. Cursor down:
1B   3D 29 51   ^J
16. Delay after positioning: 0   0A
17. Cursor home: 34. Cursor right:
         ^^   ^L
         1E   0C
                                   35. Cursor left:
ERASURE   DELAY   ^H
18. Entire screen: 08
     ^Z   0
     1A   CHARACTER SET
19. Cursor to end of screen: 36. Full upper and lower ASCII: YES
     ESC Y   0   37. Generate all control codes: YES
     1B   59   38. Bell or tone sequence:
20. Beginning of screen to cursor: ^G
                                                07

21. Cursor to end of line: EMULATION
     ESC T   0   39. Conform to ANSI X3.64?   NO
     1B   54   40. Terminals Emulated:
22. Beginning of line to cursor: TVI 912/920

23. Entire cursor line:
     ^M ESC T   0
     0D 1B   54

```
-------------------------------------------------------------------------
      Manufacturer:                    Televideo
      Terminal:                        925
-------------------------------------------------------------------------
```

41. Information provided by:
    MANUFACTURER

42. PROGRAM FUNCTION KEYS   NOTES
    1. ^A   @   ^M
       01   40   0D

    2. ^A   A   ^M
       01   41   0D

    3. ^A   B   ^M
       01   42   0D

    4. ^A   C   ^M
       01   43   0D

    5. ^A   D   ^M
       01   44   0D

    6. ^A   E   ^M
       01   45   0D

    7. ^A   F   ^M
       01   46   0D

    8. ^A   G   ^M
       01   47   0D

    9. ^A   H   ^M
       01   48   0D

   10. ^A   I   ^M
       01   49   0D

   11. ^A   J   ^M
       01   4A   0D

   12.

   13.

   14.

   15.

   16.

```
--------------------------------------------------------------------------------
  1. Manufacturer:                   Televideo
  2. Terminal:                       950
--------------------------------------------------------------------------------
```

SCREEN LAYOUT
  3. Number of rows: 24
  4. Number of columns: 80
  5. Top Row: 1
  6. Left Column: 1
  7. Printing in bottom right
     cause scroll?   YES

CURSOR ADDRESSING
  8. Lead-in sequence:
                ESC =
                1B 3D
  9. Row or column first: ROW
 10. Numeric form of row and column:
     BINARY
 11. Add offset to: Row: 1F
                          Col: 1F
 12. Separator sequence:

 13. End sequence:

 14. Cursor to top row, left column:
     ESC =   SP SP
     1B 3D   20 20
 15. 10th Row, 50th Column:
     ESC =   )   Q
     1B 3D   29 51
 16. Delay after positioning: 0
 17. Cursor home:
                ^^
                1E

ERASURE   DELAY
 18. Entire screen:
        ^Z   0
        1A
 19. Cursor to end of screen:
        ESC Y   0
        1B 59
 20. Beginning of screen to cursor:

 21. Cursor to end of line:
        ESC T   0
        1B 54
 22. Beginning of line to cursor:

 23. Entire cursor line:
        ^M ESC T   0
        0D 1B 54

VIDEO ATTRIBUTES
            ON   OFF
 24. Blinking:
     ESC G   2   ESC G   0
     1B 47 32   1B 47 30
 25. Reverse video:
     ESC G   4   ESC G   0
     1B 47 34   1B 47 30
 26. Underline:
     ESC G   8   ESC G   0
     1B 47 38   1B 47 30
 27. High intensity:
     ESC G   0   ESC G   0
     1B 47 30   1B 47 30
 28. Half intensity:
     ESC)   ESC (
     1B 29   1B 28
 29. Attributes occupy position: YES
 30. Attributes cumulative: NO
 31. All attributes off:
            ESC G   0
            1B 47 30

CURSOR CONTROL KEYS
 32. Cursor up:
                ^K
                0B
 33. Cursor down:
                ^J
                0A
 34. Cursor right:
                ^L
                0C
 35. Cursor left:
                ^H
                08

CHARACTER SET
 36. Full upper and lower ASCII: YES
 37. Generate all control codes: YES
 38. Bell or tone sequence:
                ^G
                07

EMULATION
 39. Conform to ANSI X3.64?   NO
 40. Terminals Emulated:

CONTINUED ====>

Manufacturer:	Televideo
Terminal:	950

41. Information provided by:
    MANUFACTURER

42. PROGRAM FUNCTION KEYS   NOTES
```
 1. ^A  @   ^M
    01  40  0D

 2. ^A  A   ^M
    01  41  0D

 3. ^A  B   ^M
    01  42  0D

 4. ^A  C   ^M
    01  43  0D

 5. ^A  D   ^M
    01  44  0D

 6. ^A  E   ^M
    01  45  0D

 7. ^A  F   ^M
    01  46  0D

 8. ^A  G   ^M
    01  47  0D

 9. ^A  H   ^M
    01  48  0D

10. ^A  I   ^M
    01  49  0D

11. ^A  J   ^M
    01  4A  0D

12.

13.

14.

15.

16.
```

```
------------------------------------------------------------------------
  1. Manufacturer:                  Televideo
  2. Terminal:                      970
------------------------------------------------------------------------

SCREEN LAYOUT                       VIDEO ATTRIBUTES
  3. Number of rows:       24           ON                    OFF
  4. Number of columns:    80      24. Blinking:
  5. Top Row:               1      ESC [   5    m       ESC [      m
  6. Left Column:           1      1B   5B  35  6D      1B   5B   6D
  7. Printing in bottom right      25. Reverse video:
     cause scroll?        PROG     ESC [   7    m       ESC [      m
                                   1B   5B  37  6D      1B   5B   6D
CURSOR ADDRESSING                  26. Underline:
  8. Lead-in sequence:             ESC [   4    m       ESC [      m
         ESC [                     1B   5B  34  6D      1B   5B   6D
         1B   5B                   27. High intensity:
  9. Row or column first:   ROW    ESC [   1    m       ESC [      m
 10. Numeric form of row and column:  1B   5B  31  6D      1B   5B   6D
     VARIABLE-LENGTH ASCII         28. Half intensity:
 11. Add offset to:      Row:   0  ESC [   0    m       ESC [      m
                         Col:   0  1B   5B  30  6D      1B   5B   6D
 12. Separator sequence:           29. Attributes occupy position: NO
            ;                      30. Attributes cumulative:      YES
            3B                     31. All attributes off:
 13. End sequence:                            ESC [    m
            H                                 1B   5B  6D
            48
 14. Cursor to top row, left column:  CURSOR CONTROL KEYS
ESC [   1   ;   1    H             32. Cursor up:
1B   5B  31  3B  31  48                        ESC [    A
 15. 10th Row, 50th Column:                    1B   5B  41
ESC [   1   0   ;   5   0    H     33. Cursor down:
1B   5B  31  30  3B  35  30  48                ESC [    B
 16. Delay after positioning:    0             1B   5B  42
 17. Cursor home:                  34. Cursor right:
         ESC [    H                            ESC [    C
         1B   5B  48                           1B   5B  43
                                   35. Cursor left:
ERASURE                  DELAY                 ESC [    D
 18. Entire screen:                            1B   5B  44
         ESC [   2    J       0
         1B   5B  32  4A           CHARACTER SET
 19. Cursor to end of screen:      36. Full upper and lower ASCII: YES
         ESC [   J           0     37. Generate all control codes: YES
         1B   5B  4A               38. Bell or tone sequence:
 20. Beginning of screen to cursor:            ^G
         ESC [   1    J       0                07
         1B   5B  31  4A
 21. Cursor to end of line:        EMULATION
         ESC [   K           0     39. Conform to ANSI X3.64?      YES
         1B   5B  4B               40. Terminals Emulated:
 22. Beginning of line to cursor:      970 ANSI
         ESC [   1    K       0        DEC VT100
         1B   5B  31  4B               DEC VT52
 23. Entire cursor line:
         ESC [   2    K       0
         1B   5B  32  4B
```

CONTINUED ====>

```
-----------------------------------------------------------------------
        Manufacturer:              Televideo
        Terminal:                  970
-----------------------------------------------------------------------
```

41. Information provided by:
    MANUFACTURER

42. PROGRAM FUNCTION KEYS   NOTES
    1. ESC ?   a   36. Includes soft font.
       1B 3F 61

    2. ESC ?   b
       1B 3F 62

    3. ESC ?   c
       1B 3F 63

    4. ESC ?   d
       1B 3F 64

    5. ESC ?   e
       1B 3F 65

    6. ESC ?   f
       1B 3F 66

    7. ESC ?   g
       1B 3F 67

    8. ESC ?   h
       1B 3F 68

    9. ESC ?   i
       1B 3F 69

   10. ESC ?   j
       1B 3F 6A

   11. ESC ?   k
       1B 3F 6B

   12. ESC ?   l
       1B 3F 6C

   13. ESC ?   m
       1B 3F 6D

   14. ESC ?   n
       1B 3F 6E

   15. ESC ?   o
       1B 3F 6F

   16. ESC ?   p
       1B 3F 70

```
--------------------------------------------------------------------------------
  1. Manufacturer:                        Televideo
  2. Terminal:                            Personal Terminal
--------------------------------------------------------------------------------

SCREEN LAYOUT                            VIDEO ATTRIBUTES
  3. Number of rows:            24           ON                    OFF
  4. Number of columns:         80       24. Blinking:
  5. Top Row:                    1
  6. Left Column:                1
  7. Printing in bottom right           25. Reverse video:
     cause scroll?             YES

CURSOR ADDRESSING                        26. Underline:
  8. Lead-in sequence:
          ESC =
          1B  3D                         27. High intensity:
  9. Row or column first:      ROW
 10. Numeric form of row and column:
     BINARY                              28. Half intensity:
 11. Add offset to:       Row:  1F       ESC (                ESC )
                          Col:  1F       1B  28               1B  29
 12. Separator sequence:                 29. Attributes occupy position: YES
                                         30. Attributes cumulative:      NO
                                         31. All attributes off:
 13. End sequence:                                ESC G   0
                                                  1B  47  30


 14. Cursor to top row, left column:     CURSOR CONTROL KEYS
 ESC =   SP  SP                          32. Cursor up:
 1B  3D  20  20                                      ^K
 15. 10th Row, 50th Column:                          0B
 ESC =   )   Q                           33. Cursor down:
 1B  3D  29  51                                      ^J
 16. Delay after positioning:    0                   0A
 17. Cursor home:                        34. Cursor right:
          ^^                                         ^L
          1E                                         0C
                                         35. Cursor left:
                                                     ^H
 ERASURE                      DELAY                  08
 18. Entire screen:
          ^Z                    0        CHARACTER SET
          1A                             36. Full upper and lower ASCII: YES
 19. Cursor to end of screen:            37. Generate all control codes: YES
          ESC Y                 0        38. Bell or tone sequence:
          1B  59                                     ^G
 20. Beginning of screen to cursor:                  07


 21. Cursor to end of line:              EMULATION
          ESC T                 0        39. Conform to ANSI X3.64?      NO
          1B  54                         40. Terminals Emulated:
 22. Beginning of line to cursor:


 23. Entire cursor line:
          ^M  ESC T             0
          0D  1B  54
```

CONTINUED ====>

```
--------------------------------------------------------------------------
        Manufacturer:                    Televideo
        Terminal:                        Personal Terminal
--------------------------------------------------------------------------
```

41. Information provided by:
    MANUFACTURER

42. PROGRAM FUNCTION KEYS   NOTES
    1.   4. Or 40.
                                      42. Function keys default to null.

    2.

    3.

    4.

    5.

    6.

    7.

    8.

    9.

    10.

    11.

    12.

    13.

    14.

    15.

    16.

```
--------------------------------------------------------------------------------
1. Manufacturer:                    Termiflex
2. Terminal:                        HT/1000
--------------------------------------------------------------------------------

SCREEN LAYOUT                       VIDEO ATTRIBUTES
3. Number of rows:          4            ON                    OFF
4. Number of columns:      16       24. Blinking:
5. Top Row:                 1        ^Z                   ^X
6. Left Column:             1        1A                   18
7. Printing in bottom right         25. Reverse video:
   cause scroll?           NO

CURSOR ADDRESSING                   26. Underline:
8. Lead-in sequence:
        ESC Y
        1B  59                      27. High intensity:
9. Row or column first:     ROW
10. Numeric form of row and column:
    BINARY                          28. Half intensity:
11. Add offset to:     Row:  1F
                       Col:  1F
12. Separator sequence:             29. Attributes occupy position: NO
                                    30. Attributes cumulative:      NO
                                    31. All attributes off:
13. End sequence:


14. Cursor to top row, left column: CURSOR CONTROL KEYS
ESC Y   SP  SP                      32. Cursor up:
1B  59  20  20                                       ESC A
15. 10th Row, 50th Column:                           1B   41
                                    33. Cursor down:
                                                     ESC B
16. Delay after positioning:    0                    1B   42
17. Cursor home:                    34. Cursor right:
        ESC H                                        ESC C
        1B  48                                       1B   43
                                    35. Cursor left:
ERASURE                    DELAY                     ESC D
18. Entire screen:                                   1B   44


19. Cursor to end of screen:        CHARACTER SET
        ESC J               0       36. Full upper and lower ASCII: YES
        1B  4A                      37. Generate all control codes: YES
20. Beginning of screen to cursor:  38. Bell or tone sequence:
                                            ^G
                                            07
21. Cursor to end of line:          EMULATION
        ESC K               0       39. Conform to ANSI X3.64?     NO
        1B  4B                      40. Terminals Emulated:
22. Beginning of line to cursor:


23. Entire cursor line:
```

41. Information provided by:
    MANUFACTURER

42. PROGRAM FUNCTION KEYS   NOTES
  1.   17. Home is lower left.

  2.

  3.

  4.

  5.

  6.

  7.

  8.

  9.

 10.

 11.

 12.

 13.

 14.

 15.

 16.

```
--------------------------------------------------------------------
  1. Manufacturer:                      Texas Instruments
  2. Terminal:                          931
--------------------------------------------------------------------

SCREEN LAYOUT                          VIDEO ATTRIBUTES
  3. Number of rows:        24             ON                    OFF
  4. Number of columns:     80         24. Blinking:
  5. Top Row:                1
  6. Left Column:            1
  7. Printing in bottom right          25. Reverse video:
     cause scroll?          PROG

CURSOR ADDRESSING                      26. Underline:
  8. Lead-in sequence:
         ESC Y
         1B   59                        27. High intensity:
  9. Row or column first:      ROW
 10. Numeric form of row and column:
     BINARY                             28. Half intensity:
 11. Add offset to:        Row:  1F
                           Col:  1F
 12. Separator sequence:               29. Attributes occupy position: NO
                                       30. Attributes cumulative:      NO
                                       31. All attributes off:

 13. End sequence:


 14. Cursor to top row, left column:   CURSOR CONTROL KEYS
 ESC Y    SP  SP                       32. Cursor up:
 1B   59  20  20                              ESC  [    A
 15. 10th Row, 50th Column:                   1B   5B   41
 ESC Y    )   Q                        33. Cursor down:
 1B   59  29  51                              ESC  [    B
 16. Delay after positioning:     0           1B   5B   42
 17. Cursor home:                      34. Cursor right:
         ESC H                                ESC  [    C
         1B   48                              1B   5B   43
                                       35. Cursor left:
 ERASURE                     DELAY            ESC  [    D
 18. Entire screen:                           1B   5B   44
         ESC L                  0
         1B   4C                       CHARACTER SET
 19. Cursor to end of screen:          36. Full upper and lower ASCII: YES
         ESC J                  0      37. Generate all control codes: YES
         1B   4A                       38. Bell or tone sequence:
 20. Beginning of screen to cursor:           ^G
                                              07

 21. Cursor to end of line:            EMULATION
         ESC I                  0      39. Conform to ANSI X3.64?      NO
         1B   49                       40. Terminals Emulated:
 22. Beginning of line to cursor:


 23. Entire cursor line:
```

CONTINUED ====>

| Manufacturer: | Texas Instruments |
| Terminal: | 931 |

41. Information provided by:
    MANUFACTURER

42. PROGRAM FUNCTION KEYS   NOTES
    1.   3. Also 25th status line.
                                          24.-31. Refer to manual.
                                          36. 96 ASCII characters and 32
    2.   line drawing characters. Nine
                                              international keyboards and
                                              character sets are available.
    3.   42. 12 programmable function keys.

    4.

    5.

    6.

    7.

    8.

    9.

   10.

   11.

   12.

   13.

   14.

   15.

   16.

```
-----------------------------------------------------------------------
  1. Manufacturer:              Texas Instruments
  2. Terminal:                  Professional Computer
-----------------------------------------------------------------------
```

SCREEN LAYOUT
  3. Number of rows: 24
  4. Number of columns: 80
  5. Top Row: 1
  6. Left Column: 1
  7. Printing in bottom right
     cause scroll?   NO

CURSOR ADDRESSING
  8. Lead-in sequence:
              ESC [
              1B   5B
  9. Row or column first: ROW
 10. Numeric form of row and column:
     VARIABLE-LENGTH ASCII
 11. Add offset to: Row: 0
                           Col: 0
 12. Separator sequence:
              ;
              3B
 13. End sequence:
              f
              66
 14. Cursor to top row, left column:
     ESC [1   ;   1   f
     1B   5B   31   3B   31   66
 15. 10th Row, 50th Column:
     ESC [1   0   ;   5   0   f
     1B   5B   31   30   3B   35   30   66
 16. Delay after positioning: 0
 17. Cursor home:
              ESC [H
              1B   5B   48

ERASURE   DELAY
 18. Entire screen:
         ESC [2   J   0
         1B   5B   32   4A
 19. Cursor to end of screen:
         ESC [J   0
         1B   5B   4A
 20. Beginning of screen to cursor:

 21. Cursor to end of line:
         ESC [K   0
         1B   5B   4B
 22. Beginning of line to cursor:

 23. Entire cursor line:
         ^M ESC [K   0
         0D 1B   5B   4B

VIDEO ATTRIBUTES
            ON   OFF
 24. Blinking:
     ESC [5   m   ESC [m
     1B   5B   35   6D   1B   5B   6D
 25. Reverse video:
     ESC [7   m   ESC [m
     1B   5B   37   6D   1B   5B   6D
 26. Underline:
     ESC [4   m   ESC [m
     1B   5B   34   6D   1B   5B   6D
 27. High intensity:
     ESC [1   m   ESC [m
     1B   5B   31   6D   1B   5B   6D
 28. Half intensity:

 29. Attributes occupy position: YES
 30. Attributes cumulative: YES
 31. All attributes off:
              ESC [m
              1B   5B   6D

CURSOR CONTROL KEYS
 32. Cursor up:
              ESC [A
              1B   5B   41
 33. Cursor down:
              ESC [B
              1B   5B   42
 34. Cursor right:
              ESC [C
              1B   5B   43
 35. Cursor left:
              ESC [D
              1B   5B   44

CHARACTER SET
 36. Full upper and lower ASCII: YES
 37. Generate all control codes: YES
 38. Bell or tone sequence:
              ^G
              07

EMULATION
 39. Conform to ANSI X3.64?   YES
 40. Terminals Emulated:
         IBM 3101
         IBM 3270
         TI 931

CONTINUED ====>

41. Information provided by:
    MANUFACTURER

42. PROGRAM FUNCTION KEYS   NOTES
  1.   28. Half intensity on:
                                  ESC [3 2 m
                          30. Combinations of attributes are set
  2.   by placing the specifications in
                              the ESC [Pn ; Pn ; Pn ; Pn m
                              sequence. They may be turned off
  3.   individually by sending a "set
                              sequence" without the attribute in
                              question.
  4.   40. This is a PC, not a terminal. TI
                              currently supports TTY, 3101, 3270
                              and TI 931 emulation. Application
  5.   packages could be written to
                              emulate any terminal.
                          42. 24 function keys are totally
  6.   mappable to any sequence using the
                              key-reassignment command.

  7.

  8.

  9.

10.

11.

12.

13.

14.

15.

16.

```
------------------------------------------------------------------------
1. Manufacturer:                    Tymshare
2. Terminal:                        Scanset 410, 415/HS, XL-HS
------------------------------------------------------------------------
```

SCREEN LAYOUT   VIDEO ATTRIBUTES
  3. Number of rows: 24   ON   OFF
  4. Number of columns: 80   24. Blinking:
  5. Top Row: 1
  6. Left Column: 1
  7. Printing in bottom right   25. Reverse video:
    cause scroll?   YES

CURSOR ADDRESSING   26. Underline:
  8. Lead-in sequence:
      ESC Y
      1B 59   27. High intensity:
  9. Row or column first: ROW
10. Numeric form of row and column:
    BINARY   28. Half intensity:
11. Add offset to: Row: 1F
                  Col: 1F
12. Separator sequence: 29. Attributes occupy position: NO
                        30. Attributes cumulative: NO
                        31. All attributes off:
13. End sequence:

14. Cursor to top row, left column: CURSOR CONTROL KEYS
 ESC Y   SP SP   32. Cursor up:
 1B 59 20 20   ESC A
15. 10th Row, 50th Column: 1B   41
 ESC Y   )   Q   33. Cursor down:
 1B 59 29 51   ESC B
16. Delay after positioning: 0   1B   42
17. Cursor home: 34. Cursor right:
      ESC H   ESC C
      1B 48   1B   43
                        35. Cursor left:
ERASURE   DELAY   ESC D
18. Entire screen: 0   1B   44
    ESC >
    1B 3E   CHARACTER SET
19. Cursor to end of screen: 36. Full upper and lower ASCII: YES
    ESC J   0   37. Generate all control codes: YES
    1B 4A   38. Bell or tone sequence:
20. Beginning of screen to cursor: ^G
                                07

21. Cursor to end of line: EMULATION
    ESC K   0   39. Conform to ANSI X3.64?   NO
    1B 4B   40. Terminals Emulated:
22. Beginning of line to cursor: VT52

23. Entire cursor line:

CONTINUED ====>

41. Information provided by:
    MANUFACTURER

42. PROGRAM FUNCTION KEYS   NOTES
    1.   4. Or 40.
                                  42. 12 programmable function keys.

    2.

    3.

    4.

    5.

    6.

    7.

    8.

    9.

   10.

   11.

   12.

   13.

   14.

   15.

   16.

```
-------------------------------------------------------------------------------
  1. Manufacturer:                    Vector Graphic, Inc.
  2. Terminal:                        Vector 4 & 4S & VSX
-------------------------------------------------------------------------------
```

SCREEN LAYOUT
3. Number of rows: 24
4. Number of columns: 80
5. Top Row: 1
6. Left Column: 1
7. Printing in bottom right
   cause scroll?   YES

CURSOR ADDRESSING
8. Lead-in sequence:
             ESC [
             1B 5B
9. Row or column first: ROW
10. Numeric form of row and column:
    VARIABLE-LENGTH ASCII
11. Add offset to: Row: 0
                          Col: 0
12. Separator sequence:
             ;
             3B
13. End sequence:
             H
             48
14. Cursor to top row, left column:
   ESC [1   ;   1   H
   1B 5B 31 3B 31 48
15. 10th Row, 50th Column:
   ESC [1   0   ;   5   0   H
   1B 5B 31 30 3B 35 30 48
16. Delay after positioning: 0
17. Cursor home:
             ESC [1   ;   1   H
             1B 5B 31 3B 31 48

ERASURE   DELAY
18. Entire screen:
             ESC [2   J   0
             1B 5B 32 4A
19. Cursor to end of screen:
             ESC [J   0
             1B 5B 4A
20. Beginning of screen to cursor:
             ESC [1   J   0
             1B 5B 31 4A
21. Cursor to end of line:
             ESC [K   0
             1B 5B 4B
22. Beginning of line to cursor:
             ESC [1   K   0
             1B 5B 31 4B
23. Entire cursor line:
             ESC [2   K   0
             1B 5B 32 4B

VIDEO ATTRIBUTES
          ON   OFF
24. Blinking:

25. Reverse video:
    ESC [7   m   ESC [m
    1B 5B 37 6D   1B 5B 6D
26. Underline:

27. High intensity:

28. Half intensity:

29. Attributes occupy position: NO
30. Attributes cumulative: NO
31. All attributes off:
             ESC [m
             1B 5B 6D

CURSOR CONTROL KEYS
32. Cursor up:

                8A
33. Cursor down:

                8B
34. Cursor right:

                8D
35. Cursor left:

                8C

CHARACTER SET
36. Full upper and lower ASCII: YES
37. Generate all control codes: YES
38. Bell or tone sequence:
                ^G
                07

EMULATION
39. Conform to ANSI X3.64?   YES
40. Terminals Emulated:

CONTINUED ====>

```
-------------------------------------------------------------------------
      Manufacturer:                 Vector Graphic, Inc.
      Terminal:                     Vector 4 & 4S & VSX
-------------------------------------------------------------------------
```

41. Information provided by:
    MANUFACTURER

42. PROGRAM FUNCTION KEYS   NOTES
  1.   32.-35. Shift arrow keys 9A-9D.
      C1   Ctrl arrow keys AA-AD.
                                           Shift-ctrl arrow keys BA-BD.
  2.   42. Help key   C0
      C2   Shift   D0
                                       Ctrl   E0
  3.   Shift-ctrl F0
      C3   F1-F14 shift   D1-DE
                                       F1-F14 ctrl   E1-EE
  4.   F1-F14 shift-ctrl F1-FE
      C4

  5.
      C5

  6.
      C6

  7.
      C7

  8.
      C8

  9.
      C9

 10.
      CA

 11.
      CB

 12.
      CC

 13.
      CD

 14.
      CE

 15.

 16.

```
------------------------------------------------------------------------
  1. Manufacturer:                    Visual Technology
  2. Terminal:                        V102
------------------------------------------------------------------------
```

SCREEN LAYOUT
  3. Number of rows: 24
  4. Number of columns: 80
  5. Top Row: 1
  6. Left Column: 1
  7. Printing in bottom right
     cause scroll?   YES

CURSOR ADDRESSING
  8. Lead-in sequence:
            ESC [
            1B 5B
  9. Row or column first: ROW
 10. Numeric form of row and column:
     VARIABLE-LENGTH ASCII
 11. Add offset to: Row: 0
                         Col: 0
 12. Separator sequence:
            ;
            3B
 13. End sequence:
            H
            48
 14. Cursor to top row, left column:
     ESC [1   ;   1   H
     1B 5B 31 3B 31 48
 15. 10th Row, 50th Column:
     ESC [1   0   ;   5   0   H
     1B 5B 31 30 3B 35 30 48
 16. Delay after positioning: 0
 17. Cursor home:
            ESC [H
            1B 5B 48

ERASURE   DELAY
 18. Entire screen:
            ESC [2   J   0
            1B 5B 32 4A
 19. Cursor to end of screen:
            ESC [J   0
            1B 5B 4A
 20. Beginning of screen to cursor:
            ESC [1   J   0
            1B 5B 31 4A
 21. Cursor to end of line:
            ESC [K   0
            1B 5B 4B
 22. Beginning of line to cursor:
            ESC [1   K   0
            1B 5B 31 4B
 23. Entire cursor line:
            ESC [2   K   0
            1B 5B 32 4B

VIDEO ATTRIBUTES
        ON   OFF
 24. Blinking:
     ESC [5   m   ESC [m
     1B 5B 35 6D   1B 5B 6D
 25. Reverse video:
     ESC [7   m   ESC [m
     1B 5B 37 6D   1B 5B 6D
 26. Underline:
     ESC [4   m   ESC [m
     1B 5B 34 6D   1B 5B 6D
 27. High intensity:
     ESC [1   m   ESC [m
     1B 5B 31 6D   1B 5B 6D
 28. Half intensity:

 29. Attributes occupy position: NO
 30. Attributes cumulative: YES
 31. All attributes off:
            ESC [m
            1B 5B 6D

CURSOR CONTROL KEYS
 32. Cursor up:
            ESC [A
            1B 5B 41
 33. Cursor down:
            ESC [B
            1B 5B 42
 34. Cursor right:
            ESC [C
            1B 5B 43
 35. Cursor left:
            ESC [D
            1B 5B 44

CHARACTER SET
 36. Full upper and lower ASCII: YES
 37. Generate all control codes: YES
 38. Bell or tone sequence:
            ^G
            07

EMULATION
 39. Conform to ANSI X3.64?   YES
 40. Terminals Emulated:
     DEC VT52, VT100, VT102

                    CONTINUED ====>

41. Information provided by:
    MANUFACTURER

42. PROGRAM FUNCTION KEYS

					NOTES
1.	ESC _	A	ESC \		4. Or 132.
	1B 5F	41	1B 5C		42. Default values are shown for
					PF keys. PF keys are programmable.

1. ESC _   A   ESC \
   1B 5F   41   1B 5C

2. ESC _   B   ESC \
   1B 5F   42   1B 5C

3. ESC _   C   ESC \
   1B 5F   43   1B 5C

4. ESC _   D   ESC \
   1B 5F   44   1B 5C

5. ESC _   E   ESC \
   1B 5F   45   1B 5C

6. ESC _   F   ESC \
   1B 5F   46   1B 5C

7. ESC _   G   ESC \
   1B 5F   47   1B 5C

8. ESC _   H   ESC \
   1B 5F   48   1B 5C

9. ESC _   I   ESC \
   1B 5F   49   1B 5C

10. ESC _   J   ESC \
   1B 5F   4A   1B 5C

11. ESC _   K   ESC \
   1B 5F   4B   1B 5C

12. ESC _   L   ESC \
   1B 5F   4C   1B 5C

13. ESC _   M   ESC \
   1B 5F   4D   1B 5C

14. ESC _   N   ESC \
   1B 5F   4E   1B 5C

15. ESC _   O   ESC \
   1B 5F   4F   1B 5C

16. ESC _   P   ESC \
   1B 5F   50   1B 5C

----

1. Manufacturer: Visual Technology
2. Terminal: V330 (DG D200 mode)

SCREEN LAYOUT
3. Number of rows: 24
4. Number of columns: 80
5. Top Row: 1
6. Left Column: 1
7. Printing in bottom right
    cause scroll?   YES

CURSOR ADDRESSING
8. Lead-in sequence:
        ^P
        10
9. Row or column first: COL
10. Numeric form of row and column:
    BINARY
11. Add offset to: Row: 0
                  Col: 0
12. Separator sequence:

13. End sequence:

14. Cursor to top row, left column:
^P NUL NUL
10 00   00
15. 10th Row, 50th Column:
^P 1   ^I
10 31 09
16. Delay after positioning: 0
17. Cursor home:
        ^H
        08

ERASURE   DELAY
18. Entire screen:
      ^L   0
      0C
19. Cursor to end of screen:
    ^^ J   0
    1E 4A
20. Beginning of screen to cursor:

21. Cursor to end of line:
    ^K   0
    0B
22. Beginning of line to cursor:

23. Entire cursor line:
    ^^ t   0
    1E 74

VIDEO ATTRIBUTES
        ON   OFF
24. Blinking:
  ^N   ^O
  0E   0F
25. Reverse video:
  ^^ D   ^^ E
  1E 44   1E   45
26. Underline:
  ^T   ^U
  14   15
27. High intensity:

28. Half intensity:
  ^\   ^]
  1C   1D
29. Attributes occupy position: NO
30. Attributes cumulative: YES
31. All attributes off:

CURSOR CONTROL KEYS
32. Cursor up:
                ^W
                17
33. Cursor down:
                ^Z
                1A
34. Cursor right:
                ^X
                18
35. Cursor left:
                ^Y
                19

CHARACTER SET
36. Full upper and lower ASCII: YES
37. Generate all control codes: YES
38. Bell or tone sequence:
          ^G
          07

EMULATION
39. Conform to ANSI X3.64?   NO
40. Terminals Emulated:
    VT52, ADM3A, HZ 1500, DG D200
    DG D200 codes shown here.

                     CONTINUED ====>

41. Information provided by:
MANUFACTURER

42. PROGRAM FUNCTION KEYS   NOTES
  1. ^^   q   42. Default values are shown for
      1E 71   PF keys. PF keys are programmable.

  2. ^^   r
      1E 72

  3. ^^   s
      1E 73

  4. ^^   t
      1E 74

  5. ^^   u
      1E 75

  6. ^^   v
      1E 76

  7. ^^   w
      1E 77

  8. ^^   x
      1E 78

  9. ^^   y
      1E 79

10. ^^   z
      1E 7A

11. ^^   {
      1E 7B

12. ^^ |
      1E 7C

13.

14.

15.

16.

```
-------------------------------------------------------------------------
  1. Manufacturer:                    Visual Technology
  2. Terminal:                        V500 (LSI ADM3A mode)
-------------------------------------------------------------------------

SCREEN LAYOUT                         VIDEO ATTRIBUTES
  3. Number of rows:          33           ON                    OFF
  4. Number of columns:       80     24. Blinking:
  5. Top Row:                  1         ESC ^B              ESC ^A
  6. Left Column:              1         1B  02              1B  01
  7. Printing in bottom right          25. Reverse video:
     cause scroll?           YES         ESC ^H              ESC ^G
                                         1B  08              1B  07
CURSOR ADDRESSING                      26. Underline:
  8. Lead-in sequence:                   ESC ^D              ESC ^C
            ESC =                        1B  04              1B  03
            1B  3D                     27. High intensity:
  9. Row or column first:     ROW
 10. Numeric form of row and column:
     BINARY                            28. Half intensity:
 11. Add offset to:     Row:  1F        ESC 4               ESC 3
                        Col:  1F        1B  34              1B  33
 12. Separator sequence:              29. Attributes occupy position: NO
                                      30. Attributes cumulative:    YES
                                      31. All attributes off:
 13. End sequence:


 14. Cursor to top row, left column:  CURSOR CONTROL KEYS
 ESC =   SP  SP                       32. Cursor up:
 1B  3D  20  20                                    ESC A
 15. 10th Row, 50th Column:                        1B  41
 ESC 0   )   Q                        33. Cursor down:
 1B  30  29  51                                    ESC B
 16. Delay after positioning:    0                 1B  42
 17. Cursor home:                     34. Cursor right:
            ESC H                                  ESC C
            1B  48                                 1B  43
                                      35. Cursor left:
ERASURE                      DELAY                 ESC D
 18. Entire screen:                                1B  44
            ESC w               0
            1B  77                    CHARACTER SET
 19. Cursor to end of screen:         36. Full upper and lower ASCII: YES
            ESC J               0     37. Generate all control codes: YES
            1B  4A                    38. Bell or tone sequence:
 20. Beginning of screen to cursor:                ^G
                                                   07
 21. Cursor to end of line:           EMULATION
            ESC K               0     39. Conform to ANSI X3.64?      NO
            1B  4B                    40. Terminals Emulated:
 22. Beginning of line to cursor:         VT52, LSI ADM3A, Haz 1500,
                                          DG D200, Tektronix 4010-4014
                                          graphics emulation.
 23. Entire cursor line:                  LSI ADM3A codes shown here.
            ESC t               0
            1B  74
```

          CONTINUED ====>

```
-----------------------------------------------------------------------------
      Manufacturer:                      Visual Technology
      Terminal:                          V500 (LSI ADM3A mode)
-----------------------------------------------------------------------------
```

41. Information provided by:
    MANUFACTURER

42. PROGRAM FUNCTION KEYS   NOTES
    1. ESC A   3. Or 24.
       1B 41   42. Default values are shown for
                                       PF keys. PF keys are programmable.
    2. ESC B
       1B 42

    3. ESC C
       1B 43

    4. ESC D
       1B 44

    5. ESC E
       1B 45

    6. ESC F
       1B 46

    7. ESC G
       1B 47

    8. ESC H
       1B 48

    9. ESC I
       1B 49

   10. ESC J
       1B 4A

   11. ESC K
       1B 4B

   12. ESC L
       1B 4C

   13.

   14.

   15.

   16.

---

1. Manufacturer: Visual Technology
2. Terminal: Visual 100

SCREEN LAYOUT
3. Number of rows: 24
4. Number of columns: 80
5. Top Row: 1
6. Left Column: 1
7. Printing in bottom right
   cause scroll?   PROG

CURSOR ADDRESSING
8. Lead-in sequence:
          ESC [
          1B 5B
9. Row or column first: ROW
10. Numeric form of row and column:
    VARIABLE-LENGTH ASCII
11. Add offset to: Row: 0
                         Col: 0
12. Separator sequence:
          ;
          3B
13. End sequence:
          H
          48
14. Cursor to top row, left column:
ESC [1   ;   1   H
1B 5B 31 3B 31 48
15. 10th Row, 50th Column:
ESC [1   0   ;   5   0   H
1B 5B 31 30 3B 35 30 48
16. Delay after positioning: 0
17. Cursor home:
          ESC [H
          1B 5B 48

ERASURE   DELAY
18. Entire screen:
          ESC [2   J   0
          1B 5B 32 4A
19. Cursor to end of screen:
          ESC [J   0
          1B 5B 4A
20. Beginning of screen to cursor:
          ESC [1   J   0
          1B 5B 31 4A
21. Cursor to end of line:
          ESC [K   0
          1B 5B 4B
22. Beginning of line to cursor:
          ESC [1   K   0
          1B 5B 31 4B
23. Entire cursor line:
          ESC [2   K   0
          1B 5B 32 4B

VIDEO ATTRIBUTES
          ON   OFF
24. Blinking:
ESC [5   m   ESC [m
1B 5B 35 6D   1B 5B 6D
25. Reverse video:
ESC [7   m   ESC [m
1B 5B 37 6D   1B 5B 6D
26. Underline:
ESC [4   m   ESC [m
1B 5B 34 6D   1B 5B 6D
27. High intensity:
ESC [1   m   ESC [m
1B 5B 31 6D   1B 5B 6D
28. Half intensity:

29. Attributes occupy position: NO
30. Attributes cumulative: YES
31. All attributes off:
               ESC [m
               1B 5B 6D

CURSOR CONTROL KEYS
32. Cursor up:
               ESC [A
               1B 5B 41
33. Cursor down:
               ESC [B
               1B 5B 42
34. Cursor right:
               ESC [C
               1B 5B 43
35. Cursor left:
               ESC [D
               1B 5B 44

CHARACTER SET
36. Full upper and lower ASCII: YES
37. Generate all control codes: YES
38. Bell or tone sequence:
               ^G
               07

EMULATION
39. Conform to ANSI X3.64?   YES
40. Terminals Emulated:
    DEC VT100, VT52

295

CONTINUED ====>

Manufacturer: Visual Technology
Terminal: Visual 100

41. Information provided by:
    MANUFACTURER

42. PROGRAM FUNCTION KEYS   NOTES
    1. ESC O   P   4. Or 132 (in ANSI mode only).
       1B 4F 50   7. Selectable.
                                   13. Optionally f (66H).

    2. ESC O   Q
       1B 4F 51

    3. ESC O   R
       1B 4F 52

    4. ESC O   S
       1B 4F 53

    5.

    6.

    7.

    8.

    9.

   10.

   11.

   12.

   13.

   14.

   15.

   16.

---
1. Manufacturer: Visual Technology
2. Terminal: Visual 100 (VT52 mode)

SCREEN LAYOUT
3. Number of rows: 24
4. Number of columns: 80
5. Top Row: 1
6. Left Column: 1
7. Printing in bottom right
   cause scroll?   PROG

CURSOR ADDRESSING
8. Lead-in sequence:
        ESC Y
        1B 59
9. Row or column first: ROW
10. Numeric form of row and column:
    BINARY
11. Add offset to: Row: 1F
                 Col: 1F
12. Separator sequence:

13. End sequence:

14. Cursor to top row, left column:
ESC Y   SP   SP
1B 59   20   20
15. 10th Row, 50th Column:
ESC Y   )   Q
1B 59   29   51
16. Delay after positioning: 0
17. Cursor home:
        ESC H
        1B 48

ERASURE   DELAY
18. Entire screen:
      ESC H   ESC J   0
      1B 48 1B 4A
19. Cursor to end of screen:
      ESC J   0
      1B 4A
20. Beginning of screen to cursor:

21. Cursor to end of line:
      ESC K   0
      1B 4B
22. Beginning of line to cursor:

23. Entire cursor line:

VIDEO ATTRIBUTES
            ON   OFF
24. Blinking:

25. Reverse video:

26. Underline:

27. High intensity:

28. Half intensity:

29. Attributes occupy position: NO
30. Attributes cumulative: NO
31. All attributes off:

CURSOR CONTROL KEYS
32. Cursor up:
             ESC A
             1B 41
33. Cursor down:
             ESC B
             1B 42
34. Cursor right:
             ESC C
             1B 43
35. Cursor left:
             ESC D
             1B 44

CHARACTER SET
36. Full upper and lower ASCII: YES
37. Generate all control codes: YES
38. Bell or tone sequence:
          ^G
          07

EMULATION
39. Conform to ANSI X3.64?   NO
40. Terminals Emulated:

CONTINUED ====>

41. Information provided by:
    MANUFACTURER

42. PROGRAM FUNCTION KEYS   NOTES
    1. ESC O   P   Product discontinued.
       1B 4F 50

    2. ESC O   Q
       1B 4F 51

    3. ESC O   R
       1B 4F 52

    4. ESC O   S
       1B 4F 53

    5.

    6.

    7.

    8.

    9.

    10.

    11.

    12.

    13.

    14.

    15.

    16.

```
--------------------------------------------------------------------------
1. Manufacturer:                        Visual Technology
2. Terminal:                            Visual 300 (VT100 mode)
--------------------------------------------------------------------------
```

SCREEN LAYOUT
3. Number of rows: 24
4. Number of columns: 80
5. Top Row: 1
6. Left Column: 1
7. Printing in bottom right
   cause scroll?   YES

CURSOR ADDRESSING
8. Lead-in sequence:
             ESC [
             1B 5B
9. Row or column first: ROW
10. Numeric form of row and column:
    VARIABLE-LENGTH ASCII
11. Add offset to: Row: 0
                          Col: 0
12. Separator sequence:
             ;
             3B
13. End sequence:
             H
             48
14. Cursor to top row, left column:
ESC [1   ;   1   H
1B   5B   31   3B   31   48
15. 10th Row, 50th Column:
ESC [1   0   ;   5   0   H
1B   5B   31   30   3B   35   30   48
16. Delay after positioning: 0
17. Cursor home:
             ESC [H
             1B   5B   48

ERASURE   DELAY
18. Entire screen:
        ESC [2   J   0
        1B   5B   32   4A
19. Cursor to end of screen:
        ESC [J   0
        1B   5B   4A
20. Beginning of screen to cursor:
        ESC [1   J   0
        1B   5B   31   4A
21. Cursor to end of line:
        ESC [K   0
        1B   5B   4B
22. Beginning of line to cursor:
        ESC [1   K   0
        1B   5B   31   4B
23. Entire cursor line:
        ESC [2   K   0
        1B   5B   32   4B

VIDEO ATTRIBUTES
        ON   OFF
24. Blinking:
ESC [5   m   ESC [m
1B   5B   35   6D   1B   5B   6D
25. Reverse video:
ESC [7   m   ESC [m
1B   5B   37   6D   1B   5B   6D
26. Underline:
ESC [4   m   ESC [m
1B   5B   34   6D   1B   5B   6D
27. High intensity:
ESC [1   m   ESC [m
1B   5B   31   6D   1B   5B   6D
28. Half intensity:

29. Attributes occupy position: NO
30. Attributes cumulative: YES
31. All attributes off:
             ESC [m
             1B   5B   6D

CURSOR CONTROL KEYS
32. Cursor up:
             ESC [A
             1B   5B   41
33. Cursor down:
             ESC [B
             1B   5B   42
34. Cursor right:
             ESC [C
             1B   5B   43
35. Cursor left:
             ESC [D
             1B   5B   44

CHARACTER SET
36. Full upper and lower ASCII: YES
37. Generate all control codes: YES
38. Bell or tone sequence:
             ^G
             07

EMULATION
39. Conform to ANSI X3.64?   YES
40. Terminals Emulated:
    DEC VT100, VT52

CONTINUED ====>

| Manufacturer: | Visual Technology |
| Terminal: | Visual 300 (VT100 mode) |

41. Information provided by:
    MANUFACTURER

42. PROGRAM FUNCTION KEYS   NOTES
 1. ESC O   P
    1B   4F   50

 2. ESC O   Q
    1B   4F   51

 3. ESC O   R
    1B   4F   52

 4. ESC O   S
    1B   4F   53

 5.

 6.

 7.

 8.

 9.

10.

11.

12.

13.

14.

15.

16.

---

1. Manufacturer: Visual Technology
2. Terminal: Visual 50/55 (Esprit mode)

SCREEN LAYOUT
3. Number of rows: 24
4. Number of columns: 80
5. Top Row: 1
6. Left Column: 1
7. Printing in bottom right
   cause scroll?   YES

CURSOR ADDRESSING
8. Lead-in sequence:
      ~   ^Q
     7E   11
9. Row or column first: COL
10. Numeric form of row and column:
    BINARY
11. Add offset to: Row: 0
                   Col: 0
12. Separator sequence:

13. End sequence:

14. Cursor to top row, left column:
 ~   ^Q NUL NUL
 7E 11 00 00
15. 10th Row, 50th Column:
 ~   ^Q 1   ^I
 7E 11 31 09
16. Delay after positioning: 0
17. Cursor home:
      ~   ^R
    7E 12

ERASURE   DELAY
18. Entire screen:
    ~   R   0
   7E 52
19. Cursor to end of screen:
    ~   J   0
   7E 4A
20. Beginning of screen to cursor:

21. Cursor to end of line:
    ~   K   0
   7E 4B
22. Beginning of line to cursor:

23. Entire cursor line:
    ~   E   0
   7E 45

VIDEO ATTRIBUTES
          ON   OFF
24. Blinking:
 ~   i   ~   W
 7E 69   7E 57
25. Reverse video:
 ~   j   ~   W
 7E 6A   7E 57
26. Underline:
 ~   S   s   W
 7E 53   73 57
27. High intensity:

28. Half intensity:
 ~   0   ~   W
 7E 4F   7E 57
29. Attributes occupy position: NO
30. Attributes cumulative: NO
31. All attributes off:
      ~   W
    7E 57

CURSOR CONTROL KEYS
32. Cursor up:
      ~   ^L
    7E 0C
33. Cursor down:
      ~   ^K
    7E 0B
34. Cursor right:
      ~   C
    7E 43
35. Cursor left:
      ~   D
    7E 44

CHARACTER SET
36. Full upper and lower ASCII: YES
37. Generate all control codes: YES
38. Bell or tone sequence:
      ^G
      07

EMULATION
39. Conform to ANSI X3.64?   NO
40. Terminals Emulated:
    DEC VT52, ADDS Viewpoint, Lear
    Siegler ADM3A, Hazeltine Esprit
    V55 also Hazeltine 1500-1510,
    Visual 200/210.

CONTINUED ====>

41. Information provided by:
MANUFACTURER

42. PROGRAM FUNCTION KEYS	NOTES

42. PROGRAM FUNCTION KEYS

1. ~   P
   7E 50

2. ~   Q
   7E 51

3. ~   R
   7E 52

4. ~   SP
   7E 20

5. ~   !
   7E 21

6. ~   "
   7E 22

7. ~   #
   7E 23

8. ~ $
   7E 24

9. ~   %
   7E 25

10. ~   &
   7E 26

11. ~   '
   7E 27

12. ~   (
   7E 28

13.

14.

15.

16.

NOTES
42. Default values are shown for
PF keys. PF keys are programmable.

302

```
-----------------------------------------------------------------------
1. Manufacturer:                    Visual Technology
2. Terminal:                        Visual 50/55 (VT52 mode)
-----------------------------------------------------------------------
```

SCREEN LAYOUT

3. Number of rows: 24
4. Number of columns: 80
5. Top Row: 1
6. Left Column: 1
7. Printing in bottom right
   cause scroll?   YES

CURSOR ADDRESSING

8. Lead-in sequence:
            ESC Y
            1B 59
9. Row or column first: ROW
10. Numeric form of row and column:
    BINARY
11. Add offset to: Row: 1F
                        Col: 1F
12. Separator sequence:

13. End sequence:

14. Cursor to top row, left column:
ESC Y   SP   SP
1B 59   20   20
15. 10th Row, 50th Column:
ESC Y   )   Q
1B 59   29   51
16. Delay after positioning: 0
17. Cursor home:
            ESC H
            1B 48

ERASURE   DELAY
18. Entire screen:
            ESC ^Z   0
            1B 1A
19. Cursor to end of screen:
            ESC ^   0
            1B 1F̄
20. Beginning of screen to cursor:

21. Cursor to end of line:
            ESC ^]   0
            1B 1D
22. Beginning of line to cursor:

23. Entire cursor line:
            ESC E   0
            1B 45

VIDEO ATTRIBUTES
           ON   OFF
24. Blinking:
    ESC i   ESC W
    1B 69   1B 57
25. Reverse video:
    ESC j   ESC W
    1B 6A   1B 57
26. Underline:
    ESC S   ESC W
    1B 53   1B 57
27. High intensity:

28. Half intensity:
    ESC O   ESC W
    1B 4F   1B 57
29. Attributes occupy position: NO
30. Attributes cumulative: NO
31. All attributes off:
            ESC W
            1B 57

CURSOR CONTROL KEYS
32. Cursor up:
            ESC A
            1B 41
33. Cursor down:
            ESC B
            1B 42
34. Cursor right:
            ESC C
            1B 43
35. Cursor left:
            ESC D
            1B 44

CHARACTER SET
36. Full upper and lower ASCII: YES
37. Generate all control codes: YES
38. Bell or tone sequence:
            ^G
            07

EMULATION
39. Conform to ANSI X3.64?   NO
40. Terminals Emulated:
    DEC VT52, ADDS Viewpoint, Lear
    Siegler ADM3A, Hazeltine Esprit
    V55 also Hazeltine 1510, Visual
    200-210.

                    CONTINUED ====>

41. Information provided by:
    MANUFACTURER

42. PROGRAM FUNCTION KEYS   NOTES
     1. ESC P   42. Default values are shown for
        1B 50   PF keys. PF keys are programmable.

     2. ESC Q
        1B 51

     3. ESC R
        1B 52

     4. ESC SP
        1B 20

     5. ESC !
        1B 21

     6. ESC "
        1B 22

     7. ESC #
        1B 23

     8. ESC $
        1B 24

     9. ESC %
        1B 25

    10. ESC &
        1B 26

    11. ESC ´
        1B 27

    12. ESC (
        1B 28

    13.

    14.

    15.

    16.

```
-----------------------------------------------------------------------
  1. Manufacturer:                    Wyse Technology
  2. Terminal:                        WY-100
-----------------------------------------------------------------------
```

SCREEN LAYOUT
3. Number of rows: 24
4. Number of columns: 80
5. Top Row: 1
6. Left Column: 1
7. Printing in bottom right
   cause scroll?   PROG

CURSOR ADDRESSING
8. Lead-in sequence:
                   ESC =
                   1B 3D
9. Row or column first: ROW
10. Numeric form of row and column:
    BINARY
11. Add offset to: Row: 1F
                        Col: 1F
12. Separator sequence:

13. End sequence:

14. Cursor to top row, left column:
ESC =   SP SP
1B 3D   20 20
15. 10th Row, 50th Column:
ESC =   )   Q
1B 3D   29 51
16. Delay after positioning: 0
17. Cursor home:
             ^^
             1E

ERASURE   DELAY
18. Entire screen:
       ^Z   0
       1A
19. Cursor to end of screen:
       ESC Y   0
       1B 59
20. Beginning of screen to cursor:

21. Cursor to end of line:
       ESC T   0
       1B 54
22. Beginning of line to cursor:

23. Entire cursor line:

VIDEO ATTRIBUTES
        ON   OFF
24. Blinking:
    ESC G   2   ESC G   0
    1B 47 32   1B 47 30
25. Reverse video:
    ESC G   4   ESC G   0
    1B 47 34   1B 47 30
26. Underline:
    ESC G   8   ESC G   0
    1B 47 38   1B 47 30
27. High intensity:

28. Half intensity:
    ESC G   p   ESC G   0
    1B 47 70   1B 47 30
29. Attributes occupy position: YES
30. Attributes cumulative: NO
31. All attributes off:
             ESC G   0
             1B 47 30

CURSOR CONTROL KEYS
32. Cursor up:
             ^K
             0B
33. Cursor down:
             ^J
             0A
34. Cursor right:
             ^L
             0C
35. Cursor left:
             ^H
             08

CHARACTER SET
36. Full upper and lower ASCII: YES
37. Generate all control codes: YES
38. Bell or tone sequence:
             ^G
             07

EMULATION
39. Conform to ANSI X3.64?   NO
40. Terminals Emulated:

CONTINUED ====>

41. Information provided by:
    MANUFACTURER

42. PROGRAM FUNCTION KEYS

1. ^A	@	^M
01	40	0D
2. ^A	A	^M
01	41	0D
3. ^A	B	^M
01	42	0D
4. ^A	C	^M
01	43	0D
5. ^A	D	^M
01	44	0D
6. ^A	E	^M
01	45	0D
7. ^A	F	^M
01	46	0D
8. ^A	G	^M
01	47	0D
9. ^A	H	^M
01	48	0D
10. ^A	I	^M
01	49	0D
11. ^A	J	^M
01	4A	0D
12. ^A	K	^M
01	4B	0D
13. ^A	L	^M
01	4C	0D
14. ^A	M	^M
01	4D	0D
15. ^A	N	^M
01	4E	0D
16. ^A	O	^M
01	4F	0D

NOTES
30. Multiple attributes available,
    refer to manual.
36. Plus graphics characters.
42. F1-F8 shown unshifted.
    F9-F16 refer to F1-F8 shifted.

```
--------------------------------------------------------------------------
  1. Manufacturer:                   Wyse Technology
  2. Terminal:                       WY-300
--------------------------------------------------------------------------
```

SCREEN LAYOUT   VIDEO ATTRIBUTES
  3. Number of rows: 24   ON   OFF
  4. Number of columns: 80   24. Blinking:
  5. Top Row: 1   ESC G   2   ESC G   0
  6. Left Column: 1   1B   47 32   1B   47 30
  7. Printing in bottom right   25. Reverse video:
     cause scroll?   PROG   ESC G   4   ESC G   0
                                       1B   47 34   1B   47 30
CURSOR ADDRESSING   26. Underline:
  8. Lead-in sequence: ESC G   8   ESC G   0
     ESC =   1B   47 38   1B   47 30
     1B   3D   27. High intensity:
  9. Row or column first: ROW
 10. Numeric form of row and column:
     BINARY   28. Half intensity:
 11. Add offset to: Row: 1F   ESC G   p   ESC G   0
                       Col: 1F   1B   47 70   1B   47 30
 12. Separator sequence: 29. Attributes occupy position: YES
                                     30. Attributes cumulative: NO
                                     31. All attributes off:
 13. End sequence: ESC G   0
                                            1B   47 30

 14. Cursor to top row, left column: CURSOR CONTROL KEYS
 ESC =   SP SP   32. Cursor up:
 1B   3D   20 20   ^K
 15. 10th Row, 50th Column: 0B
 ESC =   )   Q   33. Cursor down:
 1B   3D   29 51   ^J
 16. Delay after positioning: 0   0A
 17. Cursor home: 34. Cursor right:
        ^^   ^L
        1E   0C
                                     35. Cursor left:
                                            ^H
ERASURE   DELAY   08
 18. Entire screen:
        ^Z   0   CHARACTER SET
        1A   36. Full upper and lower ASCII: YES
 19. Cursor to end of screen: 37. Generate all control codes: YES
     ESC Y   0   38. Bell or tone sequence:
     1B   59   ^G
 20. Beginning of screen to cursor: 07

 21. Cursor to end of line: EMULATION
     ESC T   0   39. Conform to ANSI X3.64?   NO
     1B   54   40. Terminals Emulated:
 22. Beginning of line to cursor:

 23. Entire cursor line:

                                307   CONTINUED ====>

41. Information provided by:
    MANUFACTURER

42. PROGRAM FUNCTION KEYS   NOTES
1. ^A @   ^M   30. Multiple attributes available,
   01 40   0D   refer to manual. Color attributes
                                             available.
2. ^A A   ^M   36. Plus graphics characters. Terminal
   01 41   0D   has soft character generator into
                                             which up to 256 custom symbols may
3. ^A B   ^M   be loaded from host.
   01 42   0D   42. F1-F8 shown unshifted.
                                             F9-F16 refer to F1-F8 shifted.
4. ^A C   ^M
   01 43   0D

5. ^A D   ^M
   01 44   0D

6. ^A E   ^M
   01 45   0D

7. ^A F   ^M
   01 46   0D

8. ^A G   ^M
   01 47   0D

9. ^A H   ^M
   01 48   0D

10. ^A I   ^M
    01 49 0D

11. ^A J   ^M
    01 4A 0D

12. ^A K   ^M
    01 4B 0D

13. ^A L   ^M
    01 4C 0D

14. ^A M   ^M
    01 4D 0D

15. ^A N   ^M
    01 4E 0D

16. ^A O   ^M
    01 4F 0D

----
1. Manufacturer: Wyse Technology |
2. Terminal: WY-50

SCREEN LAYOUT   VIDEO ATTRIBUTES
3. Number of rows: 24   ON   OFF
4. Number of columns: 80   24. Blinking:
5. Top Row: 1   ESC G   2   ESC G   0
6. Left Column: 1   1B 47   32   1B   47 30
7. Printing in bottom right   25. Reverse video:
   cause scroll?   PROG   ESC G   4   ESC G   0
                                    1B 47   34   1B   47 30
CURSOR ADDRESSING   26. Underline:
8. Lead-in sequence: ESC G   8   ESC G   0
        ESC =   1B 47   38   1B   47 30
        1B   3D   27. High intensity:
9. Row or column first: ROW
10. Numeric form of row and column:
    BINARY   28. Half intensity:
11. Add offset to: Row: 1F   ESC G   p   ESC G   0
                         Col: 1F   1B 47   70   1B   47 30
12. Separator sequence: 29. Attributes occupy position: YES
                                    30. Attributes cumulative: NO
                                    31. All attributes off:
13. End sequence: ESC G   0
                                              1B   47 30

14. Cursor to top row, left column: CURSOR CONTROL KEYS
ESC =   SP SP   32. Cursor up:
1B 3D 20 20   ^K
15. 10th Row, 50th Column: 0B
ESC =   )   Q   33. Cursor down:
1B 3D 29 51   ^J
16. Delay after positioning: 0   0A
17. Cursor home: 34. Cursor right:
        ^^   ^L
        1E   0C
                                    35. Cursor left:
ERASURE   DELAY   ^H
18. Entire screen: 08
        ^Z   0
        1A   CHARACTER SET
19. Cursor to end of screen: 36. Full upper and lower ASCII: YES
                                    37. Generate all control codes: YES
                                    38. Bell or tone sequence:
20. Beginning of screen to cursor: ^G
                                              07

21. Cursor to end of line: EMULATION
                                    39. Conform to ANSI X3.64?   NO
                                    40. Terminals Emulated:
22. Beginning of line to cursor: Televideo 910/920/925
                                        Hazeltine 1500
                                        ADDS Viewpoint
23. Entire cursor line:

Manufacturer: Wyse Technology
Terminal: WY-50

41. Information provided by:
    MANUFACTURER

42. PROGRAM FUNCTION KEYS   NOTES
    1. ^A   @   ^M   4. Or 132.
       01   40   0D   8. In 132 column mode:
                                       ESC a
    2. ^A   A   ^M   10. In 132 column mode:
       01   41   0D   VARIABLE-LENGTH ASCII
                                   11. In 132 column mode:
    3. ^A   B   ^M   no offset
       01   42   0D   12. In 132 column mode:
                                       R
    4. ^A   C   ^M   13. In 132 column mode:
       01   43   0D   C
                                   14. In 132 column mode:
    5. ^A   D   ^M   ESC a 1 R 1 C
       01   44   0D   15. In 132 column mode:
                                       ESC a 10 R 50 C
    6. ^A   E   ^M   30. Multiple attributes available,
       01   45   0D   refer to manual.
                                   36. Plus graphics characters.
    7. ^A   F   ^M   42. Also shifted F1-F16. All function
       01   46   0D   keys user programmable. Default
                                       values shown.
    8. ^A   G   ^M
       01   47   0D

    9. ^A   H   ^M
       01   48   0D

   10. ^A   I   ^M
       01   49   0D

   11. ^A   J   ^M
       01   4A   0D

   12. ^A   K   ^M
       01   4B   0D

   13. ^A   L   ^M
       01   4C   0D

   14. ^A   M   ^M
       01   4D   0D

   15. ^A   N   ^M
       01   4E   0D

   16. ^A   O   ^M
       01   4F   0D

---

1. Manufacturer: Wyse Technology
2. Terminal: WY-75

SCREEN LAYOUT
3. Number of rows: 24
4. Number of columns: 80
5. Top Row: 1
6. Left Column: 1
7. Printing in bottom right
   cause scroll?   PROG

CURSOR ADDRESSING
8. Lead-in sequence:
              ESC [
              1B 5B
9. Row or column first: ROW
10. Numeric form of row and column:
    VARIABLE-LENGTH ASCII
11. Add offset to: Row: 0
                          Col: 0
12. Separator sequence:
              ;
              3B
13. End sequence:
              H
              48
14. Cursor to top row, left column:
ESC [1   ;   1   H
1B 5B   31   3B   31   48
15. 10th Row, 50th Column:
ESC [1   0   ;   5   0   H
1B 5B 31 30 3B 35 30 48
16. Delay after positioning: 0
17. Cursor home:
              ESC [H
              1B   5B 48

ERASURE   DELAY
18. Entire screen:
         ESC [2   J   0
         1B   5B 32   4A
19. Cursor to end of screen:
         ESC [J   0
         1B   5B 4A
20. Beginning of screen to cursor:
         ESC [1   J   0
         1B   5B 31   4A
21. Cursor to end of line:
         ESC [K   0
         1B   5B 4B
22. Beginning of line to cursor:
         ESC [1   K   0
         1B   5B 31   4B
23. Entire cursor line:
         ESC [2   K   0
         1B   5B 32   4B

VIDEO ATTRIBUTES
          ON   OFF
24. Blinking:
ESC [5   m   ESC [m
1B 5B   35   6D   1B 5B   6D
25. Reverse video:
ESC [7   m   ESC [m
1B 5B   37   6D   1B 5B   6D
26. Underline:
ESC [4   m   ESC [m
1B 5B   34   6D   1B 5B   6D
27. High intensity:
ESC [1   m   ESC [m
1B 5B   31   6D   1B 5B   6D
28. Half intensity:

29. Attributes occupy position: NO
30. Attributes cumulative: YES
31. All attributes off:
              ESC [m
              1B   5B 6D

CURSOR CONTROL KEYS
32. Cursor up:
              ESC [A
              1B   5B 41
33. Cursor down:
              ESC [B
              1B   5B 42
34. Cursor right:
              ESC [C
              1B   5B 43
35. Cursor left:
              ESC [D
              1B   5B 44

CHARACTER SET
36. Full upper and lower ASCII: YES
37. Generate all control codes: YES
38. Bell or tone sequence:
              ^G
              07

EMULATION
39. Conform to ANSI X3.64?   YES
40. Terminals Emulated:

311   CONTINUED ====>

| Manufacturer: | Wyse Technology |
| Terminal: | WY-75 |

41. Information provided by:
    MANUFACTURER

42. PROGRAM FUNCTION KEYS   NOTES
    1.   4. Or 132.

    2.

    3.

    4.

    5.

    6.

    7.

    8.

    9.

    10.

    11.

    12.

    13.

    14.

    15.

    16.

| 1. Manufacturer: | Zenith Data Systems |
| 2. Terminal: | ZT-10 |

SCREEN LAYOUT
3. Number of rows: 24
4. Number of columns: 80
5. Top Row: 1
6. Left Column: 1
7. Printing in bottom right
   cause scroll?   YES

CURSOR ADDRESSING
8. Lead-in sequence:
             ESC Y
             1B 59
9. Row or column first: ROW
10. Numeric form of row and column:
    BINARY
11. Add offset to: Row: 1F
                          Col: 1F
12. Separator sequence:

13. End sequence:

14. Cursor to top row, left column:
ESC Y   SP SP
1B 59   20 20
15. 10th Row, 50th Column:
ESC Y   )   Q
1B 59   29 51
16. Delay after positioning: 0
17. Cursor home:
             ESC H
             1B 48

ERASURE   DELAY
18. Entire screen:
             ESC E   0
             1B 45
19. Cursor to end of screen:
             ESC J   0
             1B 4A
20. Beginning of screen to cursor:
             ESC b   0
             1B 62
21. Cursor to end of line:
             ESC K   0
             1B 4B
22. Beginning of line to cursor:
             ESC o   0
             1B 6F
23. Entire cursor line:
             ESC I   0
             1B 49

VIDEO ATTRIBUTES
                ON   OFF
24. Blinking:
    ESC s   2   ESC s   0
    1B 73   32   1B 73   30
25. Reverse video:
    ESC s   1   ESC s   0
    1B 73   31   1B 73   30
26. Underline:

27. High intensity:

28. Half intensity:
    ESC s   4   ESC s   0
    1B 73   34   1B 73   30
29. Attributes occupy position: NO
30. Attributes cumulative: NO
31. All attributes off:
             ESC s   0
             1B 73   30

CURSOR CONTROL KEYS
32. Cursor up:
             ESC A
             1B 41
33. Cursor down:
             ESC B
             1B 42
34. Cursor right:
             ESC C
             1B 43
35. Cursor left:
             ESC D
             1B 44

CHARACTER SET
36. Full upper and lower ASCII: YES
37. Generate all control codes: YES
38. Bell or tone sequence:
             ^G
             07

EMULATION
39. Conform to ANSI X3.64?   NO
40. Terminals Emulated:
    DEC VT-52

CONTINUED ====>

Manufacturer: Zenith Data Systems
Terminal: ZT-10

41. Information provided by:
    MANUFACTURER

42. PROGRAM FUNCTION KEYS   NOTES
    1. ESC S   30. Blinking & reverse video:
       1B   53   ESC   s   3
                                          1B   73 33
    2. ESC T
       1B   54

    3. ESC U
       1B   55

    4. ESC V
       1B   56

    5. ESC W
       1B   57

    6. ESC P
       1B   50

    7. ESC Q
       1B   51

    8. ESC R
       1B   52

    9.

   10.

   11.

   12.

   13.

   14.

   15.

   16.

```
--------------------------------------------------------------------------
  1. Manufacturer:                      Zenith Data Systems
  2. Terminal:                          Z-19-HW
--------------------------------------------------------------------------


SCREEN LAYOUT                           VIDEO ATTRIBUTES
  3. Number of rows:           24             ON                    OFF
  4. Number of columns:        80      24. Blinking:
  5. Top Row:                   1
  6. Left Column:               1
  7. Printing in bottom right          25. Reverse video:
     cause scroll?             NO      ESC [   7   m        ESC [   0   m
                                       1B  5B  37  6D       1B  5B  30  6D
CURSOR ADDRESSING                      26. Underline:
  8. Lead-in sequence:
              ESC [
              1B  5B                    27. High intensity:
  9. Row or column first:      ROW
 10. Numeric form of row and column:
     VARIABLE-LENGTH ASCII              28. Half intensity:
 11. Add offset to:        Row:   0
                           Col:   0
 12. Separator sequence:                29. Attributes occupy position: NO
              ;                         30. Attributes cumulative:      NO
              3B                        31. All attributes off:
 13. End sequence:
              H
              48
 14. Cursor to top row, left column:   CURSOR CONTROL KEYS
 ESC [   1   ;   1   H                  32. Cursor up:
 1B  5B  31  3B  31  48                             ESC [   A
 15. 10th Row, 50th Column:                         1B  5B  41
 ESC [   1   0   ;   5   0   H          33. Cursor down:
 1B  5B  31  30  3B  35  30  48                     ESC [   B
 16. Delay after positioning:     0                 1B  5B  42
 17. Cursor home:                       34. Cursor right:
              ESC [   1   ;   1   H                 ESC [   C
              1B  5B  31  3B  31  48                1B  5B  43
                                        35. Cursor left:
 ERASURE                      DELAY                 ESC [   D
 18. Entire screen:                                 1B  5B  44
              ESC [   2   J        0
              1B  5B  32  4A            CHARACTER SET
 19. Cursor to end of screen:           36. Full upper and lower ASCII: YES
              ESC [   0   J        0    37. Generate all control codes: NO
              1B  5B  30  4A            38. Bell or tone sequence:
 20. Beginning of screen to cursor:                ^G
              ESC [   1   J        0                07
              1B  5B  31  4A
 21. Cursor to end of line:             EMULATION
              ESC [   0   K        0    39. Conform to ANSI X3.64?      YES
              1B  5B  30  4B            40. Terminals Emulated:
 22. Beginning of line to cursor:           VT-52
              ESC [   1   K        0
              1B  5B  31  4B
 23. Entire cursor line:
              ESC [   2   K        0
              1B  5B  32  4B
```

CONTINUED ====>

```
---------------------------------------------------------------------------
      Manufacturer:                     Zenith Data Systems
      Terminal:                         Z-19-HW
---------------------------------------------------------------------------
```

41. Information provided by:
    MANUFACTURER

42. PROGRAM FUNCTION KEYS   NOTES
 1. ESC O   S
    1B   4F   53

 2. ESC O   T
    1B   4F   54

 3. ESC O   U
    1B   4F   55

 4. ESC O   V
    1B   4F   56

 5. ESC O   W
    1B   4F   57

 6. ESC O   P
    1B   4F   50

 7. ESC O   Q
    1B   4F   51

 8. ESC O   R
    1B   4F   52

 9.

10.

11.

12.

13.

14.

15.

16.

```
-------------------------------------------------------------------------
  1. Manufacturer:                    Zenith Data Systems
  2. Terminal:                        Z-29
-------------------------------------------------------------------------
```

SCREEN LAYOUT
  3. Number of rows: 24
  4. Number of columns: 80
  5. Top Row: 1
  6. Left Column: 1
  7. Printing in bottom right
     cause scroll?   PROG

CURSOR ADDRESSING
  8. Lead-in sequence:
                ESC [
                1B 5B
  9. Row or column first: ROW
 10. Numeric form of row and column:
     VARIABLE-LENGTH ASCII
 11. Add offset to: Row: 0
                           Col: 0
 12. Separator sequence:
                ;
                3B
 13. End sequence:
                H
                48
 14. Cursor to top row, left column:
     ESC [1   ;   1   H
     1B 5B 31 3B 31 48
 15. 10th Row, 50th Column:
     ESC [1   0   ;   5   0   H
     1B 5B 31 30 3B 35 30 48
 16. Delay after positioning: 0
 17. Cursor home:
                ESC [1   ;   1   H
                1B 5B 31 3B 31 48

ERASURE   DELAY
 18. Entire screen:
                ESC [2   J   0
                1B 5B 32 4A
 19. Cursor to end of screen:
                ESC [0   J   0
                1B 5B 30 4A
 20. Beginning of screen to cursor:
                ESC [1   J   0
                1B 5B 31 4A
 21. Cursor to end of line:
                ESC [0   K   0
                1B 5B 30 4B
 22. Beginning of line to cursor:
                ESC [1   K   0
                1B 5B 31 4B
 23. Entire cursor line:
                ESC [2   K   0
                1B 5B 32 4B

VIDEO ATTRIBUTES
          ON   OFF
 24. Blinking:
     ESC [5   m   ESC [0   m
     1B 5B 35 6D   1B 5B 30 6D
 25. Reverse video:
     ESC [7   m   ESC [0   m
     1B 5B 37 6D   1B 5B 30 6D
 26. Underline:
     ESC [4   m   ESC [0   m
     1B 5B 34 6D   1B 5B 30 6D
 27. High intensity:

 28. Half intensity:
     ESC [2   m   ESC [0   m
     1B 5B 32 6D   1B 5B 30 6D
 29. Attributes occupy position: NO
 30. Attributes cumulative: NO
 31. All attributes off:
                ESC [0   m
                1B 5B 30 6D

CURSOR CONTROL KEYS
 32. Cursor up:
                ESC [A
                1B 5B 41
 33. Cursor down:
                ESC [B
                1B 5B 42
 34. Cursor right:
                ESC [C
                1B 5B 43
 35. Cursor left:
                ESC [D
                1B 5B 44

CHARACTER SET
 36. Full upper and lower ASCII: YES
 37. Generate all control codes: YES
 38. Bell or tone sequence:
                ^G
                07

EMULATION
 39. Conform to ANSI X3.64?   YES
 40. Terminals Emulated:
     Heath/Zenith H/Z-19
     ANSI X3.64-1979 (VT100)
     Lear Siegler ADM 3A
     Hazeltine 1500

317   CONTINUED ====>

Manufacturer: Zenith Data Systems
Terminal: Z-29

----

41. Information provided by:
    MANUFACTURER

42. PROGRAM FUNCTION KEYS   NOTES
 1. ESC O   S
    1B   4F   53

 2. ESC O   T
    1B   4F   54

 3. ESC O   U
    1B   4F   55

 4. ESC O   V
    1B   4F   56

 5. ESC O   W
    1B   4F   57

 6. ESC O   P
    1B   4F   50

 7. ESC O   Q
    1B   4F   51

 8. ESC O   R
    1B   4F   52

 9. ESC O   X
    1B   4F   58

10.

11.

12.

13.

14.

15.

16.

```
---------------------------------------------------------------------------
  1. Manufacturer:                     Zenith Data Systems
  2. Terminal:                         Z-49
---------------------------------------------------------------------------
```

SCREEN LAYOUT
  3. Number of rows: 24
  4. Number of columns: 80
  5. Top Row: 1
  6. Left Column: 1
  7. Printing in bottom right
     cause scroll?   PROG

CURSOR ADDRESSING
  8. Lead-in sequence:
              ESC [
              1B 5B
  9. Row or column first: ROW
 10. Numeric form of row and column:
     VARIABLE-LENGTH ASCII
 11. Add offset to: Row: 0
                             Col: 0
 12. Separator sequence:
              ;
              3B
 13. End sequence:
              H
              48
 14. Cursor to top row, left column:
     ESC [1   ;   1   H
     1B 5B 31 3B 31 48
 15. 10th Row, 50th Column:
     ESC [1   0   ;   5   0   H
     1B 5B 31 30 3B 35 30 48
 16. Delay after positioning: 0
 17. Cursor home:
              ESC [H
              1B 5B 48

ERASURE   DELAY
 18. Entire screen:
          ESC [2   J   0
          1B 5B 32 4A
 19. Cursor to end of screen:
          ESC [J   0
          1B 5B 4A
 20. Beginning of screen to cursor:
          ESC [1   J   0
          1B 5B 31 4A
 21. Cursor to end of line:
          ESC [K   0
          1B 5B 4B
 22. Beginning of line to cursor:
          ESC [1   K   0
          1B 5B 31 4B
 23. Entire cursor line:
          ESC [2   K   0
          1B 5B 32 4B

VIDEO ATTRIBUTES
              ON   OFF
 24. Blinking:
     ESC [5   m   ESC [m
     1B 5B 35 6D   1B 5B 6D
 25. Reverse video:
     ESC [7   m   ESC [m
     1B 5B 37 6D   1B 5B 6D
 26. Underline:
     ESC [4   m   ESC [m
     1B 5B 34 6D   1B 5B 6D
 27. High intensity:
     ESC [1   m   ESC [m
     1B 5B 31 6D   1B 5B 6D
 28. Half intensity:

 29. Attributes occupy position: NO
 30. Attributes cumulative: YES
 31. All attributes off:
              ESC [m
              1B 5B 6D

CURSOR CONTROL KEYS
 32. Cursor up:
              ESC [A
              1B 5B 41
 33. Cursor down:
              ESC [B
              1B 5B 42
 34. Cursor right:
              ESC [C
              1B 5B 43
 35. Cursor left:
              ESC [D
              1B 5B 44

CHARACTER SET
 36. Full upper and lower ASCII: YES
 37. Generate all control codes: YES
 38. Bell or tone sequence:
              ^G
              07

EMULATION
 39. Conform to ANSI X3.64?   YES
 40. Terminals Emulated:
     DEC VT-100

319   CONTINUED ====>

Manufacturer: Zenith Data Systems
Terminal: Z-49

41. Information provided by:
    MANUFACTURER

42. PROGRAM FUNCTION KEYS   NOTES
  1. ESC O   P   4. Optionally 132.
     1B   4F   50   36. Plus VT-100 graphics and
                                        Z-29 graphics.
  2. ESC O   Q   42. PF keys programmable.
     1B   4F   51

  3. ESC O   R
     1B   4F   52

  4. ESC O   S
     1B   4F   53

  5.

  6.

  7.

  8.

  9.

 10.

 11.

 12.

 13.

 14.

 15.

 16.

APPENDIX 1 — ASCII CODE CONVERSION CHART

Binary	Decimal	Octal	Hex	ASCII	Ctrl
0000 0000	000	000	00	NUL	^@
0000 0001	001	001	01	SOH	^A
0000 0010	002	002	02	STX	^B
0000 0011	003	003	03	ETX	^C
0000 0100	004	004	04	EOT	^D
0000 0101	005	005	05	ENQ	^E
0000 0110	006	006	06	ACK	^F
0000 0111	007	007	07	BEL	^G
0000 1000	008	010	08	BS	^H
0000 1001	009	011	09	HT	^I
0000 1010	010	012	0A	LF	^J
0000 1011	011	013	0B	VT	^K
0000 1100	012	014	0C	FF	^L
0000 1101	013	015	0D	CR	^M
0000 1110	014	016	0E	SO	^N
0000 1111	015	017	0F	SI	^O
0001 0000	016	020	10	DLE	^P
0001 0001	017	021	11	DC1	^Q
0001 0010	018	022	12	DC2	^R
0001 0011	019	023	13	DC3	^S
0001 0100	020	024	14	DC4	^T
0001 0101	021	025	15	NAK	^U
0001 0110	022	026	16	SYN	^V
0001 0111	023	027	17	ETB	^W
0001 1000	024	030	18	CAN	^X
0001 1001	025	031	19	EM	^Y
0001 1010	026	032	1A	SUB	^Z
0001 1011	027	033	1B	ESC	^[
0001 1100	028	034	1C	FS	^\
0001 1101	029	035	1D	GS	^]
0001 1110	030	036	1E	RS	^^
0001 1111	031	037	1F	US	^_
0010 0000	032	040	20	SP	
0010 0001	033	041	21	!	
0010 0010	034	042	22	"	
0010 0011	035	043	23	#	
0010 0100	036	044	24	$	
0010 0101	037	045	25	%	
0010 0110	038	046	26	&	
0010 0111	039	047	27	'	
0010 1000	040	050	28	(	
0010 1001	041	051	29	)	
0010 1010	042	052	2A	*	
0010 1011	043	053	2B	+	
0010 1100	044	054	2C	,	
0010 1101	045	055	2D	-	
0010 1110	046	056	2E	.	
0010 1111	047	057	2F	/	
0011 0000	048	060	30	0	
0011 0001	049	061	31	1	
0011 0010	050	062	32	2	
0011 0011	051	063	33	3	
0011 0100	052	064	34	4	
0011 0101	053	065	35	5	
0011 0110	054	066	36	6	
0011 0111	055	067	37	7	
0011 1000	056	070	38	8	
0011 1001	057	071	39	9	
0011 1010	058	072	3A	:	
0011 1011	059	073	3B	;	
0011 1100	060	074	3C	<	
0011 1101	061	075	3D	=	
0011 1110	062	076	3E	>	
0011 1111	063	077	3F	?	

Binary	Decimal	Octal	Hex	ASCII
0100 0000	064	100	40	@
0100 0001	065	101	41	A
0100 0010	066	102	42	B
0100 0011	067	103	43	C
0100 0100	068	104	44	D
0100 0101	069	105	45	E
0100 0110	070	106	46	F
0100 0111	071	107	47	G
0100 1000	072	110	48	H
0100 1001	073	111	49	I
0100 1010	074	112	4A	J
0100 1011	075	113	4B	K
0100 1100	076	114	4C	L
0100 1101	077	115	4D	M
0100 1110	078	116	4E	N
0100 1111	079	117	4F	O
0101 0000	080	120	50	P
0101 0001	081	121	51	Q
0101 0010	082	122	52	R
0101 0011	083	123	53	S
0101 0100	084	124	54	T
0101 0101	085	125	55	U
0101 0110	086	126	56	V
0101 0111	087	127	57	W
0101 1000	088	130	58	X
0101 1001	089	131	59	Y
0101 1010	090	132	5A	Z
0101 1011	091	133	5B	[
0101 1100	092	134	5C	\
0101 1101	093	135	5D	]
0101 1110	094	136	5E	^
0101 1111	095	137	5F	_
0110 0000	096	140	60	`
0110 0001	097	141	61	a
0110 0010	098	142	62	b
0110 0011	099	143	63	c
0110 0100	100	144	64	d
0110 0101	101	145	65	e
0110 0110	102	146	66	f
0110 0111	103	147	67	g
0110 1000	104	150	68	h
0110 1001	105	151	69	i
0110 1010	106	152	6A	j
0110 1011	107	153	6B	k
0110 1100	108	154	6C	l
0110 1101	109	155	6D	m
0110 1110	110	156	6E	n
0110 1111	111	157	6F	o
0111 0000	112	160	70	p
0111 0001	113	161	71	q
0111 0010	114	162	72	r
0111 0011	115	163	73	s
0111 0100	116	164	74	t
0111 0101	117	165	75	u
0111 0110	118	166	76	v
0111 0111	119	167	77	w
0111 1000	120	170	78	x
0111 1001	121	171	79	y
0111 1010	122	172	7A	z
0111 1011	123	173	7B	{
0111 1100	124	174	7C		
0111 1101	125	175	7D	}
0111 1110	126	176	7E	~
0111 1111	127	177	7F	DEL

INDEX BY MANUFACTURER

INDEX BY MANUFACTURER (Continued)

323

INDEX BY TERMINAL

324

INDEX BY TERMINAL (Continued)

INDEX BY CURSOR ADDRESS LEAD-IN

INDEX BY CURSOR ADDRESS LEAD-IN (Continued)

327

INDEX BY CLEAR-SCREEN SEQUENCE

INDEX BY CLEAR-SCREEN SEQUENCE (Continued)

329

INDEX BY ROW OR COLUMN FIRST IN CURSOR ADDRESS

INDEX BY FORM OF CURSOR ADDRESS

INDEX BY FORM OF CURSOR ADDRESS (Continued)

INDEX BY CURSOR KEYS